LINCOLN CHRISTIAN COLLEGE AND SEMINARY

New Ways of Classroom Assessment

James Dean Brown, Editor

New Ways in TESOL Series II

Innovative Classroom Techniques

Jack C. Richards, Series Editor

Founded 1966

Teachers of English to Speakers of Other Languages, Inc.

Typeset in Garamond Book and Tiffany Demi
by Capitol Communication Systems, Inc., Crofton, Maryland USA
and printed by
Pantagraph Printing, Bloomington, Illinois USA

Teachers of English to Speakers of Other Languages, Inc. (TESOL)
1600 Cameron Street, Suite 300
Alexandria, VA 22314 USA
Tel 703-836-0774 • Fax 703-836-7864 • e-mail: publ@tesol.edu • http://www.tesol.edu

Director of Communications and Marketing: Helen Kornblum
Managing Editor: Marilyn Kupetz
Copy Editor: Ellen F. Garshick
Cover Design: Ann Kammerer

TESOL thanks Arthur Perlstein, the staff, and the students at English for Success, Annandale, Virginia, for their assistance and participation. TESOL also appreciates the cooperation of Susan Heumann, the staff, and the students of Marymount University, Arlington, Virginia.

ISBN 0-939-791-72-2
Library of Congress Catalogue No. 97-061577

Contents

Introduction

In my years as an ESL/EFL teacher in the United States and abroad, my colleagues and I often discussed and complained about the quality of various standardized tests and the effects of those tests on our teaching. Indeed, teachers often feel helpless when confronted with large-scale standardized testing practices. In this book, teachers have been given an opportunity to answer back. Here, they have had a chance to show how they do assessment in their classrooms on an everyday basis.

My goal was to step out of the way and let teachers tell their stories about how they do assessment in their classrooms. I have a fairly strong psychometric and statistical background, which serves me well in developing norm-referenced tests for proficiency and placement purposes. But my training and work in the area of criterion-referenced tests have taught me to listen carefully to what teachers are saying about their teaching and the testing they want to do in their classrooms. As a result, my mind is not closed to new types of tests just because they do not fit well in the psychometric/statistical side of my mind. What I am trying to say is that this book offers a collection of classroom testing ideas created by teachers with as little interference as possible from a testing "expert."

At the same time, the fact that I include a particular assessment technique in this book does not constitute an endorsement of that technique on my part from a psychometric point of view. Instead, each contribution is included here because (a) a teacher found it useful, (b) this editor thought it made sense from a classroom perspective, and (c) the description was clear and it adequately explained the technique.

One of the things that I learned in doing this project was that, almost universally, the teachers who contributed to this book expressed the aims of their contributions in terms that were related directly to helping students learn. Indeed, the contributors themselves appear to have had difficulty separating the teaching from the measurement, the lesson from the assessment. I say this because I find that most of the assessment ideas described in this book also describe the teaching lessons that go with them. In some cases, the assessment activity is indistinguishable from a regular teaching lesson until the teacher, or the students themselves, do some form of scoring or other feedback.

Consequently, this book is a series of contributions from teachers that look more like assessment activities than like tests, and I will consistently refer to all of these contributions as *assessment activities*. To me, assessment *activities* are different from tests in that they are not easily distinguishable from other classroom activities because they are thoroughly integrated into the language teaching and learning processes. In other words, assessment activities do not stand out as different, formal, threatening, or interruptive. At the same time, *assessment* activities are different from ordinary classroom activities in that they provide a way of observing or scoring the students' performances and giving feedback in the form of a score or other information (e.g., notes in the margin, written prose reactions, oral critiques, teacher conferences) that can enlighten the students and teachers about the effectiveness of the language learning and teaching involved.

In each of the assessment activities, a great deal is said about feedback. But why is feedback important in the classroom? My guess is that feedback derives its importance from the fact that it is one of the teacher's most powerful tools for shaping how students approach the learning process and for finding out what is going on in the students' minds.

Traditionally, the feedback in classroom assessment settings has come from the teacher's perspective, and you will indeed find that the teachers give feedback in many of these contributions. However, many of these contributions utilize other possible feedback perspectives, including self-assessment, peer assessment, and outsider assessment strategies. Most often, these alternative scoring perspectives are used in conjunction with the teacher's feedback or in pairs, perhaps because the contributors knew intuitively that combining two or more feedback perspectives would increase the reliability (and palatability from the students' perspectives) of the resulting information.

The activities in this book are organized according to the primary or predominant emphasis of the activity, as shown in the Users' Guide to

Activities. Part I focuses on alternative methods of assessment; Part II, on alternative feedback perspectives; Part III, on alternative ways to group learners for assessment; Part IV, on alternative ways of doing classroom chores; Part V, on alternative ways of assessing written skills; and Part VI, on alternative ways of assessing oral skills.

Each assessment activity has many characteristics. For instance, an activity may be predominantly a portfolio activity but may also involve conferencing, self-assessment, and peer assessment. For your convenience, the other characteristics of each activity are indicated in the Key to Activities at the back of the book. Thus, even though all of the speaking-related activities are not found in the Speaking and Pronunciation section of Part VI, you can see at a glance that 42 of the assessment activities involve speaking, and you can tell exactly which ones they are.

Certain conventions have been followed to try to make the assessment activity descriptions as compact as possible. For instance, based on experience, I am assuming that most classrooms have blackboards and chalk (or an equivalent) and that the students have sheets of paper, pencils, and pens available. As a result, such items are not mentioned in the lists of resources needed for each assessment activity.

In browsing through this collection of assessment activities, you may notice that the contributions come from a wide variety of geographical locations. Indeed, there are contributions from teachers in the United States but also many contributions from teachers as far away as Japan, Jordan, Venezuela, Zimbabwe, and elsewhere. You may also notice that there are fairly heavy clusters of contributions from Hawai'i in the United States and from Venezuela and Japan internationally. This seemingly strange pattern results from the fact that my home base is the University of Hawai'i at Manoa. In addition, I teach regularly during the summer at Temple University Japan, and I had the good fortune to teach in the TESOL Summer Institute at the University of Carabobo in Valencia, Venezuela. Naturally, wherever I went, I tried to generate interest in contributing to this volume. Equally fortunate, however, was the fact that many contributions also arrived by mail, fax, and e-mail from many other locations.

In the end, far too many contributions were sent to include them all. Some had to be rejected because they were not clearly explained, others because they were not organized and formatted as needed, and still others because they explained an assessment activity that had been contributed earlier by another teacher.

I would like to thank all of the contributors to this book. They were universally cooperative and understanding. More importantly, they created the stuff of this book and, quite obviously, the book would not exist without them.

Users' Guide to Activities

Peer Assessment

Self-Assessment Combined With Peer Assessment

Part III: Alternative Groupings
for Assessment

Group Work

Part VI: Alternative Ways of Assessing Oral Skills

Listening and Note-Taking

Speaking and Pronunciation

Part I: Alternative Methods of Assessment

Editor's Note

The contributions in this part of the book provide good examples of alternative methods of assessment. In this case, *methods* means ways of gathering assessment information. Portfolios are one such method, and journals, logs, and conferences are three others. All four methods are fundamentally different from ordinary paper-and-pencil tests, which is why they are referred to as alternative methods of assessment.

Portfolios are collections of students' work selected by students (with the teacher's guidance) to represent their learning experiences. Portfolios usually involve students gathering together samples of their L2 use (such as compositions and video clips) into a folder or box to show to peers, parents, outsiders, and others much in the way an artist gathers paintings in a portfolio to show to prospective clients. Portfolios provide a type of personal assessment that is directly related to the activities going on in the classroom, and they are particularly appropriate for assessing language learning processes. Portfolios may also enhance students' learning, improve their view of the teacher's role in the classroom, and involve everybody in the assessment processes.

The first three contributions provide generally useful information about portfolios: a guide to planning portfolios (Planning Portfolios), a general introduction to the ideas behind using portfolios (ESL Language Portfolios: How Do They Work?), and a concrete method for assessing portfolios (Learner Self-Assessment: Preparing an *English* Portfolio). The other contributions in the portfolio section tell how to apply the portfolio method to a variety of different purposes: listening to newscasts (Portfolio Assessment of Newscast Listening), assessing business communication (The Process of Business Communication), assessing students' personal writing growth (Pretty Popular Pupil Portfolios), selecting reading texts (Using Portfolios in the EFL Reading Class), and stimulating writing (Writing Pictures).

Journal assessment activities typically require students to make regular entries in a diary or journal at home or in class. Many variations exist. Journal writing can be used to encourage students to practice writing or to assess their writing ability and its growth over time. Journal activities can also be used to collect information on students' views, beliefs, attitudes, and motivations related to a class or program or to the processes involved in learning various language skills. Two contributions tell about using journals as an assessment activity: one for self-evaluation at the midterm (Using Journals for Self-Evaluation at Midterm) and the other to help students think and write about their reading processes (Don't Talk About It, Write It Down).

Logs are somewhat different from portfolios and journals in that they afford students a chance to record experiences with English use outside the classroom. Many details may be logged, including when and where the language was used, what was involved linguistically, and why certain experiences occurred the way they did. Thus a log can document the extent to which students are using the knowledge gained from the classroom in real-world settings. Two contributions show how to use logs to encourage students to (a) figure out which learning strategies, materials, and contexts work best for them (Self-Assessment: Keeping a Language Learning Log) and (b) perform a variety of different communicative activities and keep track of what they've done (Passport: A Log).

Conferences usually involve students coming to the teacher's office alone or in groups for brief meetings to get feedback on their work. Conferences can (a) provide personalized assessment that is directly related to the learning going on in the classroom, (b) help students understand their own learning processes and strategies and develop a better self-image, and (c) let teachers elicit specific skills or tasks that students may need to review and afford teachers an opportunity to inform, mold, observe, and gather information about students. Although nine contributions in this book mention conferences in one way or another, only one focuses solely on effectively using conferences to assess students' conversational abilities in a nonthreatening environment (Eat, Drink, and Be Merry: Lunchtime Student Assessment).

In the foregoing, I discussed some of the advantages of using portfolios, journals, logs, and conferences as assessment tools. However, the psychometrician in me compels me to warn that all these advantages come at a price. A number of problems can arise (especially if these assessment methods are used on a large scale, say across an entire school district), including problems with politics, logistics, interpretation, reliability, and validity. In view of the fact that an entire literature has grown up around these issues, space does not permit discussing these problems and their solutions here (for an overview, see Norris, 1996).

References and Further Reading

Belanoff, P., & Dickson, M. (Eds.). (1991). *Portfolios: Process and product.* Portsmouth, NH: Boynton/Cook.

Herman, J. L., Aschbacher, P. R., & Winters, L. (1992). *A practical guide to alternative assessment.* Alexandria, VA: Association for Supervision and Curriculum Development.

Norris, J. M. (1996). *Performance and portfolio assessment (1985-1995): An extended annotated bibliography of sources useful for language teachers* (Research Note). Honolulu: University of Hawai'i, Second Language Teaching and Curriculum Center.

O'Malley, J. M., & Valdez Pierce, L. (1996). *Authentic assessment for English language learners: Practical approaches for teachers.* Reading, MA: Addison-Wesley.

Perrone, V. (Ed.). (1991). *Expanding student assessment.* Alexandria, VA: Association for Supervision and Curriculum Development.

◆ Portfolios
Planning Portfolios

Levels
High beginning +

Aims
Assess own progress
Teachers: Plan
instruction

Class Time
3–6 hours/week

Preparation Time
Variable

Resources
Portfolio Planning
Outline

This activity helps teachers plan assessment portfolios that can encourage students to monitor their own progress while providing teachers with feedback on instruction. This planning process helps relate assessment activities directly to instructional activities, thereby reducing the amount of time necessary for student portfolios. When portfolios are planned with assessment purposes in mind, the information is much more manageable and useful to both the teacher and the student. This planning activity and worksheet (see the Appendix) guide teachers step-by-step through the portfolio planning process, and teachers can use the completed worksheet to get started using assessment portfolios.

Procedure

1. Specify your purpose in using portfolios. Is the portfolio for assessment of oral language? Reading? Reading and writing? A content area, such as social studies? Choose a purpose that reflects your students' greatest learning needs. Starting with a clear purpose can ensure success.
2. Decide how you will use the information in the portfolio. Do you need the information to monitor students' progress? To show you where the students' greatest needs are so that you can plan activities to meet those needs? For program placement? Being clear about how you plan to use the information generated by portfolios can help you see the big picture for their use.
3. Identify the portfolio type:
   ● Collection portfolios consist of all of the students' writing or other work.
   ● Showcase portfolios contain only the students' best work.

- Assessment portfolios are selective, systematic collections of the students' work, reflection on that work, and your observations of the students' work.

  The type of portfolio you choose will help determine the entries and criteria for assessment. If you have been using collection or showcase portfolios, you may now be ready to move on to assessment portfolios, although they are not prerequisites.

4. Match the portfolio entries to your purpose. Keeping in mind your assessment purpose, think of routine classroom activities in which your students engage. Then think of how you can use these same activities for assessment. You can do this in several ways:
   - Record students' performance on a checklist, scoring rubric, or rating scale.
   - Keep anecdotal records.
   - Administer surveys and questionnaires on students' attitudes.
   - Teach the students how to engage in peer assessment and self-assessment.

5. Plan on requiring the students to collect several entries for their portfolios every quarter or semester. For year-long portfolios, you, the students, or both can maintain portfolios by keeping only selected entries from the beginning and the end of the year to pass along to the next teacher, if desired. You can also suggest optional entries that complement and broaden the scope of the required entries rather than repeat them.

6. Plan how you will record students' progress and provide feedback for each entry in the portfolio. A single letter grade is not as useful as clearly specified criteria in the form of a scoring rubric, rating scale, checklist, or anecdotal record. Surveys of the students' attitudes and peer assessment and self-assessment forms also document the students' progress. The students, their parents, and other teachers will all benefit from records that interpret and evaluate the students' performance in terms of specific criteria.

7. Involve the students in the design of their own portfolios in one or more ways:
   - Ask for their input into the criteria and standards for assessment.
   - Teach them to engage in peer assessment and self-assessment.

- Guide them in selecting entries for their portfolios.
- Invite them to participate in portfolio conferences.

8. Plan creative ways to make time for assessment portfolios. Options include
   - using learning centers, including a portfolio center
   - teaching the students how to work responsibly in cooperative learning groups
   - assessing a select number of students each day or week through staggered cycles
   - giving the students time for peer assessment and self-assessment activities.

Feedback and Scoring

1. Communicate the results to the students, parents, and other teachers.
   - Design a cover sheet with spaces for the nature of each entry, the date it was created, and comments on the portfolio as a whole.
   - Write a narrative summary indicating what the portfolio reveals about the student's strengths and weaknesses.
   - Write a letter to parents describing the portfolio process in general or providing individualized feedback on each student.
   - Hold parent-teacher conferences.

Caveats and Options

1. Beginning- or low-level students need time to acquire enough language to work with self-assessment and portfolio assessment. Give them and yourself time before involving them in these processes. Teachers of beginning-level ESL students have indicated that waiting one to two quarters (9-week grading periods) is sometimes necessary before involving them in portfolio assessment.

2. Use portfolios to gather information on how your class is progressing and to develop minilessons aimed at helping the students turn weaknesses into strengths.

3. Give yourself time to implement assessment portfolios. Initially, the process will probably take more time than it will once you have experience in managing your time, the students, and your resources.

References and Further Reading

Clemmons, J., Laase, L., Cooper, D., Areglado, N., & Dill, M. (1993). *Portfolios in the classroom, Grades 1–6.* New York: Scholastic Professional Books.

Kolls, M. R. (1992, March). *Portfolio assessment: A feasibility study.* Paper presented at the 26th Annual TESOL Convention, Vancouver, Canada.

O'Malley, J. M., & Valdez Pierce, L. (1996). *Authentic assessment for English language learners: Practical approaches for teachers.* Reading, MA: Addison-Wesley.

Appendix: Portfolio Planning Outline

Step 1: Specify purpose of portfolio (Check one.)

1. Assess oral language
2. Assess reading/writing
3. Assess content area
4. Other

Step 2: Specify use for assessment information (Check one or more.)

1. Place students
2. Monitor student growth
3. Diagnose strengths and weaknesses
4. Direct instruction

Step 3: Identify portfolio type (Check one.)

1. Showcase
2. Collection
3. Assessment

Step 4: Match entries to purpose (Propose types of entries to match your instructional goals and objectives.)

Part A: Required entries

1.
2.
3.
4.
5.

Part B: Optional entries

1.

2.

3.

4.

Step 5: Record students' progress (Specify the type of record for each portfolio entry.)

1. Scoring rubric
2. Rating scale
3. Checklist
4. Anecdotal record
5. Survey
6. Peer and self-assessment form

Step 6: Get the students involved (Check one or more.)

1. Selection of entries
2. Input into criteria or standards
3. Peer assessment
4. Self-assessment
5. Portfolio conferences

Step 7: Manage time (Check one or more.)

1. Learning centers
2. Cooperative learning activities
3. Staggered cycles
4. Peer or self-assessment, or both

Step 8: Communicate results (Check one or more.)

1. Narrative summary
2. Cover sheet or student profile
3. Letter to parents
4. Parent-teacher conference

Contributor

Lorraine Valdez Pierce teaches courses on assessment at George Mason University in Fairfax, Virginia, in the United States, and is coauthor of a book on authentic, classroom-based assessment.

ESL Language Portfolios: How Do They Work?

Levels
Any

Aims
Assess own language
use
Teachers: Assess or
place students

Class Time
Variable

Preparation Time
Minimal

Resources
Folders or containers

Language portfolios, a variation of the writing portfolios developed within both L1 and L2 teaching, are collections of selected pieces of students' work that show how they have developed in language use and understanding during a single course or for the duration of their stay in a language program. Language portfolios are much more than a folder containing students' work; the students carefully select, revise, and reflect on the pieces (e.g., compositions, homework exercises) and increase their understanding of their own language development in the process. Language portfolios can be shared with peers and can include peers' reflections as well. The primary benefit of using language portfolios is that they allow students a chance to assess their language use, which leads to greater awareness of and growth in language. The portfolios can also be used for classroom assessment or subsequent program placement.

Procedure

1. Tell the students about the language portfolios at the beginning of the course. As they do their course work, tell them to think about whether a particular assignment is one they would like to include in their portfolio or not and whether they would like to revise it.
2. Make the guidelines for the portfolio clear: whether it will include different representative examples (e.g., a listening log entry, a dialogue journal entry, a grammar assignment, a revised essay, the preparation materials for an oral report, a videotape) or whether the students have complete freedom in the choice of representative work. Either negotiate the requirements for the portfolio during the course, or determine them beforehand based on the program and its assessment needs.

3. After the students have completed a number of assignments, give them each a folder or container, and tell them to choose some examples of their work that they would like to or need to include in the language portfolio.
4. Have the students consult you and their peers and then revise the pieces if desired.
5. Make sure the students justify their choices and explain any revisions, usually by writing a letter to any readers of the portfolio about what a particular piece shows about their language development or by answering self-assessment questions (see the Appendix).

Feedback and Scoring

1. At some point, particularly if the portfolio is going to be used for more than self-assessment, give the students feedback on the developing portfolio, either from you and the students' peers or from a group of teachers within the program.
2. If either you or a group of teachers will make a final assessment (for subsequent program placement), then indicate fairly early in the course how the portfolio measures up to any established standards and what the student can do to improve it.

Caveats and Options

1. Language portfolios are not content portfolios or writing portfolios. In content-area classes (like math or social science), the students may collect examples and analyze work related to their understanding of the concepts of these fields and in the process develop a content portfolio. Similarly, writing portfolios demonstrate knowledge of writing as a discipline. In contrast, a language portfolio focuses on the language used in the students' work, that is, where the strengths and weaknesses of language use are, what the students think the pieces show about their language knowledge in various situations, and how you evaluate the language use. A portfolio that relates to content or writing knowledge could also include an analysis of language use.
2. If portfolios are used for self-assessment and credit is given for having completed the portfolio, the students have more freedom in how they pursue it. If portfolios are used for course grading, then more time will be required for evaluation, but other forms of grading can be eliminated altogether. If portfolios are used for program assessment,

then the students must meet the standards set by the program or the teacher and will have far fewer choices about what they do.

3. In some programs, placement into the next level depends partially on an exit examination and partially on the language portfolio developed in the course. In other programs, it may depend solely on the teacher's judgment, in which case the language portfolio would be a major factor, or it may depend solely on an exit examination, in which case the language portfolio would have little to do with the placement decision.

4. Language portfolios are developed throughout a course both in and outside class. Allow class time regularly for assembling and discussing the portfolios so that the students can come to appreciate what they are doing by getting clear answers to their questions about the portfolios. Looking at each other's portfolios helps the students understand what makes a good language portfolio. How much time portfolios require in class will vary with the aims of each course and with how much the portfolio affects the final grade or subsequent placement in the program.

5. Language portfolios can be used in any course designed for language teaching—speaking, reading, or writing courses; grammar, pronunciation, or vocabulary courses; and content-based or English for academic purposes courses—and can benefit all L2 learners, regardless of level or age.

6. Although language portfolios require little special preparation time, they do require you to think through how to integrate portfolios into the class process, the students' work, and the students' assessment. You must guide the process of self-assessment for it to be maximally beneficial. Initially, you will struggle with the students to define what will happen with the portfolios. Once their use has been established, ask permission to copy sample portfolios for subsequent students to examine, which will require some photocopying time at the end of the course. Evaluating the portfolios at the midpoint and end of the course will require a lot of time if the course grade depends upon this evaluation. And if teachers share evaluation duties, they will need extra time to read additional portfolios and work out shared standards of evaluation.

7. If you want to use language portfolios but have little extra time available, use them primarily for student self-assessment. Make the students largely responsible for the evaluation, which can begin in class with the students working together to provide modeling and feedback for each other. There is no set format for self-assessment, but try to develop thoughtful questions that lead the students to reflect on what they have done (see the Appendix).

References and Further Reading

Belanoff, P., & Dickson, M., (Eds.). (1991). *Portfolios: Process and product.* Portsmouth, NH: Boynton/Cook.

Black, L., Daiker, D., Sommers, J., & Stygall, G. (Eds.). (1994). *New directions in portfolio assessment.* Portsmouth, NH: Boynton/Cook.

Fradd, S., & Hudelson, S. (Eds.). (1995). [Special issue on alternative assessment]. *TESOL Journal, 5*(1).

Hewitt, G. (1995). *A portfolio primer: Teaching, collecting, and assessing student writing.* Portsmouth, NH: Heinemann.

Appendix: Sample Self-Assessment Questions

1. How would you compare your [area of language use] now with the way it was at the beginning of this course? Has your thinking about [area of language use] changed in any way? What pieces of work in your language portfolio show your development in this area? How did any revisions of these pieces contribute to your growth? In what specific ways has your language changed?
2. Everyone has a personal learning style. What kinds of activities in this course did you find useful for improving your [area of language use]? Which did you not find very useful? What pieces of work in your language portfolio show this?

Contributor

Kate Wolfe-Quintero is an assistant professor in the MA program in ESL and the PhD program in second language acquisition at the University of Hawai'i, in the United States. She is the director of the English Language Institute and the Hawai'i English Language Program.

Self-Assessment: Preparing an *English* Portfolio

Levels
High intermediate +

Aims
Reflect on progress
made in an English
course
Assess strengths and
weaknesses in learning
English
Establish goals and plans
for future independent
learning

Class Time
5 hours

Preparation Time
1 hour

Resources
Folders or binders

Many teachers have used writing portfolios to promote self-assessment among students and to focus students on progress they have made over time. Our assignment is somewhat different: It is an *English* portfolio. Done as the culminating activity for an integrated skills course, the English portfolio gives students a chance to look back over the work they have done during the course and reflect on what they have learned.

Procedure

1. Explain the concept of a portfolio to the students. If possible, bring in examples: an artist's portfolio, your own if you have one, or previous students' portfolios.
2. Describe what the students should include in their portfolio. Ask the students to go back over all the work they did during the course and decide which activities (either course work or experiences outside class) were the most meaningful for them and from which they learned the most.
3. Ask the students to choose one or two representative samples of their work during the term that show their ability to use English in each of the four skill areas: listening, reading, writing, and speaking. These samples should show their progress in English as well as their range of English use in the four skills.
4. For each piece of evidence that the students include, have them prepare a brief written explanation of what the sample shows about their progress and development as a user of English—in other words, how the sample is significant to their development in English. This written explanation is the cover sheet that introduces the evidence that they are presenting in their portfolio.

5. As part of the portfolio, have the students write a letter to you, their teacher, describing
   - the area in which they made the most progress this semester and the reason they improved so much
   - their strongest area in English and the reason they feel it is a strength
   - their weakest area in English and the reason they feel it is a weakness
   - their plan for improving their weakest area
   - an assessment of their effort in the class this term
   - the grade they would give themselves for the course
6. As a final organizing step, have the students prepare a table of contents for the portfolio and present the portfolio materials in a folder or binder.

Feedback and Scoring

1. Although you can assign a grade to the finished portfolio (see the Appendix), the true value of the activity for the students is the process of doing it; the value of the portfolio for you is the insight gained into your students' learning processes.

Caveats and Options

1. The materials in the portfolio can be direct or indirect evidence of the students' use of English. Examples of direct evidence are a list of books they read, a paper they wrote, and a videotape of an oral presentation they made. An example of indirect evidence is a short written description of a time they used English (e.g., a telephone call, a conversation with an American friend).
2. If you wish, have the students compile the materials for their portfolio outside class. We usually have them do this in class during the last week of the term.

References and Further Reading

Cohen, A. D. (1990). *Language learning: Insights for learners, teachers, and researchers*. Boston: Heinle & Heinle.

Graves, D. H., & Sunstein, B. S. (Eds.). (1992). *Portfolio portraits*. Portsmouth, NH: Heinemann.

McNamara, M. J., & Deane, D. (1995). Self-assessment activities: Toward autonomy in language learning. *TESOL Journal, 5*(1), 17–21.

Nunan, D. (1988). *The learner-centred curriculum*. Cambridge: Cambridge University Press.

O'Malley, J. M., & Chamot, A. U. (1990). *Learning strategies in second language acquisition*. Cambridge: Cambridge University Press.

Oxford, R. L. (1990). *Language learning strategies: What every teacher should know*. New York: Newbury House.

Scarcella, R. C., & Oxford, R. L. (1992). *The tapestry of language learning*. Boston: Heinle & Heinle.

Sharkey, J. (1994/1995). Helping students become better learners. *TESOL Journal, 4*(2), 18–23.

Appendix: Assessment Criteria for English Portfolios

The portfolios are read holistically with the three criteria below in mind, and a letter grade (A, B, C, D, or F) is assigned. In our course, the portfolio is equivalent to two major assignments.

1. Does the student include all the required material in the portfolio (representative samples of the student's work during the semester in listening, reading, writing, and speaking; a written explanation for each sample describing its significance to the student's progress in learning English; and a letter to the teacher describing the student's progress this semester, strong and weak areas, the student's plan for improving weak areas, and a self-assessment of work during the semester)?
2. Do the representative samples and the written explanations demonstrate the student's progress in learning English this semester?
3. Does the portfolio show evidence of the student's thoughtful reflection on the material and activities of the course and careful assessment of progress and learning in the course?

Contributors

Martha J. McNamara is a curriculum coordinator and an instructor at the English Language Institute (ELI), University of Akron, Ohio, in the United States, and Debra Deane is the director of the ELI at the University of Akron. They have both been teaching ESL for 20 years.

Portfolio Assessment of Newscast Listening

Levels
Intermediate +

Aims
Demonstrate ability to understand content and organization of TV news reports

Class Time
About 20 minutes

Preparation Time
Variable

Resources
Portfolio Record
Videotapes of news broadcasts
Video cassette players

Portfolios used to measure students' progress over time are well suited to assessing their ability to understand newscasts, which are readily available in most countries, are of high interest, and follow fairly clear organizational patterns. Over time, students can learn to recognize these patterns and develop a core of vocabulary common to newscasts. The television news–viewing portfolio was designed to measure students' progress in understanding and learning language, with repeated exposure to a set of activities.

Procedure

1. Build a library of videotaped local, national, or international news broadcasts. This step will take some time, but the advantages of selecting content and having one set of materials from which the students can choose reports will probably be worth the time.
2. Define the criteria you will use to allot points in the Portfolio Record (see the Appendix). For example, how many points will you assign for something that is factually correct but grammatically incorrect? What criteria will you set for partial credit on summaries and reactions?
3. Set the criteria for the end-of-term evaluation by determining how many total points will earn a grade of A, B, or C.
4. Give each student a copy of the Appendix or a similar Portfolio Record, and discuss each of the items and your criteria for evaluation.
5. Tell the students to watch a newscast from the video library outside class.
6. Have the students complete the portfolio record for a report as best they can during class time. Go over any difficulties the students have in understanding the activities.

7. Tell the students to continue watching newscast videos and filling out Portfolio Records. Explain that they will be assessed over time on both volume (how much they watch) and accuracy (how well they understand newscasts). Stress that the more they watch and try, the better they will become.

Feedback and Scoring

1. Throughout the course, review the students' portfolios, providing feedback on specific problems. You may need to spend classroom time on summarizing and other skills the students need to work on.
2. Base the final assessment on cumulative points as described above and in the Appendix.

Caveats and Options

1. Be sure the students have access to a video cassette player, media center, or self-access center with video systems. If all the students have access to video cassette recorders and televisions, consider allowing the students to record their own material for their portfolio. This reduces your control over content and makes assessment more difficult, but it might set the students on the road to more extensive listening.
2. At the end of the term, use the Understanding the Report section of the Portfolio Record as an achievement test of the students' abilities to get the main idea, recognize tone and organization, and summarize. Be careful, however, to avoid giving students with special content knowledge an advantage. To partially overcome this problem, have the students view at least three reports with different content.

Appendix: Portfolio Record

Directions: Complete these activities for reports from television newscasts. Write your answers on a separate sheet of paper. You do not have to do all of the activities! DO NOT FORGET TO WRITE ON YOUR ANSWER SHEET THE NAME OF THE NEWS PROGRAM, THE DATE YOU SAW THE REPORT, AND THE TIME YOU SAW THE REPORT.

Points received	Points possible		Activity
			Understanding the report
	15	1. Main idea	Write one sentence describing the main idea of the report.
	5	2. Tone	What is the tone of the report (e.g., serious, entertaining, informative, dramatic)?
	10	3. Organization	How is the report organized? ☐ Two (or more) sides of a controversy or issue are presented. ☐ One side of a controversy or issue is presented. ☐ There is no controversy in the report; something is described or talked about.
	35	4. Summary	Summarize the report in one paragraph.
	35	5. Reaction	Write one paragraph describing your reaction to the report.
			Language builders
	15	1. Listening vocabulary	Write down five words or phrases that you heard in the report. Provide a definition, a synonym or antonym, and a sentence demonstrating the meaning of each of the words or phrases.

Points received	Points possible		Activity
	15	2. Visible vocabulary	Write down in your native language the names of five things you saw in the report but do not know how to say in English. Use a dictionary to find the English word, and provide a definition or drawing. Then use the word in a sentence that demonstrates its meaning.
	20	3. Dictation	Write out 10 sentences from the report.

Contributor

Brian Asbjornson has worked in Japan as an instructor, a materials writer, and a curriculum developer. He has taught many lessons, published two textbooks, and thought a lot about how to measure his own efforts and those of his students. He is interested in the areas of testing, curriculum design, and self-access materials.

The Process of Business Communication

Levels
High intermediate +

Aims
See progress in terms of oral fluency and pragmatic competence

Class Time
Three 90-minute sessions

Preparation Time
2¹/₂ hours

Resources
Final exam
Video camera
Video cassette player
Background (e.g., pull-down screen)
Telephone
Restaurant props
Another teacher

In this activity, the students prepare written role plays in pairs or trios based on speech functions like those in the text *Speaking Naturally* (Tillit & Bruder, 1990). They learn the role plays and record them on videotape in front of their classmates, and the teacher plays the videos and provides corrective feedback. For the midterms and the final, the teacher corrects the written versions, gives corrective feedback in a follow-up session, and in a third session has the students perform the revised version of their dialogues. This procedure allows students to use a process approach to developing a communication activity and functions as a defossilization technique for students who have been in an English-speaking environment for some time. As the culminating activity of a video portfolio assembled during a 10-week English for academic purposes (EAP) session, this assessment activity enables students to see their progress in English in terms of oral fluency and pragmatic competence.

Procedure

1. At the end of the last class before finals week, distribute the final exam to the students (see the Appendix for a sample exam).
2. Administer the exam over several sessions. Use the entire week of finals, perhaps ending in a class party at the instructor's home to view the entire term's work on the video portfolios. The size of the class will determine the amount of class time needed. For an EAP class of 14–16 students working in pairs on 5- to 10-minute role plays,
   - Use a full 90-minute class to videotape the students' preliminary role plays.
   - Use another class period to give corrective feedback.
   - Use a third session for the final exam: the videotaping of the revised role plays.

Feedback and Scoring

1. Use the criteria described for the students under Grading in the Appendix to score the role plays.
2. Score with another teacher if at all possible. If you cannot find a colleague who is willing to help score the exams, consider having the students do peer evaluations to help you stay objective. I have found their assessments to be quite similar to my own on this type of activity.

Caveats and Options

1. Revise and alter the situation according to the needs and tastes of the participants.
2. Encourage creativity and ingenuity.
3. Persuade the students to rehearse their role plays enough that they do not need to use their scripts. Nothing looks worse on camera than a group of actors reading scripts. This problem should not be serious if you tell the students that they will be graded on fluency rather than memorization.
4. Have the students operate the camera so you can focus on evaluating and enjoying their performances.

References and Further Reading

Tillit, B., & Bruder, M. N. (1990). *Speaking naturally: Communication skills in American English*. Cambridge: Cambridge University Press.

Appendix: Situation and Task Description

Situation: A conversation in a U.S. restaurant between a Venezuelan businessman and a North American businesswoman. He is trying to import plastics to Venezuela from the company she represents in the United States. For the past several days, he has been taking a personal interest in her, and she has not discouraged him. In fact, after finding out that he is single, she has told him that she is divorced. However, after she gets up to go to the restroom, her cellular phone rings, the Venezuelan answers, and, of course, the woman's husband is on the line wondering why a male voice has answered the phone. When she returns to the table, she has a lot of explaining and apologizing to do. To make amends, she invites the man to play golf with her, her husband, and her sister, who is single and eligible.

Directions: With your partner, prepare a written dialogue based on the foregoing situation. Your script must include the following speech functions:

1. two openings (one in person and one on the phone)
2. thanking
3. apologizing
4. inviting
5. complimenting
6. interrupting
7. agreeing/disagreeing
8. expressing anger
9. two closings (one in person and one on the phone)
10. correct use of the English address system

Grading: Hand in your scripts at the end of the preliminary performance. At the beginning of the feedback session, I will return your corrected scripts to you as on the midterm exam. Rewrite them with the indicated corrections, practice them in the revised form, and hand them in to me on the day of the final performances. Although I will not require you to memorize your scripts perfectly, another teacher and I will grade you on the following areas:

Area	Points
1. Fluency (connected speech with appropriate hesitation sounds and gestures)	1–10
2. Accuracy (correct grammar, such as verb tenses, word order, articles and preparations; absence of global errors)	1–10
3. Pronunciation (easily intelligible; absence of global errors in pronunciation and intonation)	1–10
4. Vocabulary (correct use of words and phrases)	1–10
5. Appropriateness (correct use of each speech function)	1–10
Maximum points possible $(1–12 \times 5 = 12–60)$	100
$\times$ two instructors (2×100)	200

Note: You will have 5–10 minutes to perform your role plays, so be sure to time your practice sessions.

Contributor

J. Edward Cummins is an ESL instructor in the San Francisco Community College District, in the United States.

Pretty Popular Pupil Portfolios

Levels
Intermediate +

Aims
Assess personal writing
goals and
accomplishments

Class Time
About twelve 30-minute
sessions

Preparation Time
1–2 hours

Resources
Road map
Notebooks
Computers (optional)
Question for Precourse
Goal Setting
Portfolio Guidelines
handout
Group Activity handout
Questions for Individual
Postcourse Evaluation

Student portfolios give a more complete record of personal growth in writing than has traditionally been available, as the evaluation process includes the course as well as the degree of success and satisfaction experienced by the students. Through this approach to assessment, students learn about the writing process and develop an understanding of why they are proud of a particular piece of their writing. Attaining these goals leads in turn to learner independence.

Procedure

1. At the beginning of the writing course, give each student a notebook called a *free-writing journal*.
2. Bring a road map to class, and ask the students to name it. Discuss its functions.
   Make an analogy between the road map and goal setting: It is hard to get where you are going if you do not know where you want to go or think about how you are going to get there.
3. Pass out the Question for Precourse Goal-Setting (see Appendix A), and have the students answer the question by writing in their free-writing journal what they would like to learn in the writing course, what they would like to accomplish, or what they would like to be able to do when they finish.
4. Have the students share their answers with a partner, a small group, or the class.
5. In the last third of the course, or allowing for ten 30-minute sessions, hand out and discuss the Portfolio Guidelines (see Appendix B).
6. Have the students begin writing a showcase piece that includes an example of all the writing techniques covered in the course.

7. Have the students work as peer editors for a partner's final piece. Act as the final editor, leaving the writer's style intact and correcting only for spelling, capitalization, punctuation, and major problems in verb tenses that confuse the meaning of the piece.
8. Have the students produce final drafts of their showcase pieces and of selected portfolio pieces, answering your chosen questions about why the pieces were selected for inclusion.

Feedback and Scoring

1. During the last class meeting, display posters with the various techniques covered in the course (see Appendix C). Have the students rove around the classroom adding examples or definitions of the various techniques to the appropriate poster. Encourage collaboration.
2. During the last class, hand out class evaluation forms (see Appendix D), and have the students fill them out individually.
3. Distribute a class collection of portfolio pieces to each student.
4. Celebrate the accomplishments with a party.

Caveats and Options

1. Be sure to set aside adequate time for this form of assessment:
   - Allow two 30-minute sessions, one for precourse goal setting and one for postcourse evaluation.
   - Give the class roughly ten 30-minute sessions to select final portfolio pieces, edit them, and report why the pieces were chosen for inclusion.
   - For the assessment portion of writing workshop, set aside 1–2 hours to design the guidelines for successful portfolios, the goal-setting assignment, and the postcourse evaluation.
   - Allow additional time to assemble the finished portfolios if the students do not have access to computers.
2. This form of assessment was used in conjunction with a creative writing course for elementary school students (third through sixth grades) adapted from a program developed by Martha Clark Cummings at the Monterey Institute of International Studies, in the United States. The tasks involved in the evaluation and portfolio assessment are consistent with the types of tasks and assignments to which the students were exposed during the course of the program.

3. Rather than have the students write a final showcase piece from scratch to include in the portfolio, have the students revise an existing piece of writing to include additional techniques learned during the course.
4. Require the students to identify examples of the techniques learned in the course in various pieces in their portfolio.
5. The focus of this type of assessment is on helping the students recognize their strengths, enhancing their understanding of writing, and increasing their enjoyment of writing. An overemphasis on the editing process could defeat these goals.

References and Further Reading

Cummings, M. C. (1993, July). *Teaching your students to write creatively: How to use the techniques of professional writers in the ESL classroom.* Paper presented at a workshop at the Monterey Institute of International Studies, Monterey, CA.

Appendix A: Question for Precourse Goal Setting

Look at a road map. We need a map to get where we are going. Where do you want to go with Writing Workshop?

Appendix B: Portfolio Guidelines

To finish this class you need to put a portfolio together. For your portfolio you need three or more pieces of writing that you have done for this class. One of them should be your piece about leaving. You need to address the following about your portfolio pieces:

1. List two images or ideas in the piece that you particularly like.
2. Tell why you chose this piece: What is special about it for you? Why is it one of your best pieces, in your opinion?
3. Completely revise your leaving piece. This means you have to
   - include examples of everything you have learned about in this class
   - have a friend in class read it and tell you two things about it that she or she really likes and one thing she or she would like to know more about

- ask the teacher to write the same thing for you
- go through the *editing process*. The editing process is what you do last in writing something and includes at least checking for complete sentences and correct spelling, capitalization, and punctuation.

Checklist of Techniques Covered

These points must be included in the leaving piece. Remember: Use the new skills you've learned!

1.   Sensory details: What does it smell, sound, taste, feel and look like? Give details!
2.   Writing about emotions: Show, don't tell!
     - Use similes (e.g., *I feel like* ...; *Life is like a boat running the rapids*).
     - Use metaphors (e.g., *I was a shadow; I was a piece of paper being torn into a million pieces and thrown overboard*).
     - Describe an emotion that people are feeling by describing what they do rather than exactly what they are feeling (e.g., do not write, "He is mad" but "He looked fiercely at the letter, then slammed it down on the desk").
     - Choose one metaphor or image to use throughout the piece, such as references to the sea or a river.
     - Write *Anger is like* ... several times. Then change it in your piece of writing to *I felt like* ....
     - What emotion were you feeling? What color is that emotion for you? Make a list of things that are that color. Compare the feeling to those things (e.g., *I felt like a bull who was looking at a red flag*).
3.   Slow motion: Choose the most important part of your piece, and slow down the motion there. Describe the scene in great detail.
4.   Vivid verbs: Pick out some verbs in your piece that are not so vivid. Look in the thesaurus and replace them with vivid, strong verbs (e.g., *shriveled up, stabbed, galloped*).
5.   Repetition: Look for a line in your story that is very important. Look for somewhere else where you can repeat that line.

6. Alliteration (*sheep on a ship*): Find somewhere in your piece where you can play with the sounds in your sentences to use alliteration.

Appendix C: Group Activity for Postcourse Evaluation

Simile: Write a definition or give examples	Slow motion: Write a definition or give examples

Appendix D: Questions for Individual Postcourse Evaluation

Will you use the new skills you've learned? These are the different things you have learned about in Writing Workshop:

1.–8. [List points from Appendix C.]
9. Put words and sentences back together: We took words and made poems. We took sentences and put them in the right order.
10. Write a group story: We wrote a story about Valentine's Day in a group.
11. Dialogue journals
12. Free-writing journals: We spent 5 minutes writing whatever came into our heads about a topic.
13. Writing about music
14. Writing about a picture

What did you like the best?

What did you like the least?

What did you learn?

Contributor

Randi F. Freeman has taught EFL/ESL in Sweden and the United States. She has an MA in TESOL from the Monterey Institute of International Studies.

Using Portfolios in the EFL Reading Class

Levels
Any

Aims
Select reading texts for
the EFL class
Monitor reading process
and progress

Class Time
20-30 minutes

Preparation Time
None

Resources
Folders

One of the problems many EFL reading teachers face is that their students are bored or uncomfortable with the texts they have to read in class. Portfolios can be used to tailor reading texts to students' needs and preferences and to make students aware of their reading process and progress. Such portfolios can also serve as a text bank to help teachers write reading materials and tests.

Procedure

1. Give each student a folder. Ask the students to put in their folders copies of texts they would like to read. The texts can be selected from newspapers, magazines, textbooks, or other sources.
2. Once a week, have the students sit in a group of three, open their folders, and talk for 20-30 minutes about the texts they have collected. Make sure the students say where they found the texts and why they were selected. In addition, encourage the students to write comments to accompany the texts.
3. Ask the students to hand in their portfolios once a week. Take them home, look at the texts the students have selected, select one text from each folder, and write five content questions for each text. Put the questions in the folders.
4. Return the portfolios to the students, and give them 30 minutes to answer the questions in each of their folders.

Feedback and Scoring

1. Collect the portfolios as soon as the students finish answering the questions, and grade the reading exercises. Give 4 points for each correct and complete answer and partial credit (2 points) for each correct but ungrammatical answer. Write comments about each

student's performance on a separate sheet of paper, and put it in the folder.

2. Return the portfolios to the students. Let them look at the exercise and read your comments.
3. Set up individual biweekly interviews with the students to talk about their reading progress and performance.

Caveats and Options

1. Use some of the texts in the students' portfolios to write additional reading exercises for class and as homework or to test students in other courses. However, use other texts to write their reading tests.
   - Use the reading exercises to test vocabulary, cohesion, and other objectives in your reading program. Just be sure to select the right text for the purpose of the test. Adjust the grading system according to the number and complexity of the items.
   - Write the text contributor's name on the reading exercises and tests you use for the whole class. This will not only motivate the students to collect more reading material but also show them that you take their ideas into account.
2. Some of the texts may not fit the students' proficiency level. Adapt them, or use them in higher level courses.
3. Ask higher proficiency students to design reading exercises for the texts they have chosen (allow 30–40 additional minutes). Ask the other students to put the exercises in their folders, take the folders home, and write comments about the advanced-level students' exercises.

Contributor

Javier García is a member of the Language Department, School of Education, Central University of Venezuela. He has recently completed a master's program in EFL.

Writing Pictures

Levels
Beginning; elementary

Aims
Build skills needed in
content-class writing

Class Time
30 minutes

Preparation Time
15–20 minutes

Resources
Age-appropriate photos
or magazine cutouts

The assessment activity outlined here helps students develop their ability to use written language to communicate with an audience. Often the teacher is the only person students assume they are writing for, which can restrict the manner in which they write (Barnes, 1976). This activity gives an example of one genre of writing (description) that is consistent with many other writing tasks students encounter at the primary school level. It recycles the language and ideas from one student to two students and finally involves the whole class in each student's writing. Rather than being a source of evaluation itself, this writing activity contributes to a portfolio of writing that can serve both as a diagnostic tool, allowing the teacher to detect areas of difficulty for students during the term, and as a measure of writing achievement or proficiency at the end of the term.

Procedure

1. Give each student a photo or magazine cutout. Ask the students not to show their picture to the other students.
2. Give the students examples of the kinds of writing that this activity might produce. (The complexity of the writing will develop along with the students' writing skills.)
3. Tell the students that they will write about their picture and share that writing with the other students. Ask the students to begin writing about the picture without directly saying what is in it. Their goal is for someone who has never seen the picture to be able to understand and describe it based on what they write. Allow the students to write for approximately 10 minutes. Adjust the time allotted for writing to the age of the students.

4. Ask the students to sit with a partner, read the partner's paper, and guess what the partner's picture is or looks like.
5. Ask the students to return their partner's paper.
6. Gather the class together in a circle.
7. Have Student A read his or her paper, and then have the class decide on the best guess as to what the original picture is. Have Student A show the picture to the whole group.
8. Repeat Step 7 until each student has read his or her paper to the class.
9. Have the students attach the picture and their paper to their writing portfolios.

Feedback and Scoring

1. There are many ways to give feedback on a portfolio:
   - Give written feedback or do poster reviews (see Pretty Popular Pupil Portfolios, page 25).
   - Give feedback to parents as described in Planning Portfolios, page 6.
   - Set up a form of self-assessment like that described in ESL Language Portfolios: How Do They Work? (page 11).

Caveats and Options

1. Use this activity for any level by varying the pictures used. For advanced levels, use more complicated pictures requiring conclusions, or use pictures involving abstract ideas.
2. Reverse the process to have students demonstrate an understanding of the details or relationships in a reading passage. That is, have the students read a writing passage without seeing the corresponding picture, draw a picture or make a collage, and compare it with the original picture.
3. Ask the students to bring in pictures, or allow them to cut them out from magazines in class.

References

Barnes, D. (1976). *From communication to curriculum*. Middlesex, England: Penguin Books.

Contributor

Dana K. Petteys is an MA student in the Department of ESL, the University of Hawai'i at Manoa, in the United States.

◆ Journals, Logs, and Conferences

Using Journals for Self-Evaluation at Midterm

Levels
High beginning +;
university

Aims
Reflect on progress in
the course before formal
evaluation

Class Time
30–50 minutes

Preparation Time
None

Resources
Class syllabus

Students are often unprepared for midterm evaluations and conferences. This activity gives students the opportunity to review course goals and requirements and assess their standing in the class using the same criteria that the teacher must use.

Procedure

1. Ask the students to discuss the following questions in small groups: What is the purpose of midterm evaluations? Why are evaluations necessary? What do you like and dislike about evaluations?
2. Ask the students to review the class syllabus and discuss it in their groups.
3. Answer any questions the students have regarding the grading system. Make sure the students clearly understand the items that are considered for grading and the way the grades are computed.
4. Present the journal topic "Self-Evaluation of My Progress in This Course." Tell the students first to identify and write about their areas of strength (what they are doing well) in the course, using the syllabus to guide their writing, and, second, to identify and write about their areas of weakness (what they need to improve) in the course.
5. Allow the students to write for 20–30 minutes.

Feedback and Scoring

1. Respond to the journals either in writing or orally at the conference. Note any major discrepancies between your own evaluation and the student's self-evaluation. Discussing these differences in perception can provide the student with very valuable information.
2. After the students have received their midterm evaluations, ask the students to write in their journals on this topic: "My Plan for Improvement in This Course."

Caveats and Options

1. To help this activity proceed smoothly, ask the students to locate their syllabi in advance. Have extras on hand for students who have misplaced theirs.
2. If you do not use journal writing in your class, present this activity as a writing assignment in the form of a worksheet.
3. A good follow-up is an informal course evaluation. Ask the students to write about what has been most helpful and least helpful in the course and to suggest ways you might improve the second half of the course.
4. Consider using journal writing for a self-evaluation at the end of the course.

Contributor

Joan Blankmann teaches ESOL at Northern Virginia Community College in the United States.

Don't Talk About It, Write It Down

Levels
Any

Aims
Think and write about
the reading process and
attitudes toward reading
in English
Improve writing skills

Class Time
15–30 minutes

Preparation Time
None

Resources
Notebooks

Journal writing is no longer just a way to evaluate students' writing skills. It is also a powerful tool with which teachers can collect information on students' reading processes and strategies, assess those processes and strategies, and learn about students' attitudes toward and motivations for learning English.

Procedure

1. Distribute notebooks to the students, or ask each of them to buy one.
2. Once a week, ask the students to write in their notebooks comments, feelings, ideas, and likes and dislikes related to texts or topics in their reading class. Encourage the students to write specifically about the difficulties they encounter while reading texts written in English, the ways in which they think they can improve their reading strategies, and their attitudes toward learning English.
3. Ask the students to hand in the notebooks once a week. Read the students' comments, and write responses in the notebooks: Advise the students about their reading strategies, make comments on their reading process and progress, and add any other information you want to give your students.

Feedback and Scoring

1. If you wish, grade the students' journal writing.
2. Return the notebooks to the students so that they can read your responses, revise their written comments, and continue recording their ideas.
3. Allow the students to hand in revised versions of their English writing. Regrade them if you like, and return the journals to the students.

4. Keep a record of the students' comments. As the students become more used to writing their journals, bring up their ideas and comments as discussion points in class. Encourage other students to voice their opinions and ideas.

5. Take advantage of the students' comments to revise the objectives and materials used in your reading class to better suit the students' reading needs.

Caveats and Options

1. At first you will probably need to encourage and guide the students in writing in their journals. Be patient; they will eventually mention the topics you want to know about.

2. Have the students write in their journals at home.

3. Be sure to read and comment on the journals regularly.

4. Be careful when talking about the students' ideas and comments in class. You might be better off not mentioning the students' names but talking about the ideas and comments in general.

5. Combine the activity with the idea of a portfolio in which the students include not only written comments but also favorite texts and others they have read or plan to read.

6. Set up biweekly interviews with individual students to talk about their English reading process and progress, English writing skills, and any other topic you or the student desires.

Contributor

Javier García is a member of the Language Department, School of Education, Central University of Venezuela. He has a master's in EFL.

Self-Assessment: Keeping a Language Learning Log

Levels
High beginning +

Aims
Learn to self-assess
Identify strengths and
weaknesses in English
Determine which
language learning
strategies, materials, and
contexts work best
Document progress
Establish goals for future
independent learning

Class Time
1 hour

Preparation Time
1 hour

Resources
Handout
Spiral notebooks

This version of the language learning log is a regular, ongoing assignment. Students keep a record of situations in which they have used English (e.g., in class work, homework, or outside-of-class activities), describe them, and analyze their success or problems in comprehension and communication. Both the teacher and classmates can give feedback. Keeping a language learning log provides students with a concrete record of their activities and progress during the course.

Procedure

1. Ask the students what they think *self-assessment* means. Discuss with the students the rationale for having learners examine their own learning processes and evaluate their own abilities.
2. Explain what a learning log is and why it is helpful for the students to keep one.
3. Give the students each a notebook. Ask them to write three entries each day in their notebook about situations in which they use English in class activities, on homework assignments, or during out-of-class activities. Give examples of possible experiences that the students might describe: watching TV programs; listening to an audiotape in class; reading newspapers and magazines; writing letters, notes, or a journal in English; doing grammar homework exercises; and talking with friends or transacting business in a bank or post office. For each entry, tell the students to record the date, the activity, the amount of time they used English, the location, and a description and an analysis of their use of English. Tell the students to focus the analysis on the ease or difficulty of the activity and the reasons for that ease or difficulty.

4. Give the students about 30 minutes in class to start the first entry. To create a climate for extended, thoughtful writing, write in a notebook along with the students. In the last 10 minutes, circulate to spot-check entries and to answer individual questions.

5. At the end of each week, have the students evaluate their progress and make plans for future practice. To do this, they should reread their entries for that week, note where they succeeded and where they still have difficulties, determine their weak areas, and plan how to improve them during the following week.

6. Collect the logs and provide feedback.

Feedback and Scoring

1. Give three types of written feedback:
   - cheerleading feedback, in which you celebrate successes with the students or encourage them to persevere through difficulties
   - instructional feedback, in which you suggest strategies or materials to try, suggest ways to fine-tune strategy use, or instruct the students on their writing (e.g., help with word choice or selective grammar correction if a student requests help; we usually do not correct grammar in the entries).
   - reality-check feedback, in which you help the students set more realistic expectations for their language abilities if they are being too hard (or not hard enough) on themselves.

2. In addition to providing written feedback to the students, assess the quantity and quality of log entries:
   - For a quantity score, record the percentage of entries completed.
   - For a quality score, determine whether the students have adequately described the situations in which they used English and thoughtfully analyzed their success or difficulty in comprehending or communicating in English. We give letter grades (e.g., A, B, C) for the quality score.

Caveats and Options

1. Decide whether the students will log their experiences with English in their class work, on homework assignments, or in their extracurricular uses of English. This will depend on the environment in which the students are learning English and their access to native speakers and authentic materials outside class.

2. Determine which language skills or strategies your students will assess:
   - one language skill (e.g., reading, writing, listening, or speaking)
   - the use of a particular language learning strategy (e.g., guessing the meaning of vocabulary from context while reading or listening)
   - their success or failure with a specific teaching/learning point. For example, after writing an essay, the students could examine the way they used verb tenses in the essay and analyze the success or failure of their editing process.
3. Decide how often the students will write in their logs. Writing daily entries is a good way to begin the log assignment. Once self-assessment becomes routine for the students, they may write entries on a less frequent basis.
4. Consider how often you want to collect the logs and who will be reading the entries:
   - Collect them all once a week or every other week, or collect a few each day.
   - Develop log buddies or log study groups, and have the students read and respond to each other's log entries. These options enable the students to get peer feedback, and they lessen your paper load.

References and Further Reading

Bromley, K. (1995). Buddy journals for ESL and native-English-speaking students. *TESOL Journal, 4*(3), 7–11.

Carroll, M. (1994). Journal writing as a learning and research tool in the adult classroom. *TESOL Journal, 4*(1), 19–22.

Cohen, A. D. (1990). *Language learning: Insights for learners, teachers, and researchers*. Boston: Heinle & Heinle.

McNamara, M. J., & Deane, D. (1995). Self-assessment activities: Toward autonomy in language learning. *TESOL Journal, 5*(1), 17–21.

Nunan, D. (1988). *The learner-centred curriculum*. Cambridge: Cambridge University Press.

Nunan, D. (1995). Closing the gap between learning and instruction. *TESOL Quarterly, 29*, 133–158.

O'Malley, J. M., & Chamot, A. U. (1990). *Learning strategies in second language acquisition*. Cambridge: Cambridge University Press.

Oxford, R. L. (1990). *Language learning strategies: What every teacher should know*. New York: Newbury House.

Oxford, R. L. (1992/1993). Language learning strategies in a nutshell. *TESOL Journal, 2*(2), 18–22.

Scarcella, R. C., & Oxford, R. L. (1992). *The tapestry of language learning*. Boston: Heinle & Heinle.

Sharkey, J. (1994/1995). Helping students become better learners. *TESOL Journal, 4*(2), 18–23.

Contributors

Martha J. McNamara is a curriculum coordinator and an instructor at the English Language Institute (ELI), University of Akron, Ohio, in the United States. Debra Deane is the director of the ELI at the University of Akron. They have been teaching ESL for 20 years.

Passport: A Log

Levels
Intermediate +

Aims
Assess writing skills
through experiential
comments
Build confidence in
thinking processes
Express ideas freely
Identify learning
strategies and
weaknesses in written
communication
Lower affective filter
Get positive
reinforcement

Class Time
20 minutes

Preparation Time
1 hour

Resources
Passports
Passport Activities
handout
Weekly Feedback Form

In this assessment activity, the students improve their English writing skills and their grades by accomplishing several of a series of student-centered, communicative activities every day (or after each class). The activity is called *Passport* (after Hart, 1994) because the students bring the passports with them to class (or better yet, store them at school) and do something different with them in each activity.

Procedure

1. Tell the students they will each receive a "passport" with a list of activities. Give each of the students a passport (see Appendix A), and have them fill in their names in the place provided.
2. Read all the instructions in the passport to the students, and clarify any questions they have.
3. Pass out the Passport Activities handout (see Appendix B), and read all the activities aloud.
4. Tell the students they can begin working on any activity they want. Give them a specific deadline by which they must hand in all the passport activities, and tell them they will each receive a reinforcement award (e.g., stamps for activities done correctly and stickers for those done incorrectly) and that each activity is worth a different number of stamps or stickers depending on how well it is done.

Feedback and Scoring

1. Record the score for each task in the passport as shown in Appendix B.

2. Alternatively, score each writing assignment on the basis of the following categories, which describe the characteristics of each score between 1 and 5:

- 1 point: The writing has a personal style, and spelling and punctuation are not graded.

- 2 points: The writing has a personal style; the words chosen are clear; spelling and mechanics are correct.

- 3 points: The writing is coherent; all necessary information is included; words and phrases are combined effectively; spelling and mechanics are correct.

- 4 points: Use of supporting information is clear and convincing; the structure is clearly developed; the words chosen are clear, accurate, and precise; there are no errors in spelling or mechanics.

- 5 points: The writing shows very a complete and detailed structure; there is good use of words and expressions; words and phrases exhibit good patterns of language; there are no errors in spelling or mechanics.

Caveats and Options

1. Adjust the time limit for the activities depending on their difficulty.
2. If you wish, at the end of each week have the students write their own opinions of each week's class on a form (see Appendix C).
3. Write a response to each student's feedback form.

References and Further Reading

Hart, K. (1994). Passports give students responsibilities for their own learning. *TESOL Journal, 3*(4), 26–27.

Sharkey, J. (1994/1995). Helping students become better learners. *TESOL Journal, 4*(2), 18–22.

Appendix A: Sample Passport

Name:
Grade:
 	
PASSPORT
    PASSPORT
       PASSPORT
 	
Total grade:_____
	IMPROVE YOUR ENGLISH AND YOUR GRADE USING THE PASSPORT ACTIVITY!
	
	This is how to use it:
	1. Read all the activities you can choose from.
	2. Select the ones you prefer to do. The total number of points is 40, but you only have to complete 20.
	3. Each stamp = 1 point.
	4. Each activity is worth a number of stamps from 1 to 5.
	5. Your passport grade will be averaged with your classroom participation.
	6. Need help? Talk to the teacher. ☺

Appendix B: Passport Activities

Task 1: Talk to your teacher for a minute (free topic), and write a 25-word paragraph on what you two talked about. = 1 stamp

Task 2: Talk to any other English teacher. Write whether you understood him or her and how different it was from the conversation with your teacher. Free topic = 2 stamps; current event = 3 stamps

Task 3: Read something in the newspaper and talk about it for a minute in class. Then list those things you easily talked about as well as those that were a bit complicated for you. = 4 stamps

Task 4: Go to the library and
- Read an article and summarize it. = 4 stamps
- Read an article and write two questions that are answered in it. = 2 stamps
- Read an article and write the main idea. = 3 stamps

Task 5: Go to an English language library and look for an article in a magazine:
- Find 20 verbs in past tense. = 1 stamp
- Find 10 sentences in a specific verb tense. = 2 stamps
- Write three questions that are answered in the article. = 2 stamps

Task 6: Look for an encyclopedia and
- Write a 10-line comment about a famous personality. = 4 stamps
- Write about a concept (minimum 10 lines). = 2 stamps

Task 7: Bring the lyrics of a song (handwritten) to class. = 2 stamps. Try to write
- a description of the characters
- a description of the plot, setting, and message
- your personal opinion = 5 stamps

(Adapted from Sharkey, 1994/1995)

Appendix C: Weekly Feedback Form

Name _____ Week _____

1. How was class this week? Why? (Write complete sentences using the simple past tense and other tenses that you know.)

2. What was one activity (including one from the passport) that you liked? Why did you like it?

3. What was one activity (including one from the passport) that you did not like? Why didn't you like it?

4. How was the homework this week? Was there too much? too little?

5. Which activities (including those from the passport) would you like to do more of? Why?

6. Can you think of other activities to include in the passport?

Contributor

Jonice Tovar graduated as a teacher of English from the Universidad Pedagógica Experimental Libertador–IPB in Barquisimeto, Venezuela. Since then, she has worked with elementary, high school, and adult students in Caracas.

Eat, Drink, and Be Merry: Lunchtime Student Assessment

Levels
Any

Aims
Demonstrate
conversational ability in
a nonthreatening
environment
Teachers: Quickly
identify problem areas
and plan corrective
action

Class Time
30 minutes (lunchtime)

Preparation Time
15 minutes

Resources
Office
Chairs
Your own lunch

This activity is an evaluative or diagnostic tool that the teacher can use to gain a better picture of the students' abilities and progress. In a large conversation class, it is often difficult for the teacher to assess how the students are doing. The same few students usually volunteer to answer questions while everyone else sits quietly. By having lunch with the teacher in a relaxed atmosphere, students tend to open up more, providing a better opportunity to evaluate their progress in the class. The natural flow of the conversation allows the students to ask questions that they may have been afraid to ask in class. Students who are quiet and shy in the class tend to become less afraid of making mistakes during this time. After having lunch together, the students seem to open up more in class as well.

Procedure

Before the Class Begins

1. Prepare a sign-up sheet on which the students will schedule their lunches with you.
   - Start the lunch schedule after the first month of class to allow a better assessment of the students.
   - The number of students in the class will determine how many lunch hours to allot. To keep the assessment effective, have at least two and no more than four students sign up for each lunch hour.

First Day of Class

1. After you have explained the overall class requirements to the students, tell them that they will be required to bring a lunch and eat it with you at least once during the term (or semester, or year).

2. To reassure the students, explain that they will eat lunch in your office or in another location where they will not attract attention to themselves. Give directions to the location.
3. Show the students the sign-up sheet, and tell the students to schedule their lunches with you on a first-come, first-served basis. If your class is divided into groups, have all the members of the group come on the same day.
4. Stress that the lunch is a class requirement and that you want to have lunch to get to know the students better.

Lunch

1. Before the students arrive, make a mental list of their possible language weaknesses to help you guide the flow of the conversation and decide on areas to focus on during lunch.
2. When the students arrive, greet them and have everybody start eating. Start the conversation.
3. During lunch,
   - If necessary, ask each student questions to get the conversation going.
   - Gear the discussion to the level of the students. Control the flow and content of the conversation.
   - Keep in mind certain points you have covered or will cover in class, and manipulate the conversation to bring them in.
   - Bring subject matter covered in class into the conversation so that the students have the chance to practice using it. For example, have the students ask for and give information on such topics as their future plans, hopes, and dreams

Feedback and Scoring

1. If you wish, use this session as the basis for part of each student's grade. The grading will probably be more subjective than it is for a paper test. Because the students speak in a small group, you can more reliably evaluate their productive skills. Students whom you regard as average in class may turn out to have much higher productive skills at lunchtime because you have more time to interact and because the student-teacher ratio is much better than in class.

2. Evaluate the students' listening skills by judging the quality of the responses the students give to your questions and comments and to those of the other students.

Caveats and Options

1. I use this activity with groups of four students as my class is divided into groups. The more students there are eating lunch with the teacher, the livelier the conversation tends to be. The activity does not work well with too few students.

Contributor

David R. Neill, a lecturer at Okayama University of Science, has taught in Japan since 1983 at the university level. He graduated from the University of Hawai'i with a BA and MA in ESL. His research interests are video in the classroom, classroom design, and student motivation.

Part II: Alternative Feedback Perspectives

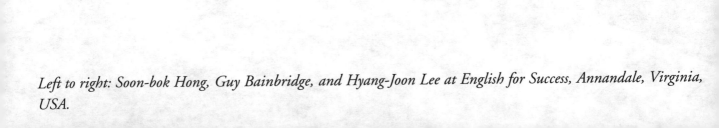

Left to right: Soon-bok Hong, Guy Bainbridge, and Hyang-Joon Lee at English for Success, Annandale, Virginia, USA.

Editor's Note

Traditionally, tests have been scored by teachers or by machines. Recently in language classrooms, some teachers have given over part of the responsibility for scoring to students. As you will see below, these student scoring methods take the form of self-assessments (in which students assess their own abilities, language production, or other aspects of their progress), peer assessments (in which students or groups of students rate or give feedback on each other's language performance, effort, or other aspects of their progress), or combinations of self-assessment and peer assessment. Note that in most of the contributions in this section, the teacher also assesses the students—probably a good idea in order to satisfy students' demand for the teacher's reactions and feedback. Below I consider each of these scoring methods in more detail.

Self-Assessment

Self-assessments are any assessments that require students to judge their own language abilities or language performance. Thus self-assessments provide some idea of how students see their own language development. Some of the advantages that advocates claim for using self-assessments are that they

- can be directly integrated into the language teaching and learning processes
- provide personalized assessments for each student
- are suitable for assessing learning processes while those processes are occurring
- require little extra time or resources
- involve students in the assessment process
- foster students' reflection on their own learning processes
- encourage student autonomy
- possibly increase students' motivation

The primary disadvantages of self-assessments are that
- the scoring is relatively subjective
- the accuracy of the scores may vary depending on skill levels (apparently, at least in some cultures, higher level students tend to underestimate their abilities)
- the scores may be particularly unreliable in high-stakes situations (e.g., final exams or placement tests)

This last issue should be less of a problem in the relatively low-stakes assessment situations typical in the classroom (where many sources of information will typically be combined in making decisions). The disadvantages can also be minimized by using a variety of other types of information (e.g., teacher assessments, peer assessments) in making decisions about the students' placement, progress, or promotion.

The section on self-assessments begins with three contributions that tell about students assessing themselves, their participation, and other aspects of their classroom performance (Assess It Yourself); integrating learner and teacher assessment (Learner Access to Assessment); and getting students to regularly assess their own oral language progress on video (Self-Evaluated Video).

Peer Assessment

Peer assessments are any assessments that require students to judge the language or language performance of one or more other students (or peers). Thus peer assessments give students some idea of how other students perceive their language performance—providing an external, yet relatively unthreatening, perspective. Some of the advantages that advocates claim for using peer assessments are that they
- can be directly integrated into the language curriculum
- provide personal feedback for each student
- require little extra time or resources
- involve students in the assessment process
- foster students' reflection on the learning processes that are going on
- encourage student cooperation

The primary disadvantages in using peer assessments are that
- The scoring is relatively subjective.
- The scores may be particularly unreliable in high-stakes situations (e.g., final exams or placement tests).
- Interpersonal problems may develop among the students over the ratings.

As with self-assessment, the problem of subjectivity can be minimized by using information from a variety of sources in making any important decisions about the students. Also like self-assessment, the problem of the unreliability of peer assessments in high-stakes decision making is probably less serious in the relatively low-stakes assessment situations typical of the classroom. However, the potential for interpersonal problems to develop out of peer assessments is very real. As mentioned above, the authors of the various contributions seem to favor two strategies for dealing with this issue: Either keep the peer assessors anonymous (which is often difficult), or train them to provide only positive and constructive feedback (a skill that might be useful in other parts of their lives).

The section on peer assessment offers five contributions that show how to give students a chance to assess their peers' voice and body language in a public speaking situation (So, How Did You Like My Presentation?), help students take an active role in constructively and positively evaluating the classroom presentations of other students (Teachers and Students Assessing Oral Presentations), encourage students to use all four skills in doing a book report (Active Book Report), involve students in being assessed while they are assessing other students (Assess the Assessors), and help create an atmosphere in which students and teachers evaluate spoken English together (Test Your Talk).

Self-Assessment Combined With Peer Assessment

Combining self-assessments and peer assessments is yet another strategy that contributors describe in this part of the book. Using both types of assessment has the advantage of providing two types of information to the students and the teacher: the students' view of themselves and the way their classmates perceive their language performance. In addition, these two sources of information are most often combined with the teacher's feedback, which provides a third perspective on the students' language performance. As mentioned twice above, combining information sources in this way is a good idea because it tends to minimize some of the disadvantages of assessments done by the students themselves or their peers.

The section on combining self- and peer assessments has 10 contributions that were designed for a variety of purposes: providing students with three-way feedback (self, peers, and teacher) on oral presentations (Oral Presentations: How Did I Do?), learning about negotiated interaction and communication breakdowns (I Said What?), practicing key skills for effective presentations (Gradually Growing Presentation Assessment), practicing communication skills in simulated systems interviews for professional purposes (How Well Did I Communicate?), reflecting on individual contributions to a group project (Self-/Peer/Teacher Assessment of Group Performance), encouraging the use of English outside the classroom (Walk-Talk Oral Tests), learning what types of public speaking will be important in their futures and developing criteria for those presentations (Interviews and Presentations for Clarifying Authentic Public Speaking Needs), effectively practicing dialogues using seven behaviors defined by the acronym SPEAKER (Peer Evaluation of Natural Communicative Behaviors With Dialogues), identifying criteria for effective writing and applying those criteria to their own writing (Activating Self-Assessment), and doing a multiskills group travel project (Self- and Peer Assessment of Group Participation).

References and Further Reading

Gardner, D. (1996). Self-assessment for self-access learners. *TESOL Journal, 5*(3), 18–23.

Lewis, J. (1990). Self-assessment in the classroom: A case study. In G. Brindley (Ed.), *The second language curriculum in action* (pp. 182–213). Sydney, Australia: National Centre for English Language Teaching and Research.

McNamara, M. J., & Deane, D. (1995). Self-assessment activities: Toward autonomy in language learning. *TESOL Journal, 5*(1), 17–21.

Murphey, T. (1994/1995). Tests: Learning through negotiated interaction. *TESOL Journal, 4*(2), 12–16.

Norris, J. M. (1996). *Performance and portfolio assessment (1985–1995): An extended annotated bibliography of sources useful for language teachers* (Research Note). Honolulu: University of Hawai'i, Second Language Teaching and Curriculum Center.

◆ Self-Assessment
Assess It Yourself

Levels
Intermediate +

Aims
Get involved in
assessment

Class Time
5–10 minutes

Preparation Time
About 2 hours

Resources
Self-assessment handout

This activity is designed to involve students in assessing themselves, their classroom participation, and other aspects of their learning. Traditionally, teachers have jealously guarded their prerogative to assess student performance. I suggest that this right can be shared if teachers are willing to trust their students to responsibly assess themselves. This assessment activity takes only a few minutes at the end of an instructional unit, course, project, semester, or academic year.

Procedure

1. Prepare a handout containing the criteria for self-assessment (ideally with input from the students).
2. Share the criteria with each class at the beginning of instructional units, the course, the project, the semester, or the academic year.
3. Have the students assess themselves at the end of the period based on the criteria.
4. Incorporate these self-assessments in your overall evaluation.

Caveats and Options

1. Have adult learners commit to self-assessment based on a learning contract (see Moskowitz, 1978; Renner, 1993).
2. For beginners, make the guidelines available and discuss them in their L1(s).
3. Apply the self-assessment to such areas as class participation, project completion, perceived progress, and skill acquisition.

References and Further Reading

Genesee, F., & Upshur, J. A. (1996). *Alternatives in second language assessment.* Cambridge: Cambridge University Press.

Jarvis, P. (1988). *Adult and continuing education: Theory and practice.* London: Routledge.

Moskowitz, G. (1978). *Caring and sharing in the foreign language class: A sourcebook on humanistic techniques*. Rowley, MA: Newbury House.

Renner, P. (1993). *The art of teaching adults: How to become an exceptional instructor and facilitator*. Vancouver, Canada: Training Associates.

Contributor

Doug Tomlinson teaches EFL at the junior college and university level in Japan. He has also taught ESL in his native Canada.

Learner Access to Assessment

Levels
Any

Aims
Become aware of own
development
Perform an integrated
teacher-learner
assessment
Produce a record of
progress
Be assessed during
classroom tasks

Class Time
40 minutes

Preparation Time
20 minutes

Resources
Listening, reading,
speaking, or writing task
Assessment Sheet

Assessment should not be separate from teaching but should be a natural step within the teaching and learning process. In fact, assessment can give teachers one more opportunity to recycle input on content and have learners put that content into practice. The difference between this kind of assessment and any other practice task is that the learners have already worked with the content and will be asked to assess their performance after carrying out the task; teachers will do the same. The advantages of this type of assessment are that it is ongoing, is built into classroom tasks, provides a record of progress for learners and teachers, and allows learners to be aware of their development.

Procedure

Listening or Reading Assessment

1. Follow the usual steps for prelistening and prereading exercises.
   - Use visual aids to help the learners forecast what the content of the task will be.
   - Guide the learners to create a hypothesis about the content by using headings, subheadings, and illustrations.
   - Elicit from the students what they think they will have to find out about the material.
   - List the questions the students will have to answer on the blackboard. At this stage, ask questions that concern a general understanding of the content.
   - Make sure the learners understand the prelistening or prereading questions.
2. Expose the learners to the material.
3. Give the learners time to answer the questions individually.
4. Check the answers with the whole group; motivate peer correction and justification of responses.

60

5. Elicit from the students some detailed information presented in the task. Have the students do a second listening or reading to look for these details.
6. Repeat Steps 3 and 4.

Speaking or Writing Assessment

1. Follow the usual steps for prespeaking and prewriting exercises.
   ● Use audiovisual aids to help the learners get ideas for carrying out the task.
   ● Guide the learners to elicit topics for discussion or writing. List these topics on the blackboard.
2. Elicit from the learners the kinds of structures and vocabulary they will need to carry out the task.
3. Review any language items necessary.
4. Give clear instructions on what the students are to do and how they are to do it.
5. In a speaking assessment,
   ● Give the learners time to think about what they are going to say. Place them either in pairs or in small groups.
   ● Be available to help the learners with any vocabulary or structures they need during the task.
   ● Have the learners discuss their performance with their peers.
6. In a writing assessment,
   ● Have the learners do the writing assignment.
   ● Have the learners exchange papers, and check the use of structures and vocabulary and the understanding of content. Caution them to give only constructive or positive feedback.
   ● Help them if necessary.

Feedback and Scoring

1. Pass out the Assessment Sheet (see the Appendix). Explain how to fill it out. For example, if the assessment is based on a listening task involving two people talking about the advantages and disadvantages of living in New York and Los Angeles, the students might fill in the Content space in the Assessment Sheet with *Comparing cities* and the Skill space with *Listening*.

2. Discuss with the students how they should assess themselves; how much of the activity they think they should have understood; and what they believe should be considered an excellent, very good, good, and fair performance. For example, for the listening task in Step 1, the following rubric might work: *Consider your performance excellent if you were able to list all the advantages and disadvantages mentioned. Consider your performance very good if you were able to list more than half of the advantages and disadvantages. Consider your performance good if you were able to list half of them.*

3. Give the students a couple of minutes to grade themselves and write about their development.

4. Collect the Assessment Sheets. After class, go over the learners' self-assessments. Write down your opinion of their performance and ways they can improve (e.g., what they need to review or practice more).

5. Return the Assessment Sheets to the learners in the next class. Make yourself available to the students during and after class to discuss their assessments.

Caveats and Options

1. Integrate the use of two or more skills in the same task and assessment (e.g., listening and speaking, reading and speaking, listening and writing).

2. A suggested schedule for doing this assessment is after every 10 hours of class.

3. Some students may resist assessing themselves, believing that assessment is only valid if it comes from the teacher. Explain that you will assess their performance but that it is essential for them and for you to know how they themselves feel about their progress.

References and Further Reading

Brindley, G. (1989). *Assessing achievement in the learner-centred curriculum*. Sydney, Australia: National Centre for English Language Teaching and Research.

Lewis, J. (1990). Self-assessment in the classroom: A case study. In G. Brindley (Ed.), *The second language curriculum in action* (pp. 187–213). Sydney, Australia: National Centre for English Language Teaching and Research.

Appendix: Assessment Sheet

Fit six copies of the sheet on one piece of paper to hand out to the students.

Student's name:

Group:

Teacher's name:

Date: Skill:

Content:

Student's assessment:

Teacher's comments:

Contributor

Magali de Moaes Menti has been an EFL teacher for 16 years and a teacher trainer for 8 years, in Brazil. Her main interests are teacher education and learning processes.

Self-Evaluated Video

Levels
Any

Aims
Use video to assess
conversational progress

Class Time
Variable

Preparation Time
10–15 minutes

Resources
One or more video
cameras
Two or more video
cassette recorders
Videotapes
Timer (optional)

In this activity, students regularly view their own conversations on video to assess themselves in the short and long term. Each week, students practice certain conversational strategies with the intention of using them in a weekly videotaped conversation. The use of technology means that the teacher can give each student a videotape to take home and evaluate immediately. The teacher keeps a master videotape of all conversations that can be used to assess the students' progress later in the course.

Procedure

1. Connect two video cassette recorders to each video camera 10–15 minutes before class.
2. Make sure the students each have a videotape with their name written on it. Ask the students to wind their videotapes to the end of the last recording and to put them on the front table at the beginning of each class.
3. Allow the students to do a warm-up conversation with their partner before anyone is videotaped.
4. Select two videotapes at random, call out the students' names, and place the videotapes in the video cassette recorders attached to Camera 1. Have the two students sit or stand in front of Camera 1.
5. Repeat Step 4 for the remaining cameras and recorders.
6. Instruct the other students to find partners to practice conversing with while they are not being videotaped and to change partners every 5 minutes. In this way, they can have six or seven partners in one class.
7. Start the cameras and recorders, and tell the students to begin. If possible, set a timer for 5 minutes.

8. After 5 minutes, stop the cameras and recorders, and give the students who have just been filmed their videotapes to view at home.

9. Repeat Steps 4, 5, 7, and 8 until all the student pairs have been videotaped.

Feedback and Scoring

1. In a class that meets three times a week for 45 minutes, for example, we teach certain material the first two classes, videotape the students using it in the third class, and have the students take their videotapes home to evaluate.

2. Give the students a focus for viewing their videos at home that encourages them to notice what they are actually doing. For example, ask them to write a short summary and answer the following questions: What did you do well? What strategies did you use? What did your partners do or say that you could use? What mistakes did you make, and what are the corrections? What specific things do you want to do differently next week?

3. In the next class, have the students share their impressions in pairs with their partners, or in groups with their partners and others.

Caveats and Options

1. Note that the procedure will vary depending on the syllabus, the number of students, and other factors. With two video cameras, the third class meeting of each week will be similar to the one described above. It usually takes about 45 minutes to go through a class of 20 students.

2. At the end of the semester, the students have about 10 segments of their conversations on one videotape. Ask them to rewind their videotapes, look at all the segments, and write a progress report (their own assessment). Look at the first week's master videotape, and compare it with that of the last week to assess the changes in the students' performance.

3. Suggest that the students view their videos with classmates or friends and family, which seems to give the students a more objective, third-person perspective on themselves.

References and Further Reading

Murphey, T., Kenny, T., & Wright, M. (1995). Learner self-evaluated video. *Academia Literature and Language, 59*, 163–201.

Contributor

Tim Murphey teaches and learns at Nanzan University in Nagoya, Japan, and does research on alternative learning forms.

◆ Peer Assessment
So, How Did You Like My Presentation?

Levels
Intermediate +

Aims
Evaluate peers on use of
voice and body in a
public-speaking course

Preparation Time
Variable

Resources
Evaluation form

Good speech presentation skills include speaking at an appropriate volume and rate, using pitch effectively, enunciating clearly, standing with a solid posture, using gestures carefully, and making good eye contact. That is a lot for a speaker to remember, but once demonstrated, each skill individually is relatively easy to evaluate. Giving students the opportunity to evaluate their peers on each of the skills above not only gives them an important sense of responsibility for their fellow students' progress, but also forces them to concentrate on the skills during their own presentations.

Procedure

1. In the first one or two meetings of the course, concentrate on voice and body skills. The voice skills are
   ● volume: The voice should be just loud enough for those in the back of the room to hear without straining.
   ● rate: Too many learners feel that better fluency means speaking faster; slow them down.
   ● pitch: Show them that the tone of the voice can be very important in conveying meaning.
   ● enunciation: Tongue twisters are an enjoyable way to practice enunciation.
   The body skills are
   ● posture: Feet should be spread shoulder-width apart, weight should be equally distributed, and students should not sway or lean.

- gestures: Gestures should be used only to make important points; students should beware of touching the hair and scratching.
- eye contact: In a class of 30 or fewer it should be possible to make eye contact with everyone, a skill that should be practiced.

2. To save paper, fit more than one evaluation form (see the Appendix) on each sheet of paper. Give each student enough evaluation forms for the day's presentations.
3. Tell the students to rate the seven voice and body skills above on a scale of 1 (meaning *room for improvement*) to 5 (meaning *excellent*).
4. Urge the students to write critical comments on the skills, especially when they assign low scores, and general comments on the presentation as a whole (e.g., "Your voice was a little too soft"; "We made eye contact five times! Great!" or "I couldn't understand some of the words").
5. Collect the evaluation forms at the end of class, giving the students extra time to add comments if needed.

Feedback and Scoring

1. Average the student-assigned scores for each of the seven skills to get peer scores for each speaker.
2. Combine all the comments on each speaker to get peer comments.
3. List the peer scores and peer comments, along with your scores and comments, on a page or two to give to the presenters at the next class meeting. Keep the peer scores and peer comments anonymous.

Caveats and Options

1. Note that your preparation time may vary considerably. It may take as little as 10–15 minutes to prepare copies of the evaluation form but an additional 5–10 minutes per student to average the scores and collate the comments.
2. Add a third category, content, to the evaluation form. Have the students evaluate their peers on, for example, their introduction, body, and conclusion and the general interest of their presentation. This part of the evaluation will be more difficult for the students and perhaps should wait until they are more competent in these areas.

3. In a debate class, use the same technique, with the addition of a persuasiveness category. As feedback, give the presenters their persuasiveness scores and those of their opponent so that they know who the winner was, but do not show them their opponent's style skill scores.
4. Use the evaluations to assess the evaluators themselves. Judge whether they really understand how to recognize good speech skills and whether their comments show that they are adequately following the presentations.

Appendix: Evaluation Form

Evaluator: _____ Presenter: _____ Title: _____

Skill	Poor	Fair	Good	Great	Excellent	Comments
Voice						
Volume	1	2	3	4	5	
Rate	1	2	3	4	5	
Pitch	1	2	3	4	5	
Enunciation	1	2	3	4	5	
Body						
Posture	1	2	3	4	5	
Gesture	1	2	3	4	5	
Eye contact	1	2	3	4	5	

General comments:

Contributor

Jeff Johnson teaches at Kanagawa Prefectural College of Foreign Languages in Yokohama, Japan.

Teachers and Students Assessing Oral Presentations

Levels
Intermediate +

Aims
Become aware of how an audience perceives a presentation
Actively evaluate oral presentations

Class Time
15–20 minutes; 5–10 minutes/presentation

Preparation Time
20 minutes

Resources
Evaluation form

In this assessment activity, students give oral presentations (of any sort), individually or in groups, while the teacher and the students in the audience share equally in evaluating them. Students are encouraged to evaluate others constructively and positively.

Procedure

1. Assign the students oral presentations of any kind (e.g., speeches, group presentations, role plays). Explain any requirements.
2. Before the presentations, talk with the students about the characteristics of a good oral presentation. For example, explain the importance of content and organization, eye contact, body language, facial expression, enthusiasm, and clarity of speech. Clearly explain your rating system and its connection to these characteristics. Give an oral presentation as a model.
3. On the day of the presentations, give the students the evaluation form that they will use to evaluate the presenter(s) (see the Appendix). Explain the scoring system. Ask them to be careful in rating each presentation and in giving comments. Tell them to point out both positive aspects of each presentation and any aspects that need improvement. In addition, ask them to remember their highest compliment to each student or group presenter.
4. Ask a student or group to give the presentation, and rate the student or group on any scale you choose with a maximum possible score of 50 points (e.g., the scales found in Mendelsohn, 1991/1992) while the students in the audience rate the student or group using the evaluation form. Allot portions of the 50 points to subsections in proportions that reflect the relative importance you attach to each.

5. After the presentation, give the students in the audience time to rate the presentation and write comments on the student evaluation forms. Collect them.

6. Repeat Steps 3–5 for additional students or groups giving oral presentations that day.

Feedback and Scoring

1. When all the presentations for the day are concluded, draw a table on the blackboard, making open spaces for each student or group that presented. Write the name of each student or group in a space. Ask all the students to come forward in a kind of free-for-all and write their highest compliment for each student or group presenter.

2. Go over the compliments, and praise both the presenters and the audience.

3. After class, tally the students' scores and take notes on the students' comments. (Use a scale such as *excellent* = 5; *very good* = 4; *good* = 3.5; *fair* = 3; *poor* = 2, depending on your grading scale.) Average the scores for each student or group presenter. Multiply the average by 10 to get the student rating. Add that number to your own rating. Write the total score on your evaluation form, and add your most important comments.

4. The next day, give the students' evaluation forms and your assessment (with the total score and your comments) to the students or groups that presented the day before. Praise all the positive aspects of the students' presentations and evaluations.

Caveats and Options

1. If your class includes more than 25–30 students, you will probably want to modify the activity to have the students work on their ratings in groups. Assign these groups to do one of the following, for example: (a) send a representative to the blackboard to write either all the compliments from group members or a single, mutually chosen compliment, (b) give compliments to different presenters, or (c) take turns in groups in coming to the blackboard.

2. Use your notes on the students' comments as the basis of further discussion of exemplary oral presentations. If possible, assign the students additional presentations so that they can put the ideas into practice.

References and Further Reading

Mendelsohn, D. J. (1991/1992). Instruments for feedback in oral communication. *TESOL Journal, 1*(2), 25–30.

Appendix: Evaluation Form for Students in the Audience

Name of student or group _____

Please rate the student or group that presented by circling the word that describes their work best:

Excellent   Very good   Good   Fair   Poor

Please add your comments:

Contributor

Kristy King has taught English in the United States and currently teaches at Asia University in Tokyo, Japan.

Active Book Report

Levels
Intermediate +

Aims
Use all four modes of
language in a book
report

Class Time
$2\frac{1}{2}$ hours

Preparation Time
2 hours

Resources
Books
Peer Assessment Sheet
Book Review Write-up
Sheet
Book-Share Presentation
Instruction Sheet
Book-Share Presentation
Evaluation Sheet
Active Book Report
Final Grade Sheet

People generally think of preparing a book report as a boring process involving a student writing a paper after reading a particular book. However, the innovative approach to book reports in this activity encourages reading in class and assesses the reading. Rather than writing just one final paper for the book report, various activities encourage students to read and enjoy reading. Students participate in the process of assessment by evaluating peers. This way, the final score that the students receive is a joint product. This practice encourages the students to perform in class to the best of their abilities.

Procedure

1. Ask the students to choose a book they want to read. If necessary, have them visit the school library to find one.
2. Allow the students an appropriate amount of time to read the book; this time may vary from class to class.
3. Train the students to ask questions of other students about a book they have read.
4. Ask the students to keep a journal on their reading. Set up a schedule so that they write in their journal about their book at least three times before completing the book.
5. Ask the students to choose a book-share partner.
6. The day the students are to have completed their reading, have them get together with their partner and share their reading by asking each other questions.
7. Pass out the Peer Assessment Sheet (see Appendix A). Have the students fill it out for their book-share partner.

8. Hand out and go over the Book Review Write-up Sheet (see Appendix B) to make sure the students understand the assignment. Assign a written book review for homework.

9. On the same day, hand out and go over the Book-Share Presentation Instruction Sheet (see Appendix C). Assign a book-share presentation for homework.

10. In the next class, have the students deliver their book-share presentations.

Feedback and Scoring

1. As you evaluate each student's presentation, have two of the student's peers evaluate along with you, using the Book-Share Presentation Evaluation Sheet (see Appendix D).

2. Calculate the students' total scores with the Active Book Report Final Grade Sheet (see Appendix E).

Caveats and Options

1. Be sure to train the students to be sharp raters. Caution them not to simply give the best possible score to their peers, disregarding the quality of the discussion or the presentation.

References and Further Reading

Freeman, Y. S., & Freeman, D. E. (1992). *Whole language for second language learners.* Portsmouth, NH: Heinemann.

Appendix A: Peer Assessment Sheet

Partner's name_____ Date_____
Title of book_____
Author_____

	No		Yes
1. My partner knows the plot of the book.	0 1 2 3
2. My partner knows the characters in the book.	0 1 2 3
3. My partner knows the personalities of the characters.	0 1 2 3
4. My partner knows the conflict of the book and how it got solved.	0 1 2 3
5. My partner knows the theme of the book.	0 1 2 3
6. My partner can tell me the events of the book sequentially (in correct time order).	0 1 2 3
7. My partner can answer my questions about the book.	0 1 2 3
8. My partner explains himself or herself clearly.	0 1 2 3
9. My partner read and understood the book.	0 1 2 3
10. Working with my partner was helpful to my understanding of the book.	0 1 2 3

Total points____ /30

Appendix B: Book Review Write-up Sheet

You have just finished reading a book of your choice. I hope you enjoyed your book! Now, it's time for you to put your enjoyment in writing. This book review, however, is a little different from other book reviews. I don't want you to tell me what the plot, characters, climax, or the theme of the book is. Rather, I want you to be creative.

You are presenting the book to the readers in a very different way. You can pretend to be the author trying to urge readers to buy the book, you can create a different character for your book, or you can write a totally different ending of the story to suit yourself! Your book review has to do with the book that you read, but the way you present the book is up to you. Be creative! Have fun with it!

Appendix C: Book-Share Presentation Instruction Sheet

Now that you have finished the book, share the story with the rest of the class through a Book-Share Presentation. The object of the presentation is to encourage your classmates to want to read the book that you read. You can accomplish this by acting out your favorite part of the book or making the class really curious by telling them just a little bit about your book. You can even turn yourself into a book and tell the class what fun you (the book) can be! Be creative! Have fun with it!

Appendix D: Book-Share Presentation Evaluation Sheet

Presenter's name_____

	No			Yes
1. The presenter got the audience's attention.	0	1	2	3
2. I could hear the presenter.	0	1	2	3
3. I could understand the presenter.	0	1	2	3
4. The presenter used appropriate gestures.	0	1	2	3
5. The presenter made good eye contact.	0	1	2	3
6. The presenter did not move around unnecessarily.	0	1	2	3
7. The presenter had all the materials necessary.	0	1	2	3
8. The presentation was creative.	0	1	2	3
9. The presentation held the audience's attention until the end.	0	1	2	3
10. I think this book would be enjoyable to read.	0	1	2	3

Appendix E: Active Book Report Final Grade Sheet

Component	Points Earned	Points Possible
1. Journal (10 points for each of three entries): _____ + _____ + _____ =		30
2. Peer Assessment Sheet (book-share with a partner): Total points _____ /2 =		15
3. Book Review (write-up)		25
4. Book-Share Presentation Evaluation: _____ + _____ + _____ /3 Points earned from Peer Peer Teacher		30
Total points		100

Contributor

Janice Lee taught ESL and Korean at International MidPac Institute for 3 years and is now teaching writing and conversation at the Hawai'i English Language Program in Honolulu, in the United States. She holds a BEd in secondary education with an emphasis in ESL.

Assess the Assessors

Levels
Intermediate +

Aims
Become aware of
assessment procedures
Recognize the
difference between
written and spoken
language
Appreciate the
importance of oral
negotiation

Class Time
Variable

Preparation Time
1 hour

Resources
Four checklist handouts

In this activity, students are assessed while they are assessing their classmates. The whole class is involved in the activity, and students have a chance to practice evaluating others' performance, which reinforces their self-esteem.

Procedure

1. Have the students each write a short essay, either in class or as homework, on a different topic that can be presented orally or in poster form. Assign half the group to prepare their essays as 3- to 5-minute oral presentations, and the other half, as small posters. Specify the date for the oral and poster presentations. If the class is small, hold both presentations on the same day.

2. Hand out one Essay Checklist (see Appendix A) to each student. Have the oral presentation students each exchange essays with a poster student and read and evaluate each other's essays, using the criteria in the checklist. Tell the students that you will be evaluating their evaluations.

3. Collect the essays and the filled-in checklists. Read the essays, and fill in your own checklist for each.

4. On the oral presentation day,
   - Remind the evaluators that they are free to ask questions.
   - Hand out one Oral Presentation Checklist (see Appendix B) to each of the poster students.
   - Have the oral presentation students give their presentations. Tell the poster students to fill in the checklist for the presentation of the student whose essay they read. During the presentations, fill in your own checklist for each speaker.

- Hand out the essays, and have the evaluators once again read the essay they previously evaluated. At the end of the activity, collect the filled-in checklists and the essays.

5. On the poster presentation day, give out one Poster Presentation Checklist (see Appendix C) to each of the oral presentation students, and have them evaluate the posters and fill in the checklist for the poster prepared by the student whose essay they read. Go around and fill in your own checklist for each poster. Have the presenters stand by their posters and answer questions from the evaluators. At the end of the activity, collect the filled-in checklists.

6. Using the Teacher's Checklist (See Appendix D), evaluate the filled-in essay, oral, and poster presentation checklists. In all, you will evaluate two checklists for each student (one for an essay and one for a presentation). Hand all the checklists (including the Teacher's Check-list) back to the evaluators in the next class meeting.

7. Lead the class in a discussion of the evaluation process, the differences between assessing written and spoken work, the importance of being able to question the presenter, and other relevant issues.

Feedback and Scoring

See Steps 3–6 of the Procedure

Caveats and Options

1. In small classes, have each student evaluate two or more presentations.
2. If you wish, cooperate with the students in preparing the checklists before you start the activity.
3. Use this activity to grade the performance of the students as writers and as presenters.

Circle a number for each item, and write your comments in the spaces provided.

Appendix A: Essay Checklist

	Excellent ↔ Poor
1. Is the *topic* clearly identified? Comment:	5 4 3 2 1 0
2. Is there a *unity* of ideas? Comment:	5 4 3 2 1 0
3. Is there *coherence*? Are the ideas presented in a logical way? Comment:	5 4 3 2 1 0
4. Is the *style* of writing interesting and attractive? Comment:	5 4 3 2 1 0
5. Is *language* used correctly? Comment:	5 4 3 2 1 0
6. What did you like about this essay?	
7. What did you dislike about this essay?	

Appendix B: Oral Presentation Checklist

Circle a number for each item, and write your comments in the spaces provided.

Excellent ↔ Poor

1. Was the *topic* clearly identified?   5 4 3 2 1 0
   Comment:

2. Was there a *unity* of ideas and *coherence*?
   Were the ideas presented in a logical and
   convincing way?   5 4 3 2 1 0
   Comment:

3. Were the speaker's *movements, gestures,*
   intonation, and use of *visual aids* (if any)
   appropriate? Was the speaker self-confident? 5 4 3 2 1 0
   Comment:

4. Did the speaker involve the *audience* in
   the presentation?   5 4 3 2 1 0
   Comment:

5. Was *language* used correctly?   5 4 3 2 1 0
   Comment:

6. What did you like about this presentation?

7. What did you dislike about this presentation?

8. Did the presentation help you understand the information given in
   the essay? Why or why not?

Appendix C: Poster Presentation Checklist

Circle a number for each item, and write your comments in the spaces provided.

Excellent ↔ Poor

1. Is the *topic* clearly identified?   5 4 3 2 1 0
   Comment:

2. Is there a *unity* of ideas and *coherence*? Are the
   ideas presented in a logical and convincing way?   5 4 3 2 1 0
   Comment:

3. Are the *graphical representations* appropriate?   5 4 3 2 1 0
   Comment:

4. Is the *design* visually attractive?   5 4 3 2 1 0
   Comment:

5. Is the poster *self-explanatory* (or did you
   have to ask questions?)   5 4 3 2 1 0
   Comment:

6. What did you like about this poster?

7. What did you dislike about this poster?

8. Did the presentation help you understand the information given in
   the essay? Why or why not?

Appendix D: Teacher's Checklist

Are all items answered appropriately and adequately?	Yes No
Are the circled grades consistent with the comments?	Yes No
Are the comments relatively consistent with your notes on the essay/presentation?	Yes No
Do the comments show an understanding and appreciation of the essay/presentation?	Yes No

Comments:

Contributors

Selda Mansour has a BA in English language teaching and has taught English for academic purposes. Wisam Mansour is an assistant professor of English at the Applied Science University in Amman, Jordan.

Test Your Talk

Levels
Any

Aims
Evaluate spoken English
with the teacher

Class Time
30-40 minutes to
collect oral data
1-2 hours for checklist
analysis

Preparation Time
10-15 minutes

Resources
Audiotape recorders and
audiotapes, or video
cameras, -tapes, and
players
Assessment Scale

Letting the students talk about what they want to talk about helps to motivate them. Limiting and extending the time students get to talk can affect their production. Evaluating the changes together and, later, with independent assessors gives students an opportunity to participate in the assessment process. This type of assessment brings the student into the evaluation process—in effect, it lets them talk about their talk.

Procedure

1. Have the students pair up and sit in two rows facing their partners, a comfortable distance apart. Place a desk or small table between the partners.
2. Give each pair a cassette recorder loaded with an audiotape (or a video camera and videotape) to place on the desk or table.
3. Assign a speaking role to the students in one row and a listening role to the students in the other. Ask the speakers to spend a few minutes selecting and thinking about a topic they would like to talk about. Tell them they have 4 minutes for their tale.
4. Tell the listeners to turn on the cassette recorders (or video cameras) and the speakers to start speaking.
5. When 4 minutes have passed, have the students shut off the cassette recorders (or video cameras).
6. Ask all the listeners to move over one seat to face a new speaker, leaving the cassette recorders (or video cameras) with the speakers.
7. Have the speakers tell their story a second time, but in 3 minutes.
8. Again ask all the listeners to move over one seat to face a new speaker, leaving the cassette recorders (or video cameras) with the speakers.

9. Tell the speakers to tell their story a third time to the new listener, but in 2 minutes.
10. Ask the students to switch roles so that the listeners become speakers and the speakers, listeners.
11. Tell the students to follow Steps 4–10 again as you time them.

Feedback and Scoring

1. Give each student a copy of the Assessment Scale (see the Appendix).
2. Have the students in groups of six to eight listen to (or watch) the six conversations on each audiotape (or videotape) and evaluate them using the Assessment Scale.
3. After the first evaluation, collect the sheets and collate the results. Distribute more Assessment Scales, and give all the students the opportunity to evaluate each of the audiotapes (or videotapes) produced.

Caveats and Options

1. Use any number of different variations of the timed sequences. I have used the above sequence of 4, 3, and 2 minutes.
2. Reverse the times: The first talk lasts 2 minutes; the second, 3 minutes; and the third, 4 minutes.
3. Use the completed Assessment Scales as the basis for individual interviews or group discussions.
4. Alter the Assessment Scale for various levels. For beginning-level students, use a scale in their L1.
5. Note that the Assessment Scale acts as a listening task for the evaluators who are the first-place speakers.

References and Further Reading

Maurice, K. (1983). The fluency workshop. *TESOL Newsletter*, no. 17, 29.

Appendix: Sample Assessment Scale

Student's name_____

Comprehensibility: Rate the speaker on a scale of 0-4. _____

0 Can't understand speaker's talk in English at all. Speaker reverts to native language.

1 Can't understand basic message. Some individual words are comprehensible.

2 Can understand basic idea. There are some pronunciation, grammar, and vocabulary problems.

3 Can understand all speech acts well. There are occasional grammatical and pronunciation errors.

4 Can understand all speech acts very well. There seem to be no errors in grammar or pronunciation.

Fluency and pronunciation: Rate the speaker on a scale of 0-3. _____

0 Speech is very halting. Message is not understandable.

1 Flow of words is slightly better; however, pronunciation is still very difficult to understand. There are many repetitions.

2 Flow is slow but smooth. Pauses between sentences and within sentences are still too numerous. Meaning is basically understandable. Mispronunciation is still marked.

3 Flow is smooth and speed is adequate. There are only a few mispronunciations. Overall message is understandable.

Contributor

Clark A. Richardson, who recently completed an MA degree at Temple University Japan, teaches and does small research projects on language learning in Tokyo, Japan. He formerly taught ESL and other subjects in Canada.

◆ Self-Assessment Combined With Peer Assessment

Oral Presentations: How Did I Do?

Levels
High beginning +

Aims
Improve speaking skills
Become more attentive
listeners
Become involved in the
evaluation procedure

Class Time
10 minutes following
each oral presentation

Preparation Time
20 minutes

Resources
Assessment form

A three-in-one assessment tool gives students complete feedback on their oral presentations while involving everyone in the class. The same simple form is used for self-evaluation, peer review, and evaluation by the teacher, so no one is left out of the evaluation process.

Procedure

1. Prepare an assessment form similar to the one in the Appendix.
2. Introduce the form to the class on a day when you do not have oral presentations scheduled. First, emphasize that the purpose of the assessment form is not to criticize another student or give false praise but to help each student improve. Point out that the presenter will fill out the form under the *Self* heading, the teacher will fill out the form under the *Teacher* heading, and the listeners will use the *Classmates* heading.
3. Explain the rating scale:
   - Make sure the students understand very clearly how each item is rated and each rating is earned so that they have specific guidelines to follow whether they are preparing a presentation or evaluating another student's presentation.
   - Show the students how to calculate the total score.

● If you wish, have the students practice writing comments that will be helpful to the presenter. Encourage the students to state specifically what the presenter did well and what the presenter might work on for the next presentation.

4. At the next scheduled presentation, hand out the form in advance so that the students can make notes while they are listening. Give the students and the presenter enough time after the presentation to complete their assessment. Fill out the form yourself at this time.

5. Collect the forms to make sure the students are filling them out properly and to keep informed on what kind of evaluations the students are receiving.

Feedback and Scoring

1. See Steps 1–5 of the Procedure and the Appendix for scoring.
2. For feedback, give all the forms to the presenter at the next class.
3. If you have the time, average the total scores of the peer reviews and keep a record of them along with your own score and the presenter's self-evaluation score. If you wish, discuss this record in a conference with each student.

Caveats and Options

1. Use an audio- or videotape of a previously recorded oral presentation to teach the students how to use the assessment form. Make sure the recorded presenter is not a member of the class.

Appendix: Three-in-One Assessment Tool

Name of presenter _____

Date_____

Subject of oral presentation _____

Rating scale: 1 = poor, 2 = needs improvement, 3 = OK,
4 = good, 5 = excellent

Item	Evaluator		
	Self	Classmates	Teacher
1. Preparation			
2. Order of ideas			
3. Pronunciation			
4. Fluency			
5. Accuracy (correct vocabulary/grammar)			
Total score (Add numbers in column; divide by 5.)			
Comments:			

Contributor

Joan Blankmann teaches ESOL at Northern Virginia Community College in the United States.

I Said What?

Levels
Intermediate +

Aims
Think about negotiated interaction
Reflect on performance
Identify communication breakdowns and use them to recognize strengths and weaknesses

Class Time
1 hour

Preparation Time
10 minutes

Resources
Problem-solving task handout
Cassette recorders and audiotapes
Student Self-Evaluation Questionnaire

Self-assessment instruments mesh well with a student-centered, communicative approach to language teaching. Through self-assessment students not only evaluate their performance but also learn from it. By having an opportunity for focused reflection (which is much facilitated by audio or video recordings of students' language use), students develop an awareness of language and the way they use it. This kind of awareness is an essential first step in learner autonomy: getting students to recognize and take responsibility for their own learning so that it is not limited by the four walls of the classroom.

Procedure

1. Group the students in pairs.
2. Set up a cassette recorder near each pair, making sure that both students' voices will be clearly recorded.
3. Describe the problem that the students will be discussing (see Appendix A). Remind them that they must come to an agreement about how they will spend their money.
4. Hand out Student Self-Assessment Questionnaire (see Appendix B). Explain that the students should pay attention to the interaction because they will be evaluating their own performance and describing their impressions of the activity.
5. When they are ready, have the students start the cassette recorder and the discussion.
6. After 5–10 minutes, have the students turn off the cassette recorder and answer the questions in the Student Self-Assessment Questionnaire, Step A. Tell them to work individually and then share their answers with their partners.

7. Have the students listen to the recording they made in order to answer the questions in the Student Self-Assessment Questionnaire, Part B. Tell them to note places where they felt their communication was successful and where problems in communication arose. Assist when needed.
8. Generate a class discussion based on the students' reactions to the task, the questionnaire, or the process as a whole.

Feedback and Scoring

See Steps 4–8 of the Procedure.

Caveats and Options

1. If the students are not averse to having peer feedback, have some pairs perform their task while other members of the class observe. Give each observer a questionnaire on which to base observations and comments on the interaction.
2. Use other problem-solving tasks or any closed two-way communication task with the self-assessment questionnaire. You may need to alter the questions to fit the task.
3. The students' self-assessment ratings become more accurate if they have more practice taking self-assessment-type tests (Oskarsson, 1980). Therefore, give the students opportunities to learn about and practice using self-rating activities before you count their ratings in the overall evaluation.
4. Use the questionnaire periodically throughout the course with various tasks, and keep it as part of the students' files or portfolios. Compare the assessments from the beginning of the term with those from the end of the term, and ask the students to write or talk about any changes they notice in their performance or in their perceptions of their performance.

References and Further Reading

Klippel, F. (1984). *Keep talking: Communicative fluency activities for language teaching*. Cambridge: Cambridge University Press. (problem-solving tasks)

Oskarsson, M. (1980). *Approaches to self-assessment in foreign language learning*. Oxford: Pergamon Press.

Appendix A: Problem- Solving Task

Student A

A Night Out *or* The Shopping Spree

You and your partner earned $100 for taking care of your neighbors' house when they were away on vacation. Decide how to spend the money together. You may buy a particular item more than once, but you must choose and agree on no more than three items totaling $100.

Suggest the following activities or items to your partner.

- throw a party ($50)
- buy tickets to a sporting event ($50)
- shop for new _____ (any amount)
- buy music: compact disc ($15) or cassette ($10)
- have lunch at a fast-food restaurant ($10)
- make a donation to a charity (any amount—which charity?)

Student B

A Night Out *or* The Shopping Spree

You and your partner earned $100 for taking care of your neighbors' house when they were away on vacation. Decide how to spend the money together. You may buy a particular item more than once, but you must choose and agree on no more than three items totaling $100.

Suggest the following activities or items to your partner.

- dinner and a movie ($50)
- ballet or concert tickets ($50)
- a bottle of fine wine ($25)
- a book ($10)
- a video rental ($3)
- a donation to a charity (any amount—which charity?)

Appendix B: Student Self-Assessment Questionnaire

A. When you finish your discussion, answer these questions. Work alone first, then compare your answers with your partner's.

1. Did you and your partner come to an agreement? What was your final decision?

2. How was the agreement reached? Did you agree all the time, or did you have to argue with or try to persuade your partner? Who do you think was more effective at persuading?

3. How often did you understand your partner's ideas well?
   100%————50%————0%
   Can you remember what caused any particular problem?

4. How often did you understand your partner's speech well?
   100%————50%————0%
   Can you remember something specific that was difficult for you to understand?

5. How often were you able to respond easily to your partner?
   100%————50%————0%
   Try to give a reason why you think it was easy or difficult.

6. Do you think your partner understood what you wanted to say?
   100%————50%————0%
   Try to give a reason why you think your partner understood you well or didn't understand you.

B. Read the following questions. Rewind the audiotape and listen to your conversation again. Look for specific examples to answer the questions. You may want to stop the audiotape so that you have time to discuss and write your answers.

1. Was the discussion balanced, or did one person speak a lot more than the other? If so, why do you think that person dominated?

2. How many new ideas did you introduce? How did you introduce them? Do you think your way of introducing them to the discussion was effective? Why or why not?

3. How did you express agreement or disagreement?

4. Did you try to persuade your partner of your opinion? How?

5. Did you give reasons to support your opinions? Were you satisfied with the way you expressed yourself?

6. Did you interrupt your partner at all? If so, what did you say? When did you interrupt? Why did you interrupt?

7. What do you think was the best thing about your performance?

8. What do you think was the least satisfying thing about your performance? How do you think you can improve for the next time?

Contributor

Mary Christianson is currently completing an MA in ESL at the University of Hawai'i at Manoa, in the United States. She has taught EFL in the Czech Republic. Her interests include task-based language learning and curriculum development.

Gradually Growing Presentation Assessment

Levels
Low intermediate +

Aims
Practice and identify key features of effective presentations

Class Time
Variable

Preparation Time
About 1 hour

Resources
Video camera
Video cassette player
Feedback sheets for each type of presentation

In this activity, students do a series of four presentations of increasing length, each of a different type: narrative (2-3 minutes), demonstration (4-5 minutes), informational (5-7 minutes), and persuasive (6-8 minutes). Feedback from the presenters (sometimes using video), their peers, and the teacher follows each presentation, using a gradually growing list of criteria, which is also specialized to the type of presentation In this way, the students' skills grow gradually from presentation to presentation.

Procedure

1. Devise an assessment sheet for four types of presentations. Include more criteria in each succeeding assessment sheet. For example,
   - narrative presentation: delivery
   - demonstration presentation: delivery and introduction
   - informational presentation: delivery, introduction, and conclusion
   - persuasive presentation: delivery, introduction, conclusion, and signposting

   The fourth feedback form (see the Appendix), which is used to evaluate the final presentation in the series, therefore includes all the target skills on it.
2. Explain the criteria before each presentation.
3. Videotape the students as they give their presentations.
4. After each student presents, ask the presenter and peers to complete the feedback sheet for the type of presentation just given.
5. Play the videotape of each presentation. Have the students give positive and constructive feedback.
6. Ask the students to make a list of areas that they will try to improve for their next presentation.

Feedback and Scoring

Appendix: Oral Presentation Feedback Form

1. As appropriate in your situation, view the videotaped presentations and rate them using the Oral Presentation Feedback Form (see the Appendix), or have the student presenters or their peers do so.

This form is used to evaluate the final presentation in the series.

Practice Task 4: Persuasive Speech   Speaker:_____

Topic: _____

Complete the questions according to the following scale and then give comments.

Excellent	Satisfactory	Weak	Unsatisfactory
3	2	1	0

Introduction
  Did the speaker attract the audience's attention? _____
  Did the speaker state the purpose of the talk? _____
  Did the speaker use blueprinting (previewing)? _____
Main Points
  Were the main points clear and complete? _____
  Did the speaker use signposting (emphasizing)? _____
Conclusion
  Did the speaker summarize? _____
  Did the speaker include a recommendation or
  concluding remarks? _____
Delivery
  Pronunciation _____
  Language use (grammar and vocabulary) _____
  Rate of speech/natural delivery _____
  Eye contact with audience _____
  Posture, gestures, energy _____

Rated by _____

Contributors

Patrick B. Gallo and George M. Jacobs teach at the SEAMEO Regional Language Centre in Singapore.

How Well Did I Communicate?

Levels
Intermediate +

Aims
Improve communication
skills

Class Time
1 hour

Preparation Time
15 minutes

Resources
Self-Reflection Sheet

In communication skills courses for professional purposes, students often engage in simulated systems interviews. During the interviews, the consultants elicit information about their clients' problems and offer them solutions. This assessment activity, which can be carried out after a simulated systems interview, gives the students a chance to reflect by themselves and to find out from the other party what their communication problems are and how they can improve their communication skills. Feedback that is based on the immediate, real, and personal experience of the participants is more realistic and better remembered than feedback given by an observer such as the teacher.

Procedure

1. Teach the students the communication skills needed to conduct a systems interview. Have the students prepare and perform in pairs a simulated systems interview between a consultant and a client.
2. Give each student 10–15 minutes to fill out a Self-Reflection Sheet (see the Appendix) based on introspection.
3. Give the parties (the consultant and the client) about 15 minutes in turn to tell the other party how they felt during the systems interview. For example, they may say,
   - "You always frowned when I talked. This made me very nervous. What did I do?"
   - "I would be less nervous if you asked me a question for clarification or asked me to speak louder rather than frowning."
   - "You were so quiet. What could I do to make you talk more?"
4. After the two parties have given feedback to each other, have them go back to the Self-Reflection Sheets that they have just filled out and use the remaining time to add information based on the feedback from

their peer and further self-reflection. These sheets become their plans for developing their oral communication skills further in upcoming oral activities.

5. If the students have a chance to conduct a second systems interview, have them check their own progress by comparing their performance as recorded on each interview's Self-Reflection Sheet.

Feedback and Scoring

See Steps 2–5 of the Procedure.

Caveats and Options

1. If necessary, provide more space in each cell on the Self-Reflection Sheet for the students to put their thoughts down. Also add more items to the Areas for Improvement column depending on the kinds of communication skills taught before the systems interview.

Appendix: Self-Reflection Sheet

Area	My performance (Circle one.)	My strengths	Areas for improvement	How I can improve
Presentation skills	1 2 3 4 5			
Questioning skills	1 2 3 4 5			
Body language	1 2 3 4 5			
Other communication skills	1 2 3 4 5			

Contributor

Belinda Ho is an assistant professor in the Department of English at the City University of Hong Kong. She has taught ESL, English for academic purposes, and English for specific purposes.

Self-/Peer/Teacher Assessment of Group Performance

Levels
Intermediate +

Aims
Reflect on contributions to a group project
Master important communication skills

Class Time
1 hour

Preparation Time
1 hour

Resources
Group Score Sheet
Individual Score Sheet

The purpose of this assessment activity is to help students reflect on their contributions to a group project and on areas that need improvement. The students also internalize important communication skills as they use the skills as criteria for assessing their performance and that of their peers, and they receive the teacher's feedback on those skills.

Procedure

1. Following a class discussion of a specific topic (generally after reading about it), have the students brainstorm for a related topic for a group project. Ask them to select one topic and work with at most five others who have chosen the same one.
2. Tell the groups to plan a presentation to the class. Let the group decide on the mode of the presentation (e.g., individual speeches, a drama, a song and dance), but be sure all members of the group participate. Encourage visual aids such as photos or graphs, and tell the groups to produce a written script for the presentation.
3. Before the presentations, remind all the students of the ground rules for being in the audience (e.g., no talking during presentations).
4. As their turn comes, ask the students in each group to go to the front of the class for their presentation.

Feedback and Scoring

1. Hand out a Group Score Sheet (see Appendix A) to each group in the audience, and explain how to score the presenting group. Tell the students that each group has to agree on one score.
2. After each group presentation, allow a few minutes for the other groups to discuss and score it.
3. After all the presentations, summarize the group scores on the blackboard (see Sample Summary of Group Scores, Appendix B). To

preserve the score givers' anonymity, ask the members of the group being scored to close their eyes. Point at the numbers on the blackboard, and have the other groups indicate their scores by raising their hands.

4. Hand out an Individual Score Sheet (see Appendix C) to each group, and explain the scoring system. Remind the students that they may write their scores in any square to preserve their anonymity.

5. Ask one student in each group to write his or her name on the Individual Score Sheet and pass the sheet to the person to the right. Tell the students to keep passing and entering scores until the sheet comes back to the originator.

6. Ask the students to add up the scores and divide by the number of scorers, thus getting the individual's average score. Averaging to get the final score is important because each group may have a different number of scorers.

7. Collect the sheets.

8. Ask the students to write their thoughts about the group work and assessment experience in their journals. Either keep the journal entries entirely open ended, or guide them by providing subtopics.

9. Collect the students' journals and group scripts.

10. Base final feedback and scoring on the group presentation scores by you and the other groups, individual scores by peers, and the score you give for the script.

11. Give the students their total project score or grade.

12. Synthesize the findings from the journal entries, and share them with the class in a discussion format. Usually the students make comments about the difficulties encountered or the benefits perceived.

Caveats and Options

1. Do not do this peer assessment activity until the students have done some group work and have some understanding of the importance of reflection and of assessment as a tool for internalizing and improving skills rather than as a judgmental device. The activity takes some degree of rapport and trust among the students.

2. Alert the students to the assessment procedure when introducing the project process so that the students know in advance about the criteria by which they will be assessed and will assess others.

3. Use different assessment criteria according to the skill-building objectives for each project. Be explicit about what the students need to practice, and link that to the assessment criteria. The criteria may be general (as in the example) or specific (such as the effectiveness of eye contact).

4. If you wish, videotape the group presentations, and play back 30-second segments of each one so that the students can see themselves in action and note their own strengths and weaknesses.

5. Use an overhead projector to summarize the group scores so that you do not have to copy them off the blackboard.

6. Decide whether to keep the identities of group and individual scorers anonymous. Whether to do so or not depends on the dynamics of the class.

7. Vary the range on the scoring scale (e.g., 1-3, 1-5). Give beginning-level scorers fewer choices.

Appendix A: Group Score Sheet

Group number_____   Date of presentation_____

Project topic_____

Circle one score for content and one for presentation.

Content		Presentation	
Makes unrelated statements	0	Not understandable	0
States a consistent opinion	1	Barely understandable	1
Gives one kind of support	2	Clear	2
Gives different kinds of support	3	Expressive	3

Total group score: Content score _____ + Presentation score _____ = _____

Appendix B: Sample Summary of Group Scores

Group	0	1	2	3	4	5	6	Total
1				///	/			13
2			//	//	/			12
3					////			16
4						///	/	21
5					/	//	/	20

Appendix C: Individual Score Sheet

Name _____ Date _____

Directions: Sit in a circle with your group members and follow the steps below.

1. Write your name and the date on the sheet.
2. Pass the sheet to the person on your right.
3. When you receive another student's score sheet, write your score (1, 2, or 3 according to the Scoring Key below) for that person in one of the squares below.
4. Continue until you get back your own sheet.
5. Total the scores and divide the total by the number of scorers. The result is your average score.

Scoring Key

1	Little participation in discussions and assignments
2	Some participation in discussions and assignments
3	A large contribution to the project

Total of all scores _____   Number of scorers _____

Your score: Total of scores ÷ Number of scorers = _____

Contributor

Genevieve Lau is a professor of language arts at Skyline College, San Francisco, in the United States. She teaches English to nonnative speakers and engages in curriculum development, program design, and evaluation.

Walk-Talk Oral Tests

Levels
Any

Aims
Learn to assess own
performance
Use English outside the
classroom
Be involved in
kinesthetic learning

Class Time
25–40 minutes

Preparation Time
30 minutes

Resources
Student-created test list

In this activity, students give each other oral tests while walking outside, and they learn to assess their own knowledge and ability.

Procedure

1. Prepare a test that reflects what you have been teaching, what the students have chosen to be tested on, or both.
2. Pass out the test lists (see Appendix A). Tell the students to underline the items they don't know and to study them, use them every day in talking to friends, and teach them to others outside class until the day of the test. Hold a mock test once or twice before the real one so that the procedure is clear (see Appendix B). Ask the students to change partners once or twice to get experience with different people.
3. On test day, explain the test and grading procedure one more time. Tell the students the amount of time they have.
4. Send the students out to do the assessment activity.
5. Walk outside and be unobtrusively available in case anyone has a question.

Feedback and Scoring

The two types of scoring that follow work with this assessment activity.

Simple Protocol for Testing and Grading

1. Demonstrate the following procedure in front of the class; simply explaining it usually confuses the students.
   - Have the students exchange their lists and take turns asking their partners a certain number of the words and expressions on the list

that they have marked (i.e., the ones they didn't know and have studied).

- Tell the students to circle the ones they ask and, after the partner answers, to write down the number of points indicated by their partner for each word or expression. Make sure the students decide for themselves the points they think they deserve and that they don't judge their partners.

2. To stress conversational interaction, tell the students that they can give themselves
   - 1 point each for (a) speaking immediately, (b) speaking continuously for at least four or five sentences, and (c) being correct in their explanation of the item (For 10 items, the maximum number of points possible is 30.)
   - 3 points if they speak only English

Someone who doesn't know the words can still get 20 points just by speaking a lot (e.g., "Strategy, umm, an interesting word, I can even remember studying it, and I'm sure it's an important word. I even remember Yuki telling me what it means. Let's see, I just can't seem to remember it right now. I guess I can only get 2 points for that one. Can you tell me what it means?"). Blackboard notes might look like this:

For each item:

Speaking immediately = 1 point

Speaking continuously = 1 point

Giving a clear and correct explanation = 1 point

Speaking English only = 3 points

---

3. Have the students write their partner's total points at the bottom of the sheet and turn it in to you for recording.

Caveats and Options

Interactive Grading

1. Have the students use a more complex grading procedure, such as the one in Appendix B.

1. A nice outdoor environment makes this assessment activity more enjoyable, but the activity also works if the students simply walk around the halls of the classroom building.
2. Vary the content, length of time, and number of points depending on the teaching objectives.
3. For clarity, demonstrate the procedure in front of the class with a student.

References and Further Reading

Murphey, T. (1994/1995). Tests: Learning through negotiated interaction. *TESOL Journal, 4*(2), 12–16.

Appendix A: Sample Student-Created Test List

The following are words and expressions chosen by the class for the conversation test. Underline only the ones you don't know and study them, use them every day in talking to friends, and teach them to others. In a few days, you will have to explain them orally (by talking).

a tip	my sight is poor	flat
he's all thumbs	follow the routine	rotate
let someone down	on my mind	squander
play around	commit suicide	slope
inspire	slam the door	get passionate about
clumsy	paste	strategy
husband-to-be/	ban	inventory
bride-to-be	night owl	addiction
rectangle	no way	nicotine
impress	turn (90, 180) degrees	kick the habit
skim the headlines	dawn is breaking	mumble
artificial versus natural	sum up	get by

potential	whisper	take a nap
switch	regress	numb
it is frowned upon	calculate	dormitory
enthusiastic	freckles	kidding
intensify	daydream	piece of cake
fascinating	so far (So far, you	decade
skip (two meaings)	are doing well.)	in good shape
flat (two meanings)	jet lag	seldom
scary	feel inhibited	keep one's word
skim	I'm behind you (idiom)	be astounded
flexible	bored with	substitute
illegal	guess	approximately
no kidding!	the rest of . . .	contagious
fabulous	dare to . . .	feel inhibited
pot luck	extraterrestrial	a valid excuse
fade	interact with	weary
rag	relative	competitive
strum		

(Based on Murphey, 1994/1995)

Appendix B: Sample Complex Interactive Grading Scheme

English I Test

A. Filled out by you

English name:

Grades: A+ A B C F   English only all the time

1. Based on what you think you know for the test, what grade would you give yourself now, before you take it?   Grade/score:_____

2. Based on how much time and effort you spent studying for the test, what grade would you give yourself now, before you take it? Grade/score:_____

Give your Vocabulary Study List to your partner, and take your partner's. Do the same with this sheet of paper.

B. Filled out by your partner

Go outside (if it is pretty) and ask your partner the following. (The partner who is the taller should answer first, and the shorter should ask; then switch.)

3. Call out every second word that is marked on your partner's sheet as being difficult, and ask your partner to explain them, use them in an example, or both. Do 10 words in this way.
   ● Make sure your partner starts to answer immediately. If your partner doesn't start answering after 5 seconds, hit the buzzer (BBBBEEEEEPPPPP! Time's up.). But give your partner all the time needed to answer completely.
   ● Write here how many words out of 10 your partner could explain adequately. Grade/score:_____

4. When both of you have finished Step 3, ask your partner to describe some object at home (without naming the object) so that you know what it is. Your partner should be able to tell you at least five things about it that allow you to know what it is. Count the number of things your partner tells you. Give your partner a score of 1–5 depending on how many things he or she told you about the object. Then exchange roles. Grade/score:_____

5. The partner with the higher student number: Choose one of the following. Give at least three reasons why it is important:
   ● the article "Try a Nonnative"
   ● shadowing/echoing
   ● loving your mistakes
   The second person speaking must not choose what the first one chose. Give a grade of 1 (poor)–5 (excellent). Grade/score:_____

6. The partner whose student number is lower: Name four ways to improve your oral English that Mr. Murphey has asked you to try outside class. Write your partner's answers below, and give your partner a score. (maximum 4 points) Grade/score:_____

The other partner: Name four songs and something you have learned from each song. Write these below and give your partner a score. (maximum 4 points)　　　　　　　　　　Grade/score:_____

Give your partner 2 points if he or she has spoken only English since walking into the classroom at 9:00 this morning.　　　　_____
Subtract points for every time your partner spoke his or her native language　　　　　　　　　　　　　　　　　　-_____

　　　　　　Total number of points out of 26 possible: _____

Now return this paper to its owner.

C. Filled out by the person who filled out Section A

1. After having taken this test, what kind of grade do you think you should get?
2. Do you think this test gave a fair picture of what you know? Was it easy, enjoyable, or what? Would you like to take other tests like this? Was it useful? Could it be improved in any way? Write some feedback below.

Thank you very much.

Contributor

Tim Murphey teaches and learns at Nanzan University in Nagoya, Japan, and does research on alternative learning forms.

Interviews and Presentations for Clarifying Authentic Public-Speaking Needs

Levels
Advanced

Aims
Determine types of public speaking used in major field
Develop individualized criteria for effective academic presentations
Teachers: Determine students' individual needs in authentic speaking situations

Class Time
30 minutes (group work)
10 minutes/student (presentations)

Preparation Time
30 minutes

Resources
Handheld cassette recorders and audio-tapes, or video cassette recorder and videotapes
Academic Speaking Interview handout
Academic Speaking Feedback handout

Early in their academic careers, L2 university students often have little idea of what kinds of academic and public-speaking situations they will be faced with over the course of their college education. Public-speaking expectations for undergraduate- as well as graduate-level students can differ substantially in various L1 backgrounds; students therefore often have a wide variety of ideas about the extent to which they will be expected to speak in the L2 college environment. This exercise enables students to gain insight into what kinds of public speaking and academic presentations are in store for them. Students use their communication skills authentically and meaningfully as they develop interview questions, defend their ideas, conduct interviews, and present their findings. The results of the interviews of expert informants provide the teacher and student with valuable, discipline-specific criteria to use in preparing, organizing, and evaluating presentations. Based on these criteria and on students' abilities in presenting them, teachers learn the kinds of public speaking students in different majors need to focus on and give evaluative feedback to students with the same majors. With the introduction of peer and self-review of the presentations, students engage in and are exposed to critical reflection based on criteria that they themselves have elucidated.

Procedure

1. Before class, prepare a handout like the Academic Speaking Interview handout (see Appendix A). Design the handout to get the students to think about the academic and public-speaking demands of their chosen field of study.

2. In class, have the students meet with a partner (preferably from a different discipline) to discuss the handout; stress that the students should describe their own perceptions of academic and public speaking (i.e., the students should not necessarily come to a consensus, as students in different academic disciplines are likely to be faced with different speaking contexts). Tell the students that they will work with these partners for the remainder of the project.

3. Have each student choose an interview informant based on the criteria found at the bottom of the Academic Speaking Interview handout. Generally, the informant should be someone in the same discipline as the student, someone at a more advanced level of study than that of the student, and someone the student respects as a public speaker.

4. Have the students each generate a set of interview questions based on (a) their specific interests, (b) the person they have chosen to interview, and (c) their own ideas about public speaking in their majors, using the questions on the Academic Speaking Interview handout as a guide. The idea is for the students to solicit relevant information about the public speaking they will face, the preparation that is involved, and the techniques that are effective in these public-speaking situations. Have the students finish this step (possibly as homework) before moving on to Step 5.

5. Schedule 10-minute conferences with the pairs of students. Tell the students to come prepared with a firm date and time for their projected interview sessions, a list of interview questions, and a rationale for their choices (of both informant and questions).

6. After commenting on and confirming the student' interview plans, make the following suggestions:
   ● Work together during the interview. The student who is not asking questions should either operate the cassette recorder (if one is available, now would be a good time to distribute it to the pair) or take a backup set of notes.
   ● Have the student conducting the interview also note the informant's answers.
   ● Estimate the amount of time required to answer each question, and realize that informants may speak with unexpected length or

brevity. Thus, be prepared to tune the interview to the informant's responsiveness.

7. Have the students conduct each of their interviews.

8. Schedule individual student presentations in class soon after the interviews have been conducted. Tell the students to organize their presentations around the interview questions, notes, and audiotapes (if available). Encourage them to incorporate into their own presentations anything they learned from their informants about academic and public speaking. Agree on time limits in advance; 5–10 minutes per student should be sufficient.

9. During the presentations,
   - Have all listeners (other than the teacher and the speaker's partner) take careful notes. Collect them directly following each presentation.
   - Along with the speaker's partner, respond to the rating scales found in the Academic Speaking Feedback handout (see Appendix B). Keep these response sheets with the collected notes.

10. Directly following each presentation, have the speakers each rate their own presentation using the Academic Speaking Feedback handout (see Appendix B).

Feedback and Scoring

Feedback on the interview presentations takes multiple forms:

1. Your ratings and comments on the Academic Speaking Feedback handout help the students understand the extent to which they have met the general criteria for academic presentations and see how well they were able to apply knowledge that they acquired from the interview.

2. The partner's ratings provide the same kind of information with the added insight of someone who witnessed the interview. Have the students compare their self-ratings with yours and their partner's to determine to what extent you, the students, and their peers envision and understand public-speaking needs within a given academic context with any degree of similarity.

3. Have the student speakers reflect on the notes taken by the other students in the class to determine how successfully they presented the findings of their interviews.
4. Have the students combine all of these sources of input and write a reflective piece on their strengths and weaknesses in presentations. Then have the students further apply the criteria provided by their informants to suggest areas for improvement on future public-speaking occasions.

Caveats and Options

1. Equipment availability and time permitting, videotape the presentations.
2. Have the students review the audiotape individually before rating themselves on the Academic Speaking Feedback handout.
3. Review the audiotape in further conferences among the student, the partner, and you. Each can comment on strengths and areas for improvement in the presentation.

References and Further Reading

Norris, J. M. (1996). *Performance and portfolio assessment (1985-1995): An extended bibliography of resources useful for language teachers* (Research Note). Honolulu: University of Hawai'i, Second Language Teaching and Curriculum Center.

Appendix A: Academic Speaking Interview

A. Think about academic speaking in your major. Meet with a partner and discuss your ideas about the following questions. Try to discover differences as well as similarities in the kinds of academic speaking in which you engage.

1. What kinds of academic speaking do you currently have to do (e.g., presentations, article critiques, comments)?
2. How do you prepare yourself for speaking in public or in class (e.g., making notes or outlines, practicing in front of a mirror or with a partner, timing yourself)?
3. What techniques do you use in order to give effective academic presentations?
4. What would you like to change about your ability to give presentations in class or in public?

B. Choose an informant. Think of someone from your field of study whom you would like to interview about academic speaking. Follow these guidelines:

1. Choose an informant from the academic area in which you study or from a related area that interests you.
2. Try to pick someone whom you respect as a public speaker. (Think about why you consider this person an effective speaker.)
3. Try to find someone who has been studying in your field for longer than you have (e.g., if you are an undergraduate in business, consider interviewing a graduate student from the MBA program).
4. Make sure the person you pick is willing and able to give you an interview. When you schedule the interview, estimate about how much time you will need (more than 30 minutes is probably too long).

Appendix B: Academic Speaking Feedback

Using the rating scales provided, respond to following statements about the presentation. Please use the space below each statement to explain your rating.

	Disagree	Agree
1. The speaker seemed well prepared for this presentation. Please explain:	1 2 3 4 5
2. The speaker used the techniques suggested by the informant. Please explain:	1 2 3 4 5
3. The presentation successfully conveyed interview findings. Please explain:	1 2 3 4 5

Contributor

John M. Norris is an ESL teacher at the University of Hawai'i at Manoa, in the United States, where he is also a doctoral student and conducts research on L2 assessment.

Peer Evaluation of Natural Communicative Behaviors With Dialogues

Levels
Any

Aims
Improve application of
the seven SPEAKER
techniques

Class Time
About 45 minutes

Preparation Time
Minimal

Resources
Copies of dialogues
SPEAKER handout
Peer Dialogue
Assessment Tool

Dialogues are a common technique used in speaking classes, but unfortunately students often rehearse a number of unnatural communicative behaviors with dialogues. For example, students often read dialogues in a monotone and with minimal body language. This assessment activity discusses seven communicative behaviors—denoted by the acronym *SPEAKER* (see Appendix A)—that low- to high-level students can practice with dialogues and provides a means of assessing these behaviors through peer evaluation. If conscientiously taught and applied, the SPEAKER techniques with their accompanying assessment tool improve the way the students practice dialogues, especially in speaking classes. The Procedure details just one of many ways to do this kind of assessment.

Procedure

1. Pass out and explain the handout Seven Communicative Behaviors for Dialogue Practice (see Appendix A).
2. Have the students break into groups of four.
3. Pass out copies of the dialogues. Ask two students to practice a given dialogue while the other two operate as peer evaluators using the assessment chart. During this step and the following ones, circulate and provide support to the groups.
4. After the students practice a dialogue, have the evaluators give feedback.
5. Have the students repeat Steps 3 and 4.
6. When they have mastered the dialogue and improved the accompanying communicative behaviors, have the pairs switch and repeat the process.

7. At the end of the dialogue practice and peer assessment, ask the students summary questions (e.g., "What technique needed the most improvement? Did you get better at it?" "Did you master the language in the dialogue?").

Feedback and Scoring

1. After the students have become familiar with all seven SPEAKER techniques, have them use the Peer Dialogue Assessment Tool (Appendix B) to evaluate their progress. In addition to the seven techniques, the assessment chart adds an eighth category related to linguistic mastery of the dialogue. The students are able to evaluate this satisfactorily because the dialogue is a controlled text that is right in front of them when they practice it.

References and Further Reading

Murphey, T. (1994, October). *ShadEchoing and reformulation: KISS principles of retention and activation.* Paper presented at the Japan Association for Language Teaching International Conference on Language Teaching/Learning, Matsuyama, Japan.

Appendix A: Seven Communicative Behaviors for Dialogue Practice

Key term	Definition
*S*hort-term memory	The ability to hold about seven bits of data briefly in memory without rehearsal
*P*rocrastination	Temporization (time-buying) techniques used when forming a response
*E*choing	Repeating what the speaker says for clarification, comprehension, and thinking time
*A*d-libbing	Creative use of the language; speaking novel sentences or ideas
*K*inesics	Body language: nonlinguistic bodily movements, such as gestures and facial expressions
*E*locution	Communicative emphasis on intonation, rhythm, stress, and pronunciation
*R*epair	Repairing mistakes naturally, as one would in real conversation, as opposed to in an evaluative encounter

Short-Term Memory

Short-term memory (STM) refers to that aspect of memory that allows us to remember briefly approximately seven chunks of information without rehearsal. For example, after hearing a seven-digit phone number, we can probably keep it in STM long enough to write it down. For dialogues, instead of reading texts to each other, the students can use STM as they practice by silently reading the text, placing a phrase in STM, and then saying it face-to-face to their partners. Thus the use of STM in dialogue practice allows the students to perform other communicative behaviors that are released as the students begin to depend less on the text and more on their memories.

Procrastination and Temporizing

These terms refer to the ways native speakers use sounds and phrases to give themselves time to formulate ideas, responses, and sentences during dialogue. There are many ways to buy time to formulate a response, but as the students say "uh . . . ," "um . . . ," and so on, they gain time to look at the dialogue, formulate their phrase, and say it in a natural way instead of waiting painfully through a period of silence. Temporizing is a key aspect of these seven techniques that works together with STM as the students move away from tunnel-visioned dependence on scripts to a more natural use of language.

Echoing and Shadowing

Echoing and shadowing refer to imitating or repeating what listeners hear speakers say for the purposes of clarification, comprehension, and thinking time. Murphey (1994) states that in *ShadEchoing*, a listener allows the words of speaker to echo in his or her mind long enough to let STM process them. In dialogue practice, listeners simply repeat (when natural or necessary) some parts or the whole of what speakers say. Thus listeners have time to process information, and they can use this shadowing as a temporizing technique as native speakers do.

Ad-Libbing and Creating

Ad-libbing refers to improvisation with dialogues. In looking at a script for skits done by the movie star Tom Hanks, I noticed that the Academy

Award winner often departed from the script. I'm not sure if this is a common practice for good actors, but it seemed natural as he personalized his script. Although students are not actors and may not possess an advanced-level ability to be creative with the target language, they still can do some creative things with dialogue. They can do this in other areas I have mentioned, such as body language and intonation, but they may also add their own ideas to the script. Moreover, if the dialogue is somewhat open-ended, motivated students may continue asking questions of their partner and begin exchanging real information.

Kinesics and Elocution

   Kinesics refers to nonlinguistic communicative behaviors. It is common in many classrooms to see very little kinesic energy put into dialogue practice, and thus the students actually rehearse negative communicative behavior. However, this problem is easy to remedy. You can model positive kinesic communication, and the students can enjoy trying to communicate nonverbally as well as verbally.

   Related to nonverbal communication is the area of elocution. In graduate school, I observed a teacher who was famous for teaching pronunciation. He used simple dialogues but turned them into dramatic productions. He would say, "Lights, camera, action!" Then, like a movie director, he had the students dramatize the dialogue. This teacher spent a lot of time working with the students on the enunciation of the phrases. It was enjoyable to watch, and the students seemed to enjoy doing the dialogues like jazz chants and minidramas. Likewise, teachers want their students to practice realistically in class, for monotone and lifeless readings of dialogues do not emulate most real-world communication.

Natural Repair

   Many of my students have studied English for years, and they often have an interesting test-taking mentality about conversation. When they make a mistake, it becomes a big event in the dialogue that they need to correct fully from the very beginning of the sentence or even the dialogue. Native speakers often make mistakes, too, but they repair them more naturally, not acting as if some major breakdown in communication has occurred. Instead, they usually repair the mistake from the place where they made it and continue naturally. Language students should also learn this: Instead of treating mistakes as failures, they need to learn to repair them as they would in their native language.

Appendix B: Peer Dialogue Assessment Tool

Check the appropriate boxes.

Name:						
Skill	Quantity			Quality		
	Unused	Too little	Enough	Poor	Good	Excellent
Short-tcrm Memory						
Procrastination						
Echoing						
Ad-libbing						
Kinesics						
Elocution						
Repair						
Speech (dialogue)						

Contributor

Joseph W. Poulshock teaches at Tokyo Christian University in Japan.

Activating Self-Assessment

Levels
High beginning +

Aims
Apply criteria for
effective writing

Class Time
45–60 minutes, several
times

Preparation Time
1–2 hours

Resources
Several effective writing
samples
Overhead projector and
transparencies
Chart paper and
markers
3-in. × 5-in. index cards

This activity helps learners identify criteria for effective writing and apply them to their own work. By reflecting on their writing and comparing it with a standard, students become more aware of how to improve their own writing. This awareness enables them to become independent learners. The teacher's role is to scaffold the self-assessment process by guiding students through a series of steps. The process proceeds from a whole-class session, to working with a partner, and finally to self-assessment, a key element of effective learning that is essential to portfolio assessment.

Procedure

1. To provide a model that is appropriate for the language proficiency and grade level of your students, select a one-page sample of good writing produced either by a former student or by a student currently in the class. Obtain the student's permission to use the writing, and remove the name from the copies and the transparency you share with the class. Enlarge the writing sample if necessary to improve its legibility, then make a transparency of it.
2. Invite the class to generate criteria for good writing: Put the transparency on the overhead projector, and ask the students, alone or with a partner, to read it and to write down as many characteristics as they can to describe what makes the writing good.
3. Make a criteria chart: After giving the students a few minutes to work, ask them to share with the whole class why they think the sample represents good writing. If the students are reticent, guide them with questions that reflect what they have learned in your class about good writing, such as "What do we know about the first letter of the first word in a sentence?" Using the overhead projector, chart paper, or

wall chart, write their comments, rephrasing the language where needed to produce short sentences (5–10 words) and to model appropriate language. The result will be a criteria chart. In the chart,

- Express each phrase in the first-person singular (e.g., *I can . . . , I put . . . , I write with . . .*) or in the imperative (e.g., *Put a period at the end of a sentence*).
- For older or more proficient learners, simply list the criteria in short phrases with bullets or check marks (e.g., *main idea in paragraph, periods, capital letters, spelling*).

4. Add to the criteria chart as you go through the modeling process several times with the whole class. Ultimately, put the chart up on the wall. It can evolve into a writer's checklist (see the example in the Appendix).

5. Give the students a copy of a different writing sample. Have them work with a partner to compare it with the criteria on the wall chart and to identify additional elements of good writing. Monitor the pairs to see that they understand the task.

6. After about 10 minutes, ask the whole class for feedback on how the second writing sample compares with the student-generated criteria chart. Engage the whole class in a discussion of the criteria, and add newly named elements to the chart.

7. Repeat Steps 1–6 at least twice more using different writing samples before proceeding to Feedback and Scoring. For the first few times, show the students models of effective writing so that they can identify the criteria for good writing. After several sessions, use models of less than effective writing written by the students in your own class as the basis for minilessons that meet the current needs of your students.

Feedback and Scoring

1. Teach the students what constructive feedback sounds like, perhaps by providing some key lead phrases such as *What I liked about this piece was . . .* or *Your writing can be improved by . . . .* Teach the students to respect each other by listening to each other's feedback and using it to improve their work.

2. Have the students apply the criteria to a peer's work in a subsequent session, perhaps 1 or 2 days later. For example, if you have taught the

students the various steps of process writing or writers' workshop, after the first or second draft ask the students to swap drafts with a partner for feedback based on the criteria chart. In many cases, the students respond much more positively to a peer's feedback than to a teacher's red ink.

3. Invite the students to apply the criteria to their own work. After a number of sessions during which the students provide feedback on a partner's work, they will be ready to apply the criteria for effective writing to their own work, the culminating step of the self-assessment process.

   ● After a writing assignment, ask the students to take a few minutes to apply the criteria on the wall chart to their own work.

   ● Ask the students to get feedback from a partner. Monitor the partners to see that they are on track, and engage all the students in a discussion of their readiness to apply the criteria to their own writing.

4. Ask the students to set learning goals for the benchmark or model sample. Begin by revisiting Step 2 of the Procedure. Returning to the original writing sample (on the transparency) used for generating criteria for good writing, ask the students what writing goals the author of the sample might set for himself or herself to work toward during a semester or quarter.

5. Have the students set learning goals for a peer. As in the process described above for setting criteria, first provide the students with several opportunities to set goals for writing models as a class. Then give the students opportunities to suggest writing goals for each other on several occasions.

6. Invite the students to set learning goals for their own work. This can occur in a writing conference with you, through a learning log or writer's journal, or by writing their goals on a 3-in. × 5-in. index card and attaching it to the writing draft. If keeping writing portfolios, the students can include the various drafts of their writing and their goal cards to share with you during portfolio conferences.

Caveats and Options

1. Help weak writers by teaming them up with a partner who will support their efforts. Research has shown that when English language learners are shown the criteria for good work along with samples of good writing (called *benchmarks*), their writing improves (Kolls, 1992).
2. This activity can be used with high-beginning-level students after they have received at least one or two semesters or quarters of instruction in your class and have acquired enough language to generate the criteria for the wall chart. Children as young as kindergartners can engage in this activity (Clemmons, Laase, Cooper, Areglado, & Dill, 1993).
3. Use the feedback from the students on their writing goals to develop minilessons aimed at helping them reach those goals.

References and Further Reading

Clemmons, J., Laase, L., Cooper, D., Areglado, N., & Dill, M. (1993). *Portfolios in the classroom, Grades 1–6.* New York: Scholastic Professional Books.

Kolls, M. R. (1992, March). *Portfolio assessment: A feasibility study.* Paper presented at the 26th Annual TESOL Convention, Vancouver, Canada.

O'Malley, J. M., & Valdez Pierce, L. (1996). *Authentic assessment for English language learners: Practical approaches for teachers.* Reading, MA: Addison-Wesley.

Appendix: Sample Student-Generated Criteria

I make a plan before I write.

I put a main idea in each paragraph.

I use words to make a picture.

I begin all sentences with a capital letter.

I end all sentences with a period, question mark, or exclamation point.

I spell words correctly.

Contributor

Lorraine Valdez Pierce teaches courses on assessment at George Mason University in Fairfax, Virginia, in the United States, and is coauthor of a book on authentic, classroom-based assessment.

Self- and Peer Assessment of Group Participation

Levels
Any

Aims
Gauge contribution to
group activities

Class Time
20–40 minutes

Preparation Time
10 minutes

Resources
Group Work Self-
Assessment Sheet

Although the type of assessment sheet used in this activity can be used for almost any group activity or project, it was designed for a multiskills group travel project. In the project, a group of four or five students compiles information on a certain city or country. The activity includes such tasks as researching historical information, writing letters to request brochures, calling for transportation costs, acting as a guide or presenter, and finding out about visa and passport requirements.

Procedure

1. Have the class complete a group project (e.g., a multiskills travel project). After the project is done, distribute a Group Work Self-Assessment Sheet (see the Appendix) to each student.
2. Tell the students to fill in
   - their name
   - their specific job for the project
   - the information they found
   - their contribution to the group, in their opinion
3. Explain the numbered grading system for the five categories, with 1 being the lowest and 5 the highest.
4. Tell the students to rate themselves, write the total score, and pass the same sheets in turn to each group member, who will also rate every other group member. Remind the students not to circle or mark the numbers because the other group members also will be using them.
5. Have the students each use the totals to see how accurately they assessed themselves.

Feedback and Scoring

See the Procedure.

Caveats and Options

1. Scramble the forms so that the students cannot guess from the order who gave whom how many points.
2. Seat the students far enough apart that they cannot see who is rating whom.
3. For grading, add the scores and compare the total scores.

Appendix: Group Work Self-Assessment Sheet

Name: _____

My job:

What I found out in the group:

What I contributed to the group:

	Low				High
Willingness to work	1	2	3	4	5
Research	1	2	3	4	5
Reading	1	2	3	4	5
Speaking	1	2	3	4	5
Helping others	1	2	3	4	5

Scores:

Student's self-assessment _____

Group member's assessment _____

Group member's assessment _____

Group member's assessment _____

Group member's assessment _____

Group member's assessment _____

Group member's assessment _____

Grand total _____

Contributor

David Progosh studied curriculum and assessment issues at the Modern Language Centre of the Ontario Institute for Studies in Education/University of Toronto, in Canada. He writes and edits ESL materials and tests. Robert West teaches at Kanda Institute of Foreign Languages, Tokyo, Japan.

Part III: Alternative Groupings for Assessment

Left to right: Sun Ok Kim and Hyang Lee at English for Success, Annandale, Virginia, USA.

Editor's Note

Traditionally tests have been administered to each student separately in paper-and-pencil format. However, that does not mean that one-by-one testing is the only way to do things. As language teaching practices have begun to change around the world in favor of communicative teaching organized around functions or tasks, pair and group activities have become increasingly common in the classroom. Apparently, judging by the contributions in this section, many teachers are also experimenting with group work and pair work for doing assessments in their classrooms. Indeed, some published articles have appeared on this topic (see, e.g., Mendelsohn, 1991/1992).

Group work assessment will be defined here as any observations or scoring done for the purpose of giving students feedback while those students are working in groups, whether the group work was specifically designed for assessment purposes or occurred naturally for other pedagogical purposes. Similarly, *pair work assessment* will be defined as any observations or scoring done for the purpose of giving students feedback while those students are working in pairs, whether those pairs were formed for assessment purposes or occurred naturally for other pedagogical reasons. These are very straightforward definitions, so no further explanation will be given.

However, one question remains: Why would teachers want to use these two ways of grouping students for assessment purposes? Group work and pair work assessments are useful because (a) they provide opportunities to assess actual language production, (b) they match the pedagogical practices going on in the classroom, (c) students may feel more relaxed and less threatened when tested in groups or pairs, and (d) such assessment can be much more efficient timewise than other techniques (e.g., oral interviews conducted individually).

Group work or pair work assessment has some disadvantages as well. For instance, scoring and feedback tend to be subjective, a problem that can be minimized by getting multiple ratings for each student (as when several teachers rate each student), by getting ratings from multiple perspectives (e.g., from the viewpoints of the students themselves, their peers, and the teacher), by making the guidelines for scoring very clear to the scorers, by doing specific training and practice in the scoring method, or ideally by using some combination of these practices.

Another set of problems associated with group work and pair work assessment is that, by chance, some students may be relegated to weak partners or contentious groups, which alone could affect their language performances and thus their scores. Naturally, comparing such students with students who have had well-matched partners and cooperative groups would not be fair. One way to address this issue is to make sure that each student participates in multiple groups or multiple pairs so that you observe all students in a variety of groupings or pairings.

In addition, group work and pair work assessments may favor the more vocal students in class. This issue can be minimized by structuring activities for equality, in the sense that you make clear from the outset that the whole group's scores will be lower if some members talk too much and others too little.

Still another problem that may arise is that, because of their personalities or other factors, some students may not speak up at all when paired or grouped with others. As a result, they will not produce enough language for you to score them or give them any kind of feedback. The solution described in the previous paragraph might help—that is, make it clear to students from the outset that their scores depend on their active participation. Or you could try making the activity competitive so that all members want to chime in. Another possibility would be to appoint the shy students as group leaders so they have to participate. In addition to the above solutions, you might want to have a backup assessment option for any students who truly cannot participate actively because they are shy or otherwise unwilling to do so. For instance, you might want to hold individual assessment conferences with groups or pairs of such students or use other assessment techniques to draw them out.

Eight of the contributions in this part of the book explain group work techniques for assessment, and as elsewhere in this book, the contributions have a variety of purposes: to develop an increased awareness of the structure, style, and other aspects of text while encouraging students to revise and edit their own writing (Author, Author! Guided Reader Response); to assess students' oral skills without using time-consuming one-on-one interviews (Group Oral Tests); to foster turn-taking and conversational repair strategies (Putting It Together: A Jigsaw Task); to foster the grouping of semantically related new and old vocabulary items (How Many Words Is a Picture Really Worth?); to improve listening comprehension while encouraging lively discussion (Mini–Talk Shows in Classroom Assessment); to assess subject-verb agreement in groups (Run and Win); to give students an opportunity to demonstrate their fluency skills while explaining a process (Let Me Explain); and to apply reading comprehension strategies to unfamiliar texts (Reciprocal Teaching: Reading Strategies at Work).

Five other contributions explain pair work techniques for assessing students' oral communication ability (Face to Face); helping students logically connect oral sentences (Three-Sentence-Speech Speaking Test [TSSST]); helping both students and teachers recognize differences in their views of speaking ability (The Audio Mirror: Reflecting on Students' Speaking Ability); encouraging students to predict, negotiate, and experiment in finding answers about colors (Using the Science and Art of Colors to Teach ESL); and helping students organize and describe sequential events in the past (Organizing Ideas With Pictures).

Three contributions in this section combine group work and pair work, again with a variety of purposes: to identify students' strengths and weaknesses and set learning goals for their spoken English (Observation, Feedback, and Individual Goal Setting); to encourage and assess conversational English directly related to course objectives (Consolidate Yourself); and to help students understand the function of pronouns (Whose Shoes Do You Use?).

References and Further Reading

Mendelsohn, D. (1991/1992). Instruments for feedback in oral communication. *TESOL Journal, 1*(2), 25–30.

Porter Ladousse, G. (1983). *Speaking personally: Quizzes and questionnaires for fluency practice.* Cambridge: Cambridge University Press.

◆ Group Work
Author, Author! Guided Reader Response

Levels
Any

Aims
Assess, revise, and edit
own writing
Increase awareness of
text structure and
expected style
Review and critique
texts

Class Time
1–2 hours

Preparation Time
20 minutes

Resources
Reader Response Guide
Drafts of students'
papers
Criterion-Referenced
Grade Sheet

In this assessment activity, students perform a guided text review and critique their peers' writing efforts. The purpose is to encourage writers to assess their own work as well as revise and edit it. The activity should also help them to develop an increased awareness of the structure of text, style, and other elements of writing.

Procedure

1. Put the students into mixed-proficiency groups of three. Make sure the students each have a completed draft of a composition and a Reader Response Guide (see the example in Appendix A).
2. Go over the instructions and the parts of the guide, and answer questions. Explain that the purpose of the activity is for the students to help each other find problems and improve their papers by seeing where more details are needed, support is inadequate, language is confusing, and the like. Confirm that the students understand the purpose of the activity and the instructions.
3. Explain that it's often easier to hear language problems when a text is read aloud. Ask one author at a time in each group to read his or her paper aloud once. Ask the other members of the group to suggest corrections in language use as they listen. Warn against overcorrecting, and ask the students to confer with you if the group disagrees on an editing point.
4. Have another student in each group, the questioner, ask the questions on the Reader Response Guide in order, and ask the author to respond. Tell the third student in the group, the recorder,

to write down on the Reader Response Guide the answers given and any problems identified.

5. After the groups have worked their way through the paper in this fashion, tell them to switch roles. Continue this process until all three papers have been reviewed and critiqued.

Feedback and Scoring

1. In addition to the feedback that is integrated into the Procedure, use the Criterion-Referenced Grade Sheet (see Appendix B) to score the final, revised version of the writing assignment.

Caveats and Options

1. As an extension activity, consider asking the students to select the best paper from their group, and have each group member rate it according to the Criterion-Referenced Grade Sheet (see Appendix B). Ask them to compare the grades given and negotiate to agree upon a grade. This activity helps them to see what you look for in a paper.

2. If you wish, collect the Reader Response Guides and review them when you go through the revised draft of the paper to see if the writer followed the suggestions given.

3. Consider giving each group a grade on the basis of effort and the quality of feedback noted on the activity. If you let the students know ahead of time that you will be giving a grade, feedback will likely be better.

Appendix A: Reader Response Guide

This guide is designed for an argumentative paper.

Directions: You will work in groups of three. One of you is the author, one a questioner, and the third a recorder. You will trade roles after going over each paper so that each of you has a turn in each role. The author will first read his or her paper aloud, and all of you should help correct and improve the language use in it (e.g., grammar, vocabulary, sentence structure). Also listen to the content. When you've finished this *surface editing* of the paper, the questioner will ask (aloud) the questions below, and the author will respond. The questioner should ask follow-up questions when necessary to get the author to clarify or better explain his or her answers. The recorder is to take notes and list the main answers given by the author. Even more importantly, the recorder should make notes to help the author improve the paper, listing weak areas and making suggestions for improving the paper. ASK YOUR TEACHER NOW IF YOUR GROUP HAS ANY QUESTIONS.

A. Ask and answer these questions, focusing on the introduction:

1. What is your paper about? (topic)
2. What does each side say about that? (issue)
3. Why is this an important (or interesting) issue?
4. Have you given details to convince me that it is important? What are some details or examples?
5. What do you think about this issue? What is your position (thesis)? What would the opposite side say?

B. Ask and answer these questions, focusing on the body of the paper:

6. What reasons or ideas have you given to support your position? (Summarize your main points.) Do these reasons make sense? Can you think of any more that you could or should include?
7. What do you want me to believe? Why should I believe that? (E.g., what is the first main point you use to support your position?) Does it make sense to the reader?
8. How does that (first main point) relate to the thesis?
9. What examples, anecdotes, quotes from experts, statistics, and other support have you given to convince me that I should believe you (because you're not an expert)?
10. Have you given me more than one type of support (e.g., statistics and expert opinion)? Sorry, one is usually not enough.
11. What is your thesis again? What is the second reason (second main point) you give to make me believe or agree with you? Remember, I won't believe you if your idea is not logical.
12. What evidence have you given to convince me that I should believe you (because you're not an expert)? In other words, what examples, anecdotes, statistics, data, counterarguments or refutation, and other support have you given?

13. Have you given me more than one type of support (e.g., statistics and expert opinion)? Sorry, one is usually not enough.
14. What is your thesis again? Do you have a third reason (third main point) to convince me that I should believe you?
15. How do you support your third main point (e.g., with examples, anecdotes, statistics, data, counter arguments and refutation)? Have you given enough support (and enough types of support)?
16. Sounds good, but what would the other side say? What main arguments would your opponents have? What have you done to *attack* their arguments? (In other words, what counterarguments have you used to refute their position?)

C. Answer these questions, focusing on the conclusion of your paper:

17. What do you want me to do about it? What action should I take?
18. What do you want me to remember (or change) after I finish reading this essay? How is this applicable or important in my life? (Sorry, a summary of the ideas you stated earlier is not enough to convince me that I should change.)

Appendix B: Sample Criterion-Referenced Grade Sheet

The following grade sheet is designed for a persuasive paper.

Writer's name and ID_____ Date _____

Content, Organization, Logic

_____(10) The introduction clearly states the issue, its importance, and the writer's position on the issue.

_____(10) The thesis statement is well developed, clear, and appropriate.

_____(10) The main reasons given clearly support the thesis and make sense logically.

_____(10) Appropriate explanations, examples, statistics, and details are given.

Composition Structure

_____(10) Topic sentences and transitions communicate clearly and effectively orient the reader.

_____(5) The paragraphs are well developed and unified. The information given is not redundant or irrelevant.

_____(10) The arguments and positions move from general to specific, are supported clearly, and are in a logical sequence.

_____(5) Logical, useful counterarguments (refutations) are provided.

Grammar/Language Use/Mechanics

_____(10) The paper shows mastery of simple sentence constructions with few grammar errors (agreement, verb tense and form, number, word order). Sentence variety is attempted with effective complex sentence constructions.

_____(10) The vocabulary range is sophisticated, word and idiom choices and usage are effective, word forms are correct, and register and tone are appropriate.

_____(5) The paper shows mastery of mechanics and form, spelling, and punctuation.

_____(5) Use of quotation, paraphrase, and citation formats is correct.

_____(100) Total (See comments on back.)

Contributors

Kim Hughes Wilhelm is an assistant professor of linguistics and the curriculum coordinator at the Center for English as a Second Language (CESL), and Marilyn Rivers is the writing coordinator and a lecturer at CESL, Southern Illinois University at Carbondale, in the United States.

Group Oral Tests

Levels
Intermediate +

Aims
Teachers: Assess oral
skills of many students
without direct teacher-
learner interviews

Class Time
15–20 minutes/group

Preparation Time
Minimal

Resources
Discussion topics

The teacher-learner oral interview can be both intimidating to students and time consuming for teachers, particularly when classes are large. One strategy for alleviating these problems is to have the students discuss a prepared topic in groups while the teacher observes and assesses.

Procedure

1. Create discussion topics, perhaps with the help of the students, and form groups (see the scheme shown in Appendix A).
2. Give the students the topic(s) and the assessment criteria (see Appendix B) in advance to allow planning time and to let the students know what they are aiming for.
3. Put the students into groups, or allow them to form groups themselves.
4. Have the students discuss the topics. Observe the students unobtrusively; make sure you can see and hear all students clearly.

Feedback and Scoring

1. Award grades according to your chosen criteria and the reason for testing. One possibility is shown in Appendix B.
2. Optionally, have the students immediately reflect on their own performances, or give them immediate feedback.

Caveats and Options

1. This approach normally depends on a cooperative attitude among the students such that they all participate in a significant way and support each other. If you doubt that this attitude prevails, consider whether this will affect the execution and validity of the group test.

2. If you wish, assess participation skills, including leadership of the group. This option might involve an element of competitiveness—making one's point strongly—alongside equitable chairing skills.
3. Give the students a range of topics or just one topic to prepare. Either tell them the composition of their groups in advance, or put them into groups at the time of testing. Avoid giving the students an opportunity to script their discussion.
4. In some cases, (e.g., if your students are trainee teachers), consider content as one component of the assessment.

Appendix A: Creating Topics and Groups

Select from the following table.

Number of topics	Topic selection	Group formation
A. One	C. Random	E. Random
B. Several	D. Decided in advance	F. Decided in advance

Possible approaches:

A, D, E	B, D, E	B, C, E
A, D, F	B, D, F	B, C, F

Appendix B: Sample Score Sheet

This score sheet presupposes a set of criteria for assessing Levels 1-5 (e.g., Voice, Audibility: frequently too quiet or too loud, 1; consistently at a comfortable level, 5). Factors such as communicativeness have been omitted as being largely unmeasurable in this way. Participation is a very subjective area to assess unless frequency counts or similar devices are used.

Accuracy		1	2	3	4	5
Fluency		1	2	3	4	5
Lexis	Range	1	2	3	4	5
	Appropriateness	1	2	3	4	5
Voice	Audibility	1	2	3	4	5
	Pitch/tone	1	2	3	4	5
	Stress	1	2	3	4	5
Content	Relevance	1	2	3	4	5
	Supporting arguments	1	2	3	4	5
Participation	Amount	1	2	3	4	5
	Leadership	1	2	3	4	5
	Support for others	1	2	3	4	5

References and Further Reading

Bygate, M. (1987). *Speaking*. Oxford: Oxford University Press.

Hughes, A. (1989). *Testing for language teachers*. Cambridge: Cambridge University Press.

Contributors

Rex Berridge, a teacher educator and formerly an English language adviser with the British Council, is the director of the Language and Learning Centre at the University of Wales Aberystwyth, in the United Kingdom. Jenny Muzambindo, a teacher educator and an expert in English teaching and the methodology of teaching across the curriculum, is a senior lecturer in English at Belvedere Technical Teachers' College, Zimbabwe.

Putting It Together: A Jigsaw Task

Levels
Beginning

Aims
Demonstrate ability to
arbitrate speaking turns
in groups
Demonstrate use of
conversational repair
strategies
Share information

Class Time
40–50 minutes

Preparation Time
1 hour

Resources
Language lab, or three
cassette recorders
Audiotapes
Tape scripts
Evaluation Checklist
Where Is It? worksheet

This activity is a jigsaw listening task that, consistent with task-based teaching and testing approaches, integrates the four language skills but also places evaluative emphasis on completing the task. The Procedure assumes that the students have already done several similar tasks for practice. Information-gap activities done in pairs, though a great improvement over the sorts of drills common in precommunicative teaching methods, are all too predictable in some unfortunate ways. Because the information is often split evenly between the students, conversational turn taking may become a matter of the two students simply alternating, and opportunities to practice more natural turn-taking skills are limited. Jigsaw activities, on the other hand, allow several students to practice negotiating turns without any one student's knowing exactly who has the necessary information. The tasks can be graded in difficulty for use even with beginning-level students to help them learn the skills they will need to negotiate conversations in groups.

Procedure

1. Before class, record three audiotapes from the tape scripts in Appendix A.
2. Hold the activity in the language lab or a similar space where three groups of students can each listen to a different audiotape at the same time. Explain to the students that they are going to draw a picture from information they get from an audiotape. Split the students into three groups, and have the students in each group move their chairs together.
3. Provide each group with a cassette recorder and with an audiotape recorded from Tapescript A, B, or C.
4. Hand out the Where Is It? worksheet (Appendix B).

5. Have the students listen to the audiotapes and take notes on (not transcribe) the content of their audiotapes on their worksheet. Provide an example on the blackboard:

Tape	Notes
The book is on the floor.	*book on floor*
	(or *book on the floor* or *a book on the floor*)

Allow the students to listen to the audiotape as many times as they need to.

6. After they have finished taking notes from their audiotapes, have the students form new groups with one at least one A, B, and C student in each. Tell any extra students to double up in an existing group or work with a teaching assistant.

7. Tell the students they are going to share the information that they heard on the audiotape and draw the objects (e.g., sofa, bookshelf, table) on the picture on their worksheets. Model a typical exchange in which one student advances an incomplete piece of information and asks a question, and another student responds:
A: The book is on the table, but where is the table?
B: The table is next to the door. Where is the door?
C: It's on the right.

8. Remind the students of some techniques for solving conversational problems (e.g., *Excuse me? Could you say that again? On the right?*).

9. Make sure to set a clear time limit (about 20 minutes), and encourage the students to draw their pictures quickly rather than beautifully.

Feedback and Scoring

1. As the students are working in their groups, circulate and check their progress. Take note of the groups' progress, their turn taking, and their conversational repair strategies. Check that individuals are participating in English.

2. Use the Evaluation Checklist (Appendix C) as part of the course's achievement testing or simply to provide feedback to the students on their strengths and weaknesses.

Caveats and Options

1. Develop similar jigsaw listening activities with a variety of formats and requirements. See Ur (1984, pp. 152-160) for a discussion of jigsaw listening techniques and Anderson and Lynch (1988, pp. 80-96) for ways to grade listening tasks.

References and Further Reading

Anderson, A., & Lynch, T. (1988). *Listening*. Oxford: Oxford University Press.

Ur, P. (1984). *Teaching listening comprehension*. Cambridge: Cambridge University Press.

Appendix A: Tapescripts

Tape A

The bookshelf is under the picture.
The CDs are on the bottom shelf.
The cat is behind the chair.
The three cushions are on the sofa, on the left.
The coat is on the floor next to the coffee table, on the right.

Tape B

The two dirty socks are next to the coat, on the right.
The coffee table is in front of the chair.
The glasses are on the bookshelf, on the top.
The clock is above the chair.
The sofa is under the window.

Tape C

The pizza is on the table.
The light is on the ceiling.
The plant is between the bookshelf and the sofa.
The book is next to the glasses.
The big chair is next to the door on the right.

Appendix B: Where Is It?

1. Divide into groups and listen to the tape. Don't write everything you hear. Write only the main ideas. For example, if you hear
   The book is on the floor.
   write
   a book on the floor

_____

_____

_____

_____

2. In groups of three, ask the other students about the things in the picture. Draw the objects in the space below.

Appendix C: Evaluation Checklist

Student's Name: _____

	Yes				No
Group					
Is the picture finished?	5	4	3	2	1
Is the picture drawn correctly?	5	4	3	2	1
Did the students take turns smoothly and appropriately?	5	4	3	2	1
Did the students fix problems in the conversation?	5	4	3	2	1
Individual					
Did the student participate in the group?	5	4	3	2	1
Did the student use English?	5	4	3	2	1

Contributor

Michael Carroll is finishing his master's degree in TESOL at Temple University Japan and teaching at Sagami Women's University High School in Kanagawa, Japan.

How Many Words Is a Picture Really Worth?

Levels
Any

Aims
Employ known lexical
items
Add new items to
lexical repertoire
Group semantically
related vocabulary

Class Time
12–50 minutes

Preparation Time
10–20 minutes

Resources
5-cm by 5-cm squares of
paper
Container (e.g., hat)
Stopwatch or watch
with second hand

Inspired by the game Pictionary, this assessment activity is designed to motivate students to learn and perform well. At least 8 students are necessary for the game to work well, and no more than 16–18 students total is recommended (although a larger class can play the game). The activity not only helps reinforce the items in the students' memory by communicative and task-based exposure, but also creates a semantically related set of words in the students' minds. The game serves as both a very powerful learning strategy and a useful assessment guide: The students learn how to group semantically related vocabulary items, a skill that may be very useful, and the teacher sees generally where the class's lexical strengths and weaknesses lie.

Procedure

1. On each of 15–20 pieces of paper, write one lexical item that is appropriate to the level of the class. Use any items you choose, such as nouns or verbs, experiment with such abstract items as articles, or choose words that simply seem to fit nicely together or that are part of a hierarchical structure (e.g., *flower, rose, tulip*). Fold the papers twice so as to hide the contents.
2. Put the squares into a hat.
3. Divide the class into two groups.
4. Give the students the following instructions, and have them play the game:
   - For each turn, a different student draws for the group, and another student, the recorder, writes on the blackboard every guess that is given by members of the group.
   - To begin, one of the drawers picks a square from the hat, being careful that no one else sees the word, and shows the word to the opposing drawer.

- The timer is set for 1 minute. When the timer is started, the drawers begin to elicit the correct answer from their respective group's members (except for the recorder, who sits out during this turn) by drawing on the blackboard. The drawer may use any pictorial strategy except numbers and letters and may not use vocal cues.
- When the timer rings, if neither group has guessed correctly, no points are allotted, and the turn is finished. Whether a group has succeeded or not, the recorders write on the blackboard the options suggested by each group and return to their seats.

5. With the students, discuss the options and divide them into the categories *possible* and *impossible*. Also discuss items with which many of the students are unfamiliar.
6. If more than one turn is played, repeat the game, with different students taking the roles of drawer and recorder.

Feedback and Scoring

1. In perhaps the most important part of the activity, have the students, either in small groups or as a class, attempt to find ways that different words relate to one another (e.g., *horse* and *dog* are both animals; *laughing* and *crying* both show emotion).

Caveats and Options

1. When deciding which lexical items to use for the exercise, you may want to avoid *mixing*, that is, including, for example, both nouns and verbs in the hat. Mixing may defeat the purpose of trying to increase the students' skill in grouping certain types of lexical items.
2. If appropriate, tell the students beforehand which lexical category their skills are being tested in.
3. Keep track of the lexical items to use in future vocabulary exercises and tests.
4. If the class consists of students with mixed proficiency levels, as some English for specific purposes classes do, maintain an equal ratio of proficient to nonproficient students when dividing the students into teams. Also make sure that the more proficient students don't end up dominating.

References and Further Reading

Long, M. H., & Crookes, G. (1993). Units of analysis in syllabus design: The case for task. In G. Crookes & S. M. Gass (Eds.), *Tasks in a pedagogical context: Integrating theory and practice* (pp. 9–54). Clevedon, England: Multilingual Matters.

Pica, T., Kanagy, R., & Falodun, J. (1993). Choosing and using communication tasks for second language instruction and research. In G. Crookes & S. M. Gass (Eds.), *Tasks and language learning: Integrating theory and practice* (pp. 9–34). Clevedon, England: Multilingual Matters.

Contributor

Kayleigh Garman, an MA student in the Department of ESL at the University of Hawai'i at Manoa, teaches business English at Intercultural Communications College in Honolulu, in the United States.

Mini–Talk Shows in Classroom Assessment

Levels
Intermediate +

Aim
Recall content of a movie
Engage in a lively verbal exchange of ideas

Class Time
40 minutes

Preparation Time
Previewing: 10-15 minutes
Viewing: 1-1½ hours
Postviewing: 10-15 minutes

Resources
Movie on videotape
Video cassette player
Television monitor
List of topics

Visuals are often said to increase students' comprehension of language material. However, I find that, after seeing a film for the first time, the students retain only about 5% of what they see. This activity combines purposeful watching, group work, and creative expressions in an effort to improve the rate of comprehension.

Procedure

Previewing

1. Tell the students that you will show them a movie (or a part of it). Explain the mechanics of a talk show, and tell the students that, after viewing the movie, each of them will be a panel member on a talk show for a preset time limit.
2. Pass out a list of information you want the students to gather while they watch. Examples are
   - what the sequence of events is and how it is developed
   - who the actors are and what their roles in the film are
   - what the style of the film is
   - whichever useful English expressions they can pick out
   Attending to the items in the list should help the students increase their comprehension of the material.
3. Divide the class into groups of four or five depending on the size of the class and the number of topics you assign. Remind the students of the time limit for each talk show presentation.
4. Assign one topic to each group, or allow the students to choose from a list.

Viewing and Postviewing

1. Show the film.
2. Give the students time to organize their thoughts, individually or as a group.

The Talk Show

1. Ask the students to present their talk show (i.e., speak on their chosen topic) in any order you think appropriate.
2. Stress interactive presentation by encouraging other members of the class to ask questions after each talk show.

Feedback and Scoring

1. Although students at this level usually have a high level of motivation, encourage them to do their best by grading them on the work done, perhaps using the feedback sheet for group presentations described in Mendelsohn (1991/1992, p. 27). Alternatively, base the grades on a variation of Mendelsohn's feedback sheet.
2. Because this activity requires quite a long time from previewing to presenting the talk shows, it is best used as an end-of-term or end-of-school-year assessment device.

Caveats and Options

1. Adjust the choice of the movie to the level and interests of the class. Don't choose a film that is too long, as it will tend to drag, or cut it into parts.
2. At times, the students may not know how to divide the work among themselves in order to address the assigned topic. Assign or suggest tasks as follows, for example:
   ● On the topic *characters*, assign each member one or two of the characters to analyze and talk about.
   ● On the topic *sequence of events*, suggest that the group cut the movie into parts, with each member taking charge of one part.
3. Either decide on the order of presentations yourself, ask the students to volunteer, or decide the order via some sort of lottery.

References and Further Reading

Mendelsohn, D. (1991/1992). Instruments for feedback in oral communication. *TESOL Journal, 1*(2), 25-30.

Nelson, W. R. (1993). Increasing student-initiated communication and responses. *The Language Teacher, 17*, 39-42.

Schmidt, R. (1993). Psychological mechanisms underlying second language fluency. *Studies in Second Language Acquisition, 17*, 357-385.

Contributor

Cecilia B. Ikeguchi holds an MA in English education and educational systems and a PhD in educational theory. Currently a lecturer at Dokkyo University and Tsukuba University in Japan, she conducts research on language acquisition and testing, and comparative education.

Run and Win

Levels
Beginning

Aims
Learn present tense
subject-verb agreement

Class Time
30 minutes

Preparation Time
1 hour

Resources
Magnetic cards
containing subjects and
verbs
One blue and one pink
envelope

One of the biggest problems for beginning-level students in English is subject-verb agreement. This activity is designed to see if the students understand the third-person singular present tense form correctly, but in a way that students should enjoy. This assessment is done in groups but can serve as an individual assessment, as the students perform one or two at a time.

Procedure

1. Put the subject cards into the blue envelope, and put the verb cards into the pink envelope (see Appendix A).
2. Divide the students into two groups. Stand by the blackboard with the two envelopes.
3. Divide the blackboard into two parts by drawing a line.
4. Have two students (one from each group) run up to the blackboard and pull out a card from each envelope. Tell the students to put the cards on the blackboard and write a sentence in the present tense using the subject and verb on the card. For example,

Subject card   Verb card

| he | | read |

Sentence: He reads a book.

5. If the sentence is correct, allow the student to be seated; if the sentence is incorrect, have the student correct the mistake; if the student doesn't know how to correct the sentence, ask the next student from the same group to come up and help.

150

6. Have the students take turns as in Steps 4 and 5 in a sort of relay race until every student in a group has done the activity. The first group to have every student do the activity wins the game.

Feedback and Scoring

1. Assess the students while they are doing the activity. One way is to use the following scoring method:

   5   Correct sentence including spelling
   4   Two or fewer spelling mistakes
   3   Some mistakes in constructing the sentence
   2   Mistake in inflection of the verb
   1   Mistakes in inflection and construction of the sentence

Caveats and Options

1. Choose some verbs and subjects from the words the students have already learned, but include some verbs the students do not know to see how well they understand the inflection rule.
2. Select verbs of these three types:
   - V + -s (*work—works*)
   - V + -es (*watch—watches*)
   - V*y* + *ies* (*study—studies*)
3. Write the subject cards in ink of one color and the verb cards in ink of another.
4. Vary the game by changing the subject cards and verb cards into noun cards, adjective cards, or others to see how well the students understand the rules for making nouns plural, placing adjectives, and so forth.
5. Do this activity at least twice to give the students more opportunities to perform. These multiple opportunities will in turn help you to assess the students' understanding more fairly.

References and Further Reading

Celce-Murcia, M., & Larsen-Freeman, D. (1983). *The grammar book*. Boston: Heinle & Heinle.

Appendix A: Subject and Verb Cards

Subject cards		Verb cards	
I	Jack	be	sing
you	Jane	eat	study
he	Jane and Jack	fly	wait
she	Ken	listen	wash
it	Sally	live	watch
we	Spot and Tiger	play	work
they		rush	

Contributor

Misako Ohtani teaches at Koen Girl's School in Warabi, Saitama Prefecture, Japan.

Let Me Explain

Levels
Low intermediate +

Aims
Demonstrate fluency in explaining a process

Class Time
15–30 minutes to introduce
7–10 minutes/workshop

Preparation Time
1 hour

Resources
Scoring forms
Stopwatch

In this assessment activity, students give miniworkshops or short lessons to explain a hobby or teach a skill to a group of fellow students. The activity assumes that the students have studied how to give instructions, are familiar with the appropriate lexis and grammatical structures (e.g., *first, then, next, finally,* imperatives), and are familiar with asking for repetition and clarification. The activity requires students to demonstrate their ability to give instructions logically and clearly, examines their control over appropriate vocabulary, and checks their fluency.

Procedure

1. (about 15 minutes) Explain the activity to the students.
   - Have the students each select a topic (e.g., how to play a sporting activity, draw a picture, make pottery, play a musical instrument, arrange flowers) and prepare a miniworkshop in which they explain or teach some aspect of that topic. Encourage the students to bring realia (e.g., a putter, a cutout of a piano keyboard) when possible so that the other students can actually practice what they are being taught.
   - Inform the students that some of them will be trainees who will act out the instructions as they are being given. Tell them to ask for clarification or repetition any time they are unsure of the instructions or confused about what to do.
2. (10–15 minutes) The following week, have the students confirm their workshop topics. If necessary, help them with ideas for realia.
3. A week or so later, on the day of the workshops, divide the class into groups of 5–10 students. Have the students in each group arrange their chairs in a semicircle.

4. Designate one or two of the students from each group as trainees. To evaluate fluency as well as the ability to explain a process, encourage appropriate communication between the presenter and the trainees. Give the students useful prompts, for example,
   - Sorry, could you repeat that?
   - I beg your pardon?
   - Did you say _____?
   - [a brief reiteration of what the presenter says]
   Have the remaining group members write down the instructions as they are being explained using the target structures (e.g., *first, then*). Encourage the students to ask questions if they are unsure of the instructions.
5. Have the presenter and the trainees stand up and begin the workshops.

Feedback and Scoring

1. Using a scoring form (see the Appendix), circulate among the groups, and quickly circle the appropriate number for each student's performance level in each category. Total the four scores.

Caveats and Options

1. If the class is large, schedule the workshops over a few weeks.
2. Expect the students to give their workshops without notes. Depending on the complexity of the task, however, you may want to permit the students to write down a short list of vocabulary items.

References and Further Reading

Liskin-Gasparro, J. (1987). *Testing and teaching for oral proficiency*. Boston: Heinle & Heinle.

Weir, C. (1994). *Understanding and developing language tests*. Upper Saddle River, NJ: Prentice Hall.

Appendix: Sample Scoring Form

Student's name _____

1. Structures	1	2	3	4	5
2. Vocabulary	1	2	3	4	5
3. Strategic skills (repetition/reiteration, circumlocution, fielding and answering questions)	1	2	3	4	5
4. Communicative effectiveness (pronunciation, voice quality, intelligibility, paralinguistics)	1	2	3	4	5
Total					_____

Acknowledgments

The author thanks Sophia Wisener and Eric Bray for their helpful comments.

Contributor

Robin Russ has taught in Australia and in Spain and is currently teaching at Kansai University in Osaka, Japan.

Reciprocal Teaching: Reading Strategies at Work

Levels
Intermediate +

Aims
Apply reading
comprehension
strategies to unfamiliar
texts

Class Time
30–60 minutes, several
times

Preparation Time
1–2 hours

Resources
Overhead projector
Transparencies
Reading passages
unfamiliar to students
Reading Strategies
Group Record or
Anecdotal Record

This activity helps students routinely apply the reading comprehension strategies of summarizing, predicting, and asking questions for clarification to unfamiliar texts. English language students tend to need lots of support in activating these strategies and using them consistently. Through effective teacher modeling and repeated opportunities for practice in small groups, students learn to formulate questions reflecting literal and inferential comprehension, analysis, and other critical thinking skills. The importance of modeling cannot be overstated. When the activity is used for instruction, the teacher can assess reciprocal teaching as students work in small groups with a Reading Strategies Group Record (see Appendix A) or an Anecdotal Record (see Appendix B).

Procedure

1. Select several reading passages unfamiliar to the students that are at a challenging or instructional reading level (not too easy, not too hard) and that are of interest to them. The passages can be either excerpts or entire texts consisting of several paragraphs. Enlarge the first four paragraphs of each, and put them on transparencies.
2. Give each student a copy of one of the transparencies. Using the overhead projector, model the activity several times with the whole class as follows:
   - Ask all the students to read the first paragraph silently. Give them three purposes for reading: (a) to summarize the paragraph, (b) to ask questions for clarification of something in the paragraph that is unclear or that provokes a personal response, and (c) to predict what will appear in the following paragraph of the text.
   - When the students finish reading, (a) produce a one-sentence summary of the first paragraph; (b) ask yourself and the students

one question for clarification posed by the first paragraph, perhaps a point that is difficult to understand; and (c) predict what you think the author(s) will say in the second paragraph. Discuss possible answers.

- Repeat the modeling process with the second paragraph.
- For the third paragraph, ask for student volunteers to do each step (one step per student). Restate each student's response to model appropriate language where necessary.
- Repeat the modeling process with the fourth paragraph.

3. At intervals of several days, repeat the entire modeling sequence (Step 2) with a different reading passage until the students appear comfortable with it. When the students begin to be comfortable with the process, name the three strategies (summarizing, predicting, and questioning) as you model them, and encourage the students to name each strategy when they use it.

4. Give the students a printed copy of the three steps of reciprocal teaching, or display them on the overhead projector.

5. Tell the students they will follow the three-step reciprocal teaching process in small groups as follows:
- A leader reads the first paragraph and applies the three reading strategies.
- The next student applies the strategies to the second paragraph, and so on.
- Each student in the group gets a turn at being the leader. In this way, each student has an opportunity to practice and get feedback from peers and is held accountable for using the strategies.

6. Form small groups of four to five students.

7. Ask each group to pick a leader and begin the reciprocal teaching process.

8. Monitor each group to see that the students are following the process appropriately. Use either the Reading Strategies Group Record (see Appendix A) or the Anecdotal Record (see Appendix B).

9. Encourage the students to use the three strategies in their independent reading and to report back on their success, their difficulties, and the way they overcame any obstacles to effective strategy use.

Feedback and Scoring

1. Use the information generated on the Reading Strategies Group Record or Anecdotal Records to revisit this activity and to provide additional modeling or instruction in the application of reading strategies.
2. The Reading Strategies Group Record provides space for comments on each student's application of the reading strategies. Give feedback to groups or individual students in conferences or in a short write-up.

Caveats and Options

1. Support weak readers in one of several ways:
   - Form heterogeneous groups for the activity.
   - Team up weak readers with buddies who will support their efforts.
   - Ask each team to assist students who need it.
   - Allow weak readers to opt out of the activity if they do not feel comfortable. They will still be exposed to continuous modeling of both the reciprocal teaching process and the language involved.
2. With large classes, monitor only a few groups, perhaps those with the weakest readers, each time you conduct this activity.

References and Further Reading

O'Malley, J. M., & Valdez Pierce, L. (1996). *Authentic assessment for English language learners: Practical approaches for teachers*. Reading, MA: Addison-Wesley.

Palincsar, A. S., & Brown, A. L. (1984). Reciprocal teaching of comprehension-fostering and comprehension-monitoring activities. *Cognition and Instruction, 1*, 117–175.

Appendix A: Reading Strategies Group Record

Date _____

Students	Reading strategies			Comments
	Summarizes effectively	Asks questions for clarification	Makes predictions based on text and prior knowledge	
1. Carmen				
2. Hussein				
3. Harpreet				
4. Emma				
5. Carlos				

Appendix B: Anecdotal Record

Student's name:			
	Use of reading strategies		
Date	Reading strategies applied effectively	Reading strategies not applied	Additional instruction needed

Contributor

Lorraine Valdez Pierce teaches courses on assessment at George Mason University in Fairfax, Virginia, in the United States, and is coauthor of a book on authentic classroom-based assessment.

◆ Pair Work
Face to Face

Levels
Low beginning–high
intermediate

Aims
Demonstrate ability to
use descriptive
adjectives orally

Class Time
10 minutes

Preparation Time
10 minutes

Resources
Watch or timer

Are you tired of having to call on your students to get them to answer a question? This assessment activity gets students speaking English right away, and the teacher hardly has to utter a word. It's enjoyable and competitive, and the teacher can concentrate on a number of areas (e.g., grammar points, vocabulary reviews, assessments of strengths and weaknesses).

Procedure

1. Have the students count off by number. Break up the class into pairs of one odd- and one even-numbered student.
2. Have the odd-numbered students arrange their desks with their backs to the blackboard. Have the even-numbered students arrange their desks so that they face their partners' desks. Have all the students sit down.
3. Tell the students that you are going to write words on the blackboard, one at a time and that they must describe the word on the blackboard to their partner within a certain time limit. Also tell the students that they (a) cannot use hand gestures and (b) must speak only English.
4. Model a word for the students. For example, write the word *apple* on the blackboard. Describe the word to a model partner whose back is to the blackboard: "It is a fruit. It is round. It is green or red . . . ." Continue until the student answers correctly or the time limit is called.
5. To begin the assessment, give the pairs names or numbers for identification purposes. Write *A* and *B* on the blackboard to represent the students in each pair.

6. Write a word on the blackboard, and tell the students to begin. Tell the students when the time has expired. If the word is guessed correctly, award 1 point to the student who does the explaining.
7. Have the students switch seats (and roles) after several words have been played.

Feedback and Scoring

1. Tally the number of words each student has successfully described, as indicated by the other student's guessing it.

Caveats and Options

1. In a class with varying levels, avoid pairing students with relatively strong English skills. Instead, form pairs made up of a strong student and a weaker one so that there are no overly dominant pairs.
2. If you are teaching a class with students of varying nationalities, avoid pairing people who speak the same language to minimize the students' temptation to speak their L1.
3. If any strong or weak pairs disturb the flow of the activity, give one of the students a list of words. Have that student come to the blackboard and take your role in writing the words. Have the other partner team up with another pair to make a threesome, or you take the student's vacated seat and join the students.
4. This activity can assess the students' listening comprehension skills, too: Simply award points to the student who has guessed the correct word.

Contributor

Juergen J. Bulach has taught ESL in Germany, the United States, and Japan. He is an ESL instructor at Seattle International College Japan in Tokyo, Japan.

Three-Sentence-Speech Speaking Test (TSSST)

Levels
Beginning

Aims
Logically connect
sentences orally

Class Time
20 minutes/class for
every six students

Preparation Time
5 minutes

Resources
None

This activity gives quiet students something to talk about and gets them to speak out as much as possible, with the positive washback effect of process assessment. The more students speak, the more logically they speak, and the more natural they sound, the more points they can earn.

Procedure

1. Ask the students to arrange their chairs in a circle. Assign each student a number.
2. Have the students form a pair with the student beside them.
3. Have one partner ask the other partner a question (e.g., *What did you do last weekend?*).
4. Tell the partner to answer the question in at least three sentences.
5. When the first partner is finished with the three-sentence response, tell the answering partner to ask the same question of the other partner by saying, "How about you? What did you do last weekend?"
6. Choose one pair of students, and assess the two students' speaking ability while they are doing this dialogue exchange.
7. When the exchange is finished, ask the odd-numbered students to stand up and look for a new dialogue partner to their left.
8. Have the new pairs repeat the dialogue exchange. Assess another pair's speaking ability while they are performing their dialogue.
9. When the second exchange is finished, ask the students with odd numbers to stand up and look for a new dialogue partner to their left.
10. Let the new pairs perform the same dialogue. Assess another pair's speaking ability while they are performing their dialogue.

11. When the third pair's exchange is finished, tell the students go back to their original seats.
12. One by one, call on the six students you assessed during the dialogue exchange, and while the other students listen, have them attempt a narrative discourse on what their partners in the last pair did over the weekend.

Feedback and Scoring

1. Assess each student's narration ability (third-person narration using *he* or *she*). Try to focus your evaluations on the students' efforts to make sentences, then on the quality of the sentences they make.

Caveats and Options

1. Choose relevant topics for the dialogue exchange (e.g., *What will you do during winter vacation? What do you usually do on weekends?*) so that the students will be motivated to speak out.
2. Be patient with the students' frequent pauses.
3. Advise the students to repeat the last sentence or the last word of the previous sentence a couple of times when they cannot come up with a new sentence immediately.

Contributor

Yuji Nakamura is an associate professor of English at Tokyo Keizai University, Japan. His interests include listening and oral proficiency testing, and item response theory.

The Audio Mirror: Reflecting on Students' Speaking Ability

Levels
Advanced

Aims
Reflect on field-specific
speaking abilities
Demonstrate
conceptions of language
abilities
Identify differences
between students' and
teachers' conceptions of
speaking ability
Teachers: Determine
students' speaking needs
in authentic language
contexts

Class Time
2 hours

Preparation Time
30 minutes

Resources
Listening Handouts
Cassette recorders
Audiotapes

This assessment activity mirrors students' and teachers' attitudes toward the speaking process so that they can more clearly see and understand them. In this sense, the mirror reflects in multiple directions—it is not just a one-way (or even a two-way) mirror. By listening to themselves speaking on academic topics from their fields, students get to hear what they sound like when talking about subjects that interest them. By analyzing and critiquing their own speech, students reveal their ideas about their speaking ability and about what they think of as their strengths and weaknesses. The mirror also reflects a teacher's impressions. By conducting the same kind of analysis as the students, teachers reveal their attitudes toward individual students' ability and toward what they think constitutes effective speaking. In comparing these points of view in conferences, the teacher and the student can come to agreement on the student's goals for contextualized speaking needs. The entire reflective process generates an image of an effective academic speaker that is a helpful reference point for both students and teachers.

Procedure

1. In the class before you begin the assessment, tell the students to come to the next class meeting prepared to give a brief (5- to 10-minute) explanation of a single concept that they consider essential in their major academic area. Give a sample explanation. (See Caveats and Options, No. 1.)
2. Before the next class, set up enough recording stations to allow your class, working in pairs, to record a conversation without disturbing the other groups. A language lab is ideal for this activity.

3. To encourage authentic explanation and questioning, pair students with different areas of study; that is, pair students with someone who does not share their own major.

4. Make sure the students understand the functioning of the cassette recorders. Tell the students to turn on the cassette recorders and explain their chosen concept to their partner, assuming no previous understanding, as follows:
   - Tell the students to give a definition of the concept, explain how it applies to their major field of academic interest, and give reasons why it is an important concept to know.
   - Encourage the listening partners to question the speaker at any stage of the explanation. The students might request repetition of misunderstood speech, clarification of ideas, or definitions of words used.

5. Give the students 30 minutes in which to record the concept explanations of both partners.

6. Collect the audiotapes.

7. For the next class, make sure you have enough listening stations for all students to individually listen to their audiotapes.

8. In class, redistribute the audiotapes to their owners. Have the students begin by listening to the audiotape once through to give them an idea of what they sound like while speaking on their areas of academic interest.

9. Pass out the Listening Handout (see the Appendix). Have the students address the questions on it as they listen to their audiotapes again. Advise the students to be as specific as they can when answering the questions on the handout. Give them plenty of time (one class period), and tell them to listen to their audiotapes several times, rewinding, stopping, and analyzing as they go.

10. Collect the audiotapes and answers at the end of class. Do not read the students' answers until you have completed Step 11.

11. Listen to and reflect on the student's audiotapes. For each student, give your own answers to the questions on the Listening Handout.

12. Retain copies of both forms for yourself, and return copies of both forms to the students.

Feedback and Scoring

1. Schedule individual conferences with the students to compare your assessments with theirs.
2. In the conference, note similarities between your responses: Do you agree on the student's strengths and weaknesses? Do you make similar suggestions with respect to improving the student's speaking abilities?
3. Move on to disagreements. Try to decide to what extent disagreements stem from field-specific knowledge that the students have (and to which you may not be privy) and to what extent preconceptions about speaking needs and speaking ability are operating (for both of you).
4. Probe the students for deeper information on their individual academic speaking needs. Do they think their performance was representative of how they generally speak in academic situations? Do they think the explaining function was typical of the academic speaking they are faced with? Do they notice a difference between academic and everyday speaking requirements?
5. In class, address the range of comments and their similarities and differences across the different speakers.

Caveats and Options

1. Give an sample explanation before Step 1 of the Procedure, but not on taping day. That way the students can get an idea of what kind of discourse you are looking for, but the form of their explanations won't be modeled so much on yours. I usually give a 5-minute explanation of standardized testing—what it means and how it influences my work.
2. Use this assessment activity at the beginning of the semester. After holding conferences with all of the students, compile sets of field-specific speaking criteria from your notes, and share them with the students. Or form the students into groups by areas of academic similarity to create speaking standards based on contextualized speech, the students' individual reflections, and your reflections. Building these student-teacher-negotiated criteria transfers ownership of the assessment process from class-external or top-down sources to the individuals involved in the assessment process.

3. Follow up this activity by giving the students the opportunity to re-record their concept explanations. This encourages the students to plan and revise.

References and Further Reading

Norris, J. M. (1996). *Performance and portfolio assessment (1985-1995): An extended annotated bibliography of sources useful for language teachers* (Research Note). Honolulu: University of Hawai'i, Second Language Teaching and Curriculum Center.

Appendix: Listening Handout

Directions: Listen once to the audiotape of your explanation. Then read the following questions and listen again. Try to give detailed responses to all of the questions. Feel free to rewind and listen again as you see fit.

1. Do you think you gave a good enough explanation of the concept to your partner? Why or why not?
2. Were you able to give reasonable and clear answers to your partner's questions?
3. On this occasion, what were your major strengths when speaking about your academic interests?
4. On this occasion, what were your major weaknesses when speaking about your academic interests?
5. Based on this exercise, what should you do to improve your academic speaking abilities?

Contributor

John M. Norris is a doctoral student, teaches ESL, and conducts research on L2 assessment at the University of Hawai'i at Manoa, in the United States.

Using the Science and Art of Colors to Teach ESL

Levels
Intermediate; ages 7–11

Aims
Use English communicatively
Heighten consciousness of colors in the environment, in print, and in oral communication
Use prediction, negotiation, and experimentation skills to find answers
Work with primary and secondary colors

Class Time
1 hour

Preparation Time
20 minutes (with classroom aides)

Resources
Story, poem, or passage
Materials in Appendix A
Worksheets

Color plays an important part in everyday life. It can alter moods, can express ideas and feelings, and is a key descriptor used in spoken, visual, and written communication. This introductory color assessment activity gives children hands-on experience with how colors are formed and how they are related.

Procedure

Preparation

1. Before class, list the materials required for the activity on the chalkboard or chart paper (see Appendix A).

Introduction

1. In class, read the students a story, poem, or passage that includes color as a descriptor.
2. Conduct a short discussion with the students about how color is used in the text, and ask them for their own examples of where they see colors (e.g., in television commercials, clothing, makeup, cars).
3. Tell the students what primary colors are, and ask if anyone knows what *primary* means.
4. Group the students into pairs, designating one person as *Diamond* and the other person as *Heart*.
5. Ask the Diamonds to get the materials preceded by a diamond on the chart paper or blackboard, and ask the Hearts to get the materials preceded by a heart. Tell the students how much time they have to do this.
6. Inform the students that the newsprint will be the easel on which they will experiment with blending colors. Explain that the Dia-

monds will be responsible for spooning a dime-sized glob of paint onto the newsprint and that the Hearts will be responsible for blending the paint on the newsprint with the paintbrush.

7. Tell the students to paint a red, silver-dollar-sized dot in Section 1, a blue dot in Section 3, and a yellow dot in Section 5 of the paper-plate color wheel (see Appendix D).

Worksheet 1

1. Inform the students that they will work in pairs to complete Worksheet 1 (see Appendix B). Pass out a copy of Worksheet 1 to each student, read the directions aloud, and give an example for each activity. Ask the students if they have any questions.
2. Tell the students to fill in the remaining three of the six sections of the color wheel with a blend or secondary color made by mixing the two adjacent primary colors.
3. Have the students clean up their work areas and recycle the plastic spoons.

Worksheet 2

1. Pass out a copy of Worksheet 2 (see Appendix C) to each student, read the directions aloud, and give an example for each activity. Tell the students to look at their color wheel (see Appendix D) for hints on the answers.

Feedback and Scoring

1. Collect Worksheets 1 and 2 and the color wheel from each pair. Comment on the accuracy of their observations about color.
2. If you wish, comment on the accuracy of the language the students used in expressing their observations.
3. Return the materials to the students.

Caveats and Options

1. As a follow-up game, divide the class into two groups (Diamonds and Hearts), and choose one student from each group. Ask such questions as "What primary colors are used to make the color orange?" and "What is a complementary color of blue?"

2. In a variation of the follow-up game, have each student write down the answers and turn them in.

References and Further Reading

Blanton, L. L. (1992). A holistic approach to college ESL: Integrating language and content. *ELT Journal, 46*, 285–293.

Crandall, J. (1993). Content-centered learning in the United States. *Annual Review of Applied Linguistics, 13*, 111–126.

Davis, C., & Brown, C. (1988). *How to use color*. Tustin, CA: Walter Foster.

Mohan, B. A. (1979). Relating language teaching and content teaching. *TESOL Quarterly, 13*, 171–182.

Appendix A: Materials

Each pair of students will need
- ♦ newspaper to cover the work area
- ♦ a container of water
- ♦ an egg carton with red, blue, yellow, and white paint in four separate compartments*
- ♦ four plastic spoons

- ♥ one worksheet
- ♥ one paintbrush
- ♥ one sheet of newsprint
- ♥ one paper plate that has lines dividing it into sixths, labeled clockwise as Sections 1–6* (See Appendix D.)
- ♥ paper towels

*Requires extra preparation before class.

Appendix B: Worksheet 1

1. Record all observations on the table below.
2. Brainstorm a list of six objects that are not black, white, brown, gray, or a primary color.
3. Predict how to make the color, or a close approximation of the color, of the objects using a blend of two primary colors. For a hint on making your predicting easier, look at the color wheel with the three primary colors.
4. Experiment with the primary-color paints to produce the colors of the objects.

5. Fill in the last column with a name of the color that you have blended.
6. Predict and experiment to create the following colors: brown, black, gray, and white. You can use white and more than two primary colors.

Name of object	Colors to blend		Color of object
	Prediction	Actual	
1. grass			
2.			
3.			
4.			
5.			
6.			
7. —			brown
8. —			black
9. —			gray
10. —			white

Appendix C: Worksheet 2

1. List five objects and their color. Then write the two primary colors blended to make that color.

	Object and color	Primary colors blended
1.		
2.		
3.		
4.		
5.		

2. Give two examples for each of the following:
   ● primary colors
   ● secondary colors
   ● complementary colors (any two colors directly across from each other on the color wheel)

Note: Any two complementary colors mixed together will make brown!

Appendix D: Color Wheel

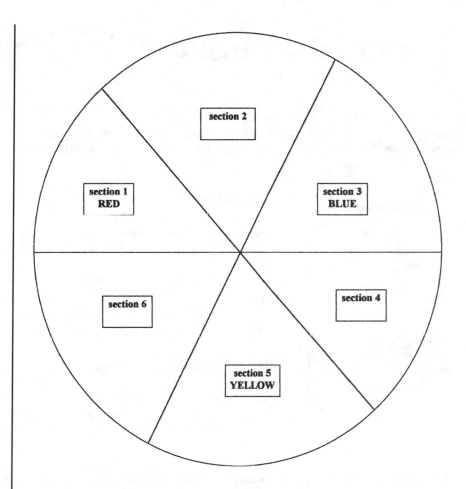

Contributor

Sharon F. Okano, a graduate student at the University of Hawai'i, in the United States, received her degree in elementary education and has taught in Hawai'i.

Organizing Ideas With Pictures

Levels
Intermediate

Aims
Organize ideas
Describe events in the
past

Class Time
2 hours

Preparation Time
1 hour

Resources
Sets of sequential
picture cards
Envelopes
Scoring sheet

Caveats and Options

Sequential pictures can help students speak coherently and organize ideas related to one topic. In this activity, they are used to describe events in the past.

Procedure

1. Select sets of sequential pictures showing different events (see Appendix A), and arrange them in the wrong order. Put the sets in envelopes.
2. Give each student one envelope. Ask the students to organize the pictures into a logical order.
3. After a few minutes of observation, ask each student to describe the events shown in the pictures orally, as if they occurred yesterday.

Feedback and Scoring

1. Score the students' performances on this activity in the areas of organization of ideas, coherence, fluency, pronunciation, accuracy, and appropriateness, as shown in the Model Scoring Sheet (Appendix B).

1. Instead of small pictures, make big cards, and have the whole class describe a single series of events.
2. Have the students discuss different ways to describe the same events.
3. Based on this oral description of the events, have the students write a short composition about what they have described.
4. The Model Scoring Sheet gives more weight to organization of ideas and appropriateness than to the other categories. Weight the categories equally by using 4-point scales for all of them.

Appendix A: Model Sequential Picture Cards

Appendix B:
Model
Scoring Sheet

Student's name: _____

Criterion			Score		
Organization	0	1	2	3	4
Coherence	0	1	2	3	
Fluency	0	1	2	3	
Pronunciation	0	1	2	3	
Accuracy	0	1	2	3	
Appropriateness	0	1	2	3	4
Total					

Contributor

Ilse A. Rodriguez, who works in the Department of Modern Languages at the Universidad de Carabobo in Valencia, Venezuela, is a teacher of English in a teacher training program.

◆ Group Work Combined With Pair Work

Observation, Feedback, and Individual Goal Setting

Levels
Beginning +

Aims
Demonstrate strengths
and weaknesses in oral
interaction tasks
Set individual learning
goals based on teacher's
assessment

Class Time
30–45 minutes

Preparation Time
15 minutes

Resources
Oral communication
task
Observation Schedule
Assessment Criteria for
Oral Interaction

Recent years have seen important changes in how students' L2 development is reported on and assessed. In particular, attention to the notions of communicative performance testing and "evaluation as an aid to learning" (Brindley, 1989, p. 5) in L2 classrooms has increased. The assessment tasks here aim to draw these concerns together. In this activity, the teacher observes and evaluates the students' oral performance and gives detailed feedback based on specific, performance-related criteria. The students draw on this evaluation and feedback to set individual language learning goals.

Procedure

1. Choose a pair or group oral communication task, or a series of tasks, linked to the aims of the course of study your students are undertaking and the aspect of language use they are currently focusing on (see Klippel, 1984; Nolasco & Arthur, 1987; Porter Ladousse, 1983).
2. Make a copy of the Observation Schedule in Appendix A for each of the students in your class.
3. Set up the communication task(s) you have chosen so that the whole lesson takes about 30–45 minutes to complete. If you wish to use only one task for the lesson, ask the students to perform it a number of times with different partners or in a different group, depending on the nature of the task.

4. Observe the students' oral interactions pair by pair or group by group, as appropriate.

Feedback and Scoring

1. Make notes about individual students' performance according to the categories on the Observation Schedule (see Appendix A). Use the criteria in Appendix B as the basis for the comments you write.
2. Hold a general feedback session on the activity for the class as a whole, highlighting the positive aspects of the students' performance as well as areas of their performance that they could improve.
3. Write up individual assessments of each student's performance under the categories listed in Appendix A. Use the Assessment Criteria for Oral Interaction (see Appendix B) to refer to specific areas of the students' performance that would benefit from attention.
4. Give the students your assessments in a subsequent lesson. Then make appointments for the students to discuss their assessments with you individually. When discussing the assessments with individual students, ask them to identify one area from the assessment they will work on for their next in-class observation and assessment. In this way, you can help each student establish learning goals.

Caveats and Options

1. Repeat this assessment activity after a further period of instruction, using the previous assessment as the starting point for your observation and feedback.
2. Assign the students a grade for each of the areas of assessment as well as an overall score for their performance. Then use the grades as a reference point against which to measure future assessments and as a way of showing the students how they are progressing toward the learning goals they have set.
3. Give higher level students copies of the criteria you use for your assessment, and write your feedback in light of the terminology that they employ. Be sure, however, to spend time explaining the meaning of some of the more technical terms used in the criteria sheet. The criteria are explained in detail in Paltridge (1992).
4. Give the students an opportunity to assess each other's performance in the same way that you have observed and assessed theirs. Then

have them give each other feedback as you have done and help each other establish individual learning goals based on these assessments.

References and Further Reading

Brindley, B. (1989). [Editorial]. *Prospect, 4,* 5–8.

Klippel, F. (1984). *Keep talking: Communicative fluency activities for language teaching.* Cambridge: Cambridge University Press.

Nolasco, R., & Arthur, L. (1987). *Conversation.* Oxford: Oxford University Press.

Paltridge, B. (1992). EAP placement testing: An integrated approach. *English for Specific Purposes, 11,* 243–268.

Porter Ladousse, G. (1983). *Speaking personally: Quizzes and questionnaires for fluency practice.* Cambridge: Cambridge University Press.

Appendix A: Observation Schedule

Name:	
Focus of assessment	Comments
Overall impression	
Accuracy	
Fluency	
Appropriateness	
Intelligibility	
Comprehension	
Strength(s) of your spoken English	
Area(s) for improvement	

Appendix B: Assessment Criteria for Oral Interaction

Level	Overall impression	Accuracy	Fluency
0: Beginner	Nonuser. Cannot communicate in English at all.		
1: Elementary	Intermittent user. Communication occurs only sporadically.	Very limited grasp of lexical, grammatical and relational patterns and functional language use.	Utterances consist of isolated words or short, memorized phrases. Frequent pauses may occur. Lack of range, subtlety, and flexibility.
2: Intermediate	Limited user. Neither productive skills nor receptive skills allow continuous communication.	Limited grasp of lexical, grammatical, and relational patterns. Initial grasp of functional language use.	Speech hesitant but self-correction occurs. Little ability to take the initiative in developing a conversation. Limited range, no subtlety or flexibility.
3: Upper intermediate	Moderate user. Can get by without serious breakdowns. However, misunderstandings and errors may still occur.	Moderate grasp of lexical, grammatical, and relational patterns, enabling the expression of a broader range of meanings and relationship between those meanings.	Can sustain conversation but reformulation sometimes necessary. Moderate range, subtlety, and flexibility.
4: Advanced	Competent user. Copes well in most situations. Will have occasional misunderstandings or errors.	Competent grasp of lexical and grammatical, patterns and functional language use. Relationships between meanings generally well expressed.	Can generally engage in spontaneous conversation on most general purpose topics. Competent range, subtlety, and flexibility.
5: Special purpose	Good user. Copes well in most situations. Can perform competently within own special purpose areas.	Confident and generally accurate use of lexical and grammatical patterns and functional language use. Relationships between meanings well expressed.	Can engage in spontaneous conversation on general topics as well as matters relevant to own special purpose interests. Good range, subtlety, and flexibility.

Appropriateness	Intelligibility	Comprehension
Use of language minimally appropriate to context, function, and intention.	Can convey only very simple meanings. Concentration and constant verification necessary on the part of the listener. Lacking strategies to compensate for low level of language ability.	Can understand only slow, careful speech. Frequently requires repetition.
Use of language appropriate to function, context, and intention within a limited range of situations.	Can convey basic meanings. Can be understood with effort but patient understanding necessary. Simple mastery of basic communication strategies.	Can understand speech related to familiar topics phrased simply. Repetition may still be required.
Use of language generally appropriate to function, context, and intention within a moderate range of situations.	Can be understood without undue difficulty when discussing familiar topics but problems may arise with detailed explanations. Moderate command of a range of communication strategies.	Can generally understand and interpret meanings related to familiar subjects spoken by a native speaker at normal speed.
Use of language generally appropriate to function, context, and intention within a range of situations.	Communicates meanings competently in general communication contexts. Competent command of a range of communication strategies.	Can understand and extract information from native-speaker speech at normal speed. Some repetition may be required in special purpose areas.
Use of language mainly appropriate to function, context, and intention within a good range of situations.	Communicates meanings well in general and within own special purpose areas. Good command of a range of communication strategies.	Can understand and extract information from most native-speaker speech. Will also have some competency within own special purpose areas.

Contributor

Brian Paltridge is a senior lecturer in applied linguistics at the University of Melbourne, Australia. He has taught ESL/EFL in Australia, New Zealand, and Italy.

Consolidate Yourself

Levels
Any

Aims
Review course
objectives in an
enjoyable way
Receive feedback and a
score on performance

Class Time
30-60 minutes

Preparation Time
15-30 minutes

Resources
Game boards
Dice
Small objects to use as
tokens
Direct Assessment Form
or
Teacher's Assessment of
Students Form

Because I teach within a curriculum that has an achievement test scheme, I am pressed to get my students to show a gain on the final test. To do this, I use the Consolidate Yourself game board (a) periodically during the course as reinforcement and (b) as a review of course objectives toward the end of the course. My students enjoy the visual aspect of this game, and I reach my teaching objective: The students show a gain. Also, the game lends itself to free (real) conversation in an English classroom in Japan—something not easily done.

Procedure

Making the Game Board

1. Choose items from the course objectives that you think the students need to review.
2. Make a game board like the one in Appendix A. Fill in the spaces with tasks that are based on the objectives you have chosen. Several times on the game board, repeat tasks based on one objective that you especially want to concentrate on assessing, for example, comparing Japan with other countries. The sample game board in Appendix B contains this objective four times on the board so that the teacher can assess every student.

Playing the Game

1. Put the students in pairs or in groups of three or four students each. If you form groups of three, you can monitor them more easily and, if so desired, surreptitiously.

2. Distribute one game board, one die, and objects that serve as tokens (e.g., coins, erasers) to each pair or group. Do not read the game board to the students before they play. To prepare the students to play, tell them to
   - supply details, not short answers
   - start again when they finish the game (The game lends itself to digressions.)
   - not play to win
3. Have the students roll the die and move their selected token across the game board.

Feedback and Scoring

1. Assess the students' responses with the Direct Assessment Form (see Appendix C).
2. Either return the form to the students at the end of class, or record the assessment on the Teacher's Assessment of Students Form for your own records (see Appendix D). Returning the form to the students immediately prevents you from forgetting to do it later and, more importantly, the students really appreciate it.

Caveats and Options

1. Vary the design of the game board each time you make a new one by using different colors, sizes, and so on. This prevents both you and the students from becoming bored.
2. Either use computer-designed game boards, or make them by hand.
3. Don't assess the students during the first part of the game; let them warm up. When they answer the same question more than once, the students naturally tend to give better and better answers, showing that they are taking advantage of the learning environment.
4. This assessment activity, initially designed for adults and high school students in Japan, can be adapted to any level.
5. Instead of using one type of game board, give each group a different one.
6. After the students have gone through the game board once, rotate one student from each group into another group. This option gives the groups a chance to communicate and compare their English with more combinations of students and gives the students more chances to learn.

Appendix A: Blank Game Board

CONSOLIDATE YOURSELF

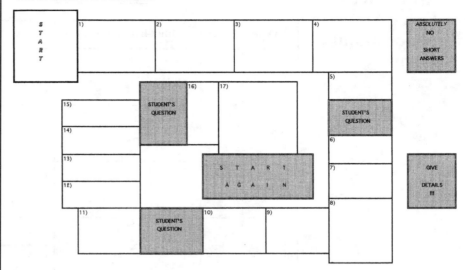

Appendix B: Sample Game Board

CONSOLIDATE YOURSELF: THE BASICS

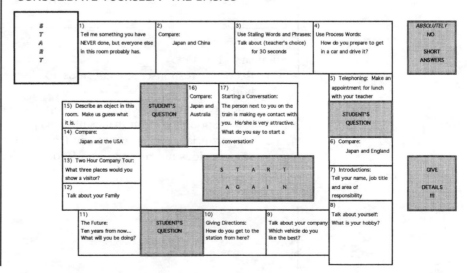

Appendix C: Direct Assessment Form

Student: _____

Date	Rater	Objective assessed	Scores	Average
			1 2 3 4 5	
			1 2 3 4 5	
			1 2 3 4 5	
			1 2 3 4 5	
			1 2 3 4 5	
			1 2 3 4 5	
			1 2 3 4 5	
			1 2 3 4 5	
			1 2 3 4 5	
			1 2 3 4 5	

Summary of Scores

5 Excellent response; student adds to discussion, involves others, or both.

4 Good response; student responds appropriately.

3 Fair response; student makes obvious grammar and fluency errors.

2 Inappropriate response; student tries to respond or clarify.

1 Student does not respond or ask for clarification; uses Japanese.

Appendix D: Teacher's Assessment of Students Form

Date:

Class:

Teacher:

Student	Objective assessed	Scores	Average
		1 2 3 4 5	
		1 2 3 4 5	
		1 2 3 4 5	
		1 2 3 4 5	
		1 2 3 4 5	
		1 2 3 4 5	
		1 2 3 4 5	
		1 2 3 4 5	
		1 2 3 4 5	
		1 2 3 4 5	

Summary of Scores

5   Excellent. Student answers appropriately, freely adds to response, and involves others in his or her discourse.

4   Good. Student answers appropriately; minor mistakes—if any—don't hamper comprehension.

3   Fair. Student gives fair response and makes obvious grammar and fluency errors.

2   Poor. Student tries to respond, but response is inappropriate.

1   Student doesn't understand, ask for clarification, or respond in any way; uses Japanese profusely.

Contributor

Chris Samsell is an English teacher in Zushi City, Kanagawa, Japan.

Whose Shoes Do You Use?

Levels
Intermediate +

Aims
Understand and
demonstrate functions
and uses of pronouns

Class Time
1 hour

Preparation Time
15–20 minutes

Resources
Directions and list of
items
Role-play descriptions
Realia (optional)
Assessment form
(optional)

Procedure

Preparation

1. If you wish, collect realia (e.g., household items: clocks, toothbrushes, dishes, food items, shoes, books) to bring to class.
2. Based on the realia, fill in the List of Items (see Appendix A) so that all the items are listed next to the characters who own them.

Explanation

1. Tell the students that they will do an activity to help them learn the use of pronouns.
2. Go over the basic pronouns: *I, me, my, he, him, his, she, her, her, they, them, their, we, us, our, you, you, your.*
3. Practice some of the pronouns by having the students make sentences using themselves, you, or their classmates as subjects.

Warm-up Activity

1. Ask the students to form groups of three to five and to list conversational situations in which they might use pronouns.
2. Regroup the class and discuss each group's findings.
3. Explain that the students will be doing a role play about college housemates who are all moving away after graduating.

Assessment Activity

1. Form pairs of students.
2. Pass out the directions and list of items (see Appendix A).

3. Go over the role-play directions, and discuss new vocabulary (using the realia to stimulate discussion) and any questions that arise.
4. Assign each student a role description from Appendix B, and help individual students understand their parts.
5. Have the students perform their role plays. Observe and make notes on how they use pronouns.

Feedback and Scoring

1. After the role play is complete, give the students feedback on their use of pronouns.
2. If you wish, record the interaction while noting nonverbal communication, and fill out the assessment form in Appendix C.

Caveats and Options

1. Use the students' ideas to design a similar role play.
2. If finding realia proves difficult, draw items on paper, or simply have the students use their imaginations.
3. This type of role-play activity is also good for practicing the use of modals and the language of negotiation.

References and Further Reading

Ellis, R. (1993). Interpretation tasks for grammar teaching. *TESOL Quarterly, 29*, 87–105.

Nunan, D. (1995). Closing the gap between learning and instruction. *TESOL Quarterly, 29*, 133–158.

Pica, T., Canoga, R., & Fellation, J. (1993). Choosing and using communication tasks for second language instruction and research. In G. Crookes & S. M. Gass (Eds.), *Tasks and language learning: Integrating theory and practice* (pp. 9–34). Clevedon, England: Multilingual Matters.

Appendix A: Directions and List of Items

Directions: You are all roommates who have been living in the same house while going to college. It is now the end of the school year, so everybody will be graduating and moving away to start jobs in different cities. There are lots of things in the house that need to be packed, but it isn't clear which things belong to which roommate. Try to sort out everybody's belongings.

Item	Owner
[Add names of items here.]	[Add names of owners here.]

Appendix B: Role Descriptions

Ahmad: You have been living in the house for 4 years. Because you have been living there so long, you have more things than everybody else. You are a leader of the house, so make sure you and everybody else gets their things sorted out as peacefully as possible. Below is a table of things in the house and who owns them. This should help you sort out the household items.

Item	Yours	Somebody else's	Not sure whose

Sharon: You have lived in the house for 1 year. You brought a lot of things to the house when you moved in, so be sure to get them back. You're not too fond of Richard because he's really forgetful. Below is a table of things in the house and who owns them. This should help you sort out the household items.

Item	Yours	Somebody else's	Not sure whose

Nolan: You've lived in the house for only 6 months, and you didn't bring so many things to the house. Because you've lived in the house for such a short time, you don't have so many things and you remember exactly what is yours and what isn't. Below is a table of things in the house and who owns them. This should help you sort out the household items.

Item	Yours	Somebody else's	Not sure whose

Yoko: Richard is your boyfriend. You have lived in the house for a year and a half. Richard is forgetful, so he might not be so accurate about what he owns and what you own together. Be sure to get what is yours, and try to do it as smoothly as possible. Below is a table of things in the house and who owns them. This should help you sort out the household items.

Item	Yours	Somebody else's	Not sure whose

Richard: You and your girlfriend Yoko have lived in the house for a year and a half. You're not so sure about what is yours and what isn't, so try to get as many things as possible just to be sure. Sharon doesn't like you because she thinks you're forgetful. Below is a table of things in the house and who owns them. This should help you sort out the household items.

Item	Yours	Somebody else's	Not sure whose

Appendix C: Assessment Form

1. Does the student use pronouns that correspond to their antecedents?
2. Does the student use pronouns in appropriate places within sentences?
3. Does the student use pronouns as frequently as possible?
4. Does the student use pronouns appropriately within discourse?
5. Does the student use means of clarification, such as circumlocution and gesturing, when difficulties with pronouns arise?
6. Does the student get the items that belonged to him or her? If not, is it because of a lack of proficiency in using pronouns?
7. Does the student's use of pronouns contribute to settling the entire group's situation?
8. Does the student use pronouns while speaking to individuals as well as with the entire group?

Contributor

Mark D. Stafford holds a master's degree in ESL and has taught in Japan and in Hawai'i, in the United States.

Part IV: Alternative Ways of Doing Classroom Chores

Editor's Note

Traditionally, preparing students for tests, creating assessment procedures, grading, and evaluating curriculum have all been prerogatives of the teacher. Yet a number of the contributions to this book clearly offer alternative ways of doing these classroom chores. In some cases, the contributors appear to be trying to save teachers work by using the students' energy to get things done. In other cases, the contributors appear to have a genuine and healthy interest in involving students in the decision-making processes as part of their learning experience. In most cases, the teachers who contributed to this book seem to be recognizing the central role of assessment in curriculum development (for more on this issue, see Brown, 1995). Regardless of their motivations, the contributors are advocating that students be involved in (a) preparing themselves for tests, (b) making their own assessment procedures, (c) helping make grading easier, and (d) evaluating their own curriculum.

As elsewhere in this book, the three contributions involving the students in the processes of preparing themselves for tests have a variety of purposes: to help students appraise their multiple-choice test-taking skills (Test-Wiseness Minitest), anticipate essay exam questions and create appropriate answers by putting themselves in the place of university professors ("Now You're the Professor!" Anticipating Essay Exam Questions), and identify answers in their returned tests that warrant reconsideration by the teacher and encourage them to politely reason and negotiate with the teacher about those answers (It's OK to Argue).

The four contributions that show how students can develop their own assessment procedures also focus on different goals: to assess students' reading comprehension and question formation abilities based on questions they themselves formulate about a reading passage (U Test U), to provide a bridge between what teachers and students think should be learned (Let Them Make Quizzes: Student-Created Reading Quizzes), to introduce students to the assessment of their work using their own rubrics (Developing a Student-Centered Scoring Rubric), and to create criteria and standards for assessing aspects of language that are seldom evaluated through student involvement (A Continuous Assessment Framework).

The three contributions that help make grading easier do so with several purposes in mind: to assess students' abilities to understand a reading and answer questions on it (Raise Your Hand and Be Counted); to assess students' abilities to integrate and sequence events (Course of Events); and to help students better understand, control, and predict their grades (Getting the Point(s): An Adaptable Evaluation System).

Finally, the three contributions that utilize students in evaluating their own curriculum do so for different reasons: to assess students' degree of satisfaction with and involvement in various classroom activities (Thermometer), to assess students' understanding of classroom activities and involve students regularly in evaluating those activities (Multiple Assessment Action Logging), and to get teachers to learn from students what works and what doesn't (Wow! Marvelous Task).

References and Further Reading

Allan, A. (1992). Development and validation of a scale to measure test-wiseness in EFL/ESL reading test takers. *Language Testing, 9*, 101–122.

Brown, J. D. (1995). *The elements of language curriculum: A systematic approach to program development*. Boston: Heinle & Heinle.

Fuji, T. (1993). Classroom management: Creating motivation by use of a clear grading system. *The Language Teacher, 17*, 37, 39.

Murphey, T. (1994/1995). Tests: Learning through negotiated interaction. *TESOL Journal, 4*(2), 12–16.

◆ Preparing Students for Tests
Test-Wiseness Minitest

Levels
Intermediate +

Aims
Estimate skill at taking
multiple-choice tests

Class Time
15–20 minutes

Preparation Time
5 minutes

Resources
Test-Wiseness Minitest

Quite often, items on classroom tests, especially multiple-choice tests, contain unintended clues to the correct answers. Students who are test-wise are able to exploit these weaknesses and select the correct answers without necessarily possessing the knowledge or skills that the items are intended to measure. The Test-Wiseness Minitest gives a broad indication of test-wiseness. Low-scoring students are sensitized to their possible lack of this skill and can be suitably counseled and trained.

Procedure

1. Tell the students to that they are to work individually on a test. Remind them to use their skill, judgment, experience, and any tactics they can think of (apart from copying from each other!) to find the correct answers.
2. Hand out the Test-Wiseness Minitest (see Appendix A).
3. Tell the students to select the best option (a, b, c, or d) for each question.

Feedback and Scoring

1. When the students have completed the test, read out the correct answers (see Appendix B) so they can mark their responses. The higher the students' total scores, the more test-wise they are. Anyone scoring higher than 3 (the level expected from blind guessing) has some amount of test-wiseness.
2. Have the students in pairs or threesomes try to identify the items making up the three subscales, each measuring one aspect of test-wiseness, in the test (see Appendix C).

Caveats and Options

1. Remind the students not to take their scores too seriously. The test should produce valid scores, but it is very short, so the scores may not be reliable. They are merely suggestive.
2. Have the students note the strategies they use when responding to each item and compare them with their classmates'.

References and Further Reading

Allan, A. (1992). Development and validation of a scale to measure test-wiseness in EFL/ESL reading test takers. *Language Testing, 9,* 101–122.

Appendix A: Test-Wiseness Minitest

1. Anna looked at the bowl of fruit then chose an
   a. banana.
   b. orange.
   c. mango.
   d. pear.

2. The herb called Eyebright was traditionally used
   a. to treat weak eyesight.
   b. for flower arrangements.
   c. in cooking vegetarian food.
   d. as a perfume.

3. A copper beech is a
   a. police dog.
   b. tree.
   c. mineral deposit.
   d. coin.

4. Steve has consulted many chiromancers, but only one
   a. are willing to give him advice.
   b. seems to understand him.
   c. charge him reasonable fees.
   d. offer to help him.

5. Mr. Park was dismissed from his job unfairly. This made his friends
   a. going on strike.
   b. to be sad.
   c. sympathizing.
   d. angry.

6. The leaves of the copper beech
   a. must be turned over every day.
   b. look similar to the leaves of most other trees.
   c. are the color of copper.
   d. should be used for protecting house walls from heavy rain.

7. My teacher, Mrs. Lee, said that my handwritten essay was a good example of cacography. This means
   a. my essay was too short.
   b. I had included some interesting ideas.
   c. I had written on the wrong topic.
   d. my handwriting was hard to read.

8. The Ashcan School was a
   a. old school that was closed down because it was so bad.
   b. ugly, unpleasant place used temporarily as a school.
   c. group of artists who painted scenes of city life in the early 20th century.
   d. organization that wanted to reform society by destroying poor-quality buildings.

9. Mrs. Lee
   a. was a ballet dancer.
   b. was a music lover.
   c. worked in a school.
   d. worked in a bank.

10. Small lakes found in mountainous areas are known as
    a. turns.
    b. tarns.
    c. terns.
    d. tiryns.

11. Jenny's crazy about books. She collects dozens of them. You could call her
    a. a woman.
    b. a person.
    c. Jenny.
    d. a bibliomaniac.

12. While climbing in the mountains, my brother Vic found a tarn and
    a. nearly fell into it.
    b. wore it all day to keep off the rain.
    c. kept it as a pet.
    d. sold it later for a large sum of money.

13. My parents have gone out for a preprandial walk. This means
    a. a healthy walk.
    b a long walk.
    c. a walk for pleasure.
    d. a walk before dinner.

14. I told my dog to keep quiet, but it barked
    a. loud and loud.
    b. even louder.
    c. ever loud.
    d. too loud.

15. Who among the following sometimes goes on hiking holidays?
    a. Anna.
    b. Mr. Park.
    c. Vic.
    d. Mrs. Lee.

Appendix B: Answer Key

1 (b) orange. ("*an* orange")
2 (a) to treat weak eyesight. ("*Eye*bright")
3 (b) tree. (See clue in Question 6(b), "most other *trees*.")
4 (b) seems to understand him. ("only *one* seem*s* to understand him")
5 (d) angry. (The phrase "made his friends" must be followed by an adjective [angry].)
6 (c) are the color of copper. ("*copper* beech")
7 (d) my handwriting was hard to read. ("*hand*written" . . . "*hand*writing")
8 (c) group of artists who painted scenes of city life in the early 20th century. (Indefinite article *a* should be followed by a word beginning with a consonant.)
9 (c) worked in a school. (See clue in Question 7, "my *teacher*, Mrs. Lee.")
10 (b) tarns. (See clue in Question 12, "climbing in the mountains.")
11 (d) a bibliomaniac. ("*crazy* . . . biblio*maniac*")
12 (a) nearly fell into it. (See clue in Question 10(b), *tarns*.)
13 (d) a walk before dinner. ("*pre*prandial . . . before dinner")
14 (b) even louder. (This is the only grammatically correct option.)
15 (c) Vic. (See clue in Question 12.)

Appendix C: Subscales

The three item groups (subscales) in the test measure different aspects of test-wiseness, as follows.

Ability to	Items
1. Recognize a clue in the question stem	2, 6, 7, 11, 13
2. Recognize that the grammar in the question stem or in one of the options points to the correct answer	1, 4, 5, 8, 14
3. Recognize that a word or phrase in the stem or options in one question gives a clue to the answer in a different question	3, 9, 10, 12, 15

Contributor

Alastair Allan is an associate professor in the English Department at the City University of Hong Kong.

"Now You're the Professor!" Anticipating Essay Exam Questions

Levels
High intermediate +

Aims
Anticipate essay exam
questions
Determine salient
features of appropriate
essay exam answers
Gain insight into the
creation of essay
questions and the
evaluation of answers
Improve study habits for
exams

Class Time
2-3 hours over three to
four classes

Preparation Time
30-60 minutes

Resources
Overhead projector,
transparencies, and
markers
Self-Assessment
Worksheet

Students often have difficulty predicting what a professor will ask them on exams and knowing how to study effectively. Essay exams can be particularly problematic for ESL students. In this activity, the tables are turned: The students imagine they are professors and write essay exam questions while the teacher takes the role of the student and writes essay answers to the questions written by the students. The professors then evaluate the answers and give feedback to the students. In this way, ESL students not only learn strategies to prepare for and succeed on essay exams but also come to understand better the material they are studying.

Procedure

1. After the students have completed a content unit, ask them to imagine that they are professors, that they have just given their students the lectures and readings in the unit, and that they are now ready to test their students on their understanding of the material.
2. (30-50 minutes) Ask the "professors" to form groups three to four and, using their lecture notes and academic readings, to write essay exam questions on the material they've taught their students.
3. After class, choose the four or five best questions from the groups and, in your new role as student, write answers to the essay questions. Make some answers appropriate and correct; in others, include erroneous information and write in a confused manner. Make photocopies of your answers for the class.
4. At the next class, give your answers to the professors. For homework, ask them to grade the answers and write positive and negative feedback, pointing out what is good in the answers and where you have made errors or seem confused.

5. (30–50 minutes) Have the professors meet again in their original groups and discuss their grades and feedback. Ask the group members to come to a consensus and then to put their grades and written feedback for each answer on an overhead transparency.

6. (30–50 minutes) Ask each group of professors to come to the front of the class and use their transparencies on the overhead projector to present their grades and written feedback to the rest of the class, justifying their decisions using the information from the content unit and specific details in the essay answers.

7. (approximately 30 minutes) At the end of the presentations, elicit from the students the characteristics of good essay exam answers. Then examine these essay questions and the other questions generated by the groups earlier, and elicit characteristics of typical university essay exam questions. Also note which of the students' questions would probably not be asked in a university course and why.

Feedback and Scoring

1. As a culminating activity, have the students evaluate the following (see the Self-Assessment Worksheet in the Appendix):
   ● their abilities to anticipate essay exam questions and recognize acceptable answers
   ● their understanding of the main ideas of the content unit

Caveats and Options

1. Before doing this activity, discuss the terminology typically used in essay exam questions and the types of questions frequently asked.

2. If your class is quite advanced, have the students read, evaluate, and write feedback on the answers in class instead of assigning these activities for homework. This option allows lower level or reticent students to think about their opinions and be prepared for the group work in class; it also gets the students to think for themselves first without being influenced by the other group members' opinions.

3. Depending on their cultural backgrounds, the students may be hesitant or uncomfortable about evaluating and grading their teacher. The structure of the activity alleviates this problem: The students take the role of professors, work in groups to discuss their grading of the teacher, come to a consensus, and present it to the class. Humor can

also defuse the situation; say things students have said to you, such as "Please don't make your test too hard! I haven't had a chance to study enough!" When the students understand the purpose of the activity, they usually enjoy turning the tables on their teacher.

References and Further Reading

Leki, I. (1989). *Academic writing: Exploring processes and strategies* (2nd ed.). New York: St. Martin's Press. (See chapters 15 and 16 for tips on helping students prepare for and practice taking essay exams.)

McNamara, M. J. (1994). *Work in progress*. Boston: Heinle & Heinle. (See chapter 6 for an explanation of types of essay questions and strategies to help students prepare for essay exams and cope with test-day anxiety.)

Appendix: Self-Assessment Worksheet

1. I rate my ability to anticipate essay exam questions as follows.
Excellent_____ Very good_____ Satisfactory_____ Needs more practice_____
Explanation:

2. I rate my ability to recognize good essay exam answers as follows:
Excellent_____ Very good_____ Satisfactory_____ Needs more practice_____
Explanation:

3. As a result of this activity, my understanding of the important information in this content unit has: (Choose one.)
Increased_____ Stayed the same_____
Explanation:

Contributor

Debra Deane is the director of the English Language Institute, University of Akron, Ohio, in the United States, and has taught ESL in academic programs for 20 years.

It's OK to Argue

Levels
Any

Aims
Be aware of ambiguous
answers and poor
questions on tests
Politely negotiate with
the teacher over test
answers
Take responsibility for
learning and assessment

Class Time
1 hour

Preparation Time
10 minutes

Resources
Completed test
Test Self-Evaluation
Sheet

The primary purposes of this assessment activity are to encourage students to identify answers that warrant reconsideration by the instructor, make students aware of ambiguous answers and poor questions, and encourage students to politely reason and negotiate with the teacher by explaining reasons for their answers and problems with the questions. In the activity, students also assess their knowledge of content, use of strategies, and failure to follow directions on unit tests; develop their metacognitive awareness; and become motivated to improve their use of language and study strategies. In addition, the activity encourages students to be responsible for their own learning and reinforces a collaborative approach to assessment.

Procedure

1. When introducing the course and again before you give the first major test,
   - Tell the students that your policy is to give them 1 day in class to argue with you about their test grade.
   - Explain that you consider this a survival skill for academic work and that it is appropriate as long as students are polite and able to explain their thinking process.
   - Assure them that you will not consider them impolite or disrespectful if they question an item on a test, because different people think in different ways and you need their help to identify confusing test questions.
2. As soon as possible after you give a test, bring the graded tests to class, and list at least the range of scores on the chalkboard from high to low. If you wish, also include the following in your analysis of the students' performance on the test:

- the range of scores by section so that the students can compare their scores on each section with those of other students and assess their own abilities and needs. The range of scores also tells you which skills and content are most difficult for the students (and require more work) and which the students have mastered.
- a question analysis (which questions were particularly good and which may have been ambiguous or poor questions)
- the number of students who missed a particular question and the breakdown of incorrect answers given

Feedback and Scoring

1. Hand out the Test Self-Evaluation Sheet (see the Appendix), and tell the students to fill it out as you go through the test section by section.
2. Hand back the test, section by section if possible, and go over it section by section.
   - If necessary, prompt the students to fill out the form for the first section. Discuss possible reasons for incorrect answers—for example, "just didn't know the answer" (hadn't studied well enough), "spent more time on the reading than on the film" (should have watched the film again), or "didn't follow directions."
   - List the range of scores for that section on the blackboard, and discuss any patterns you notice (e.g., say, "Most people did well on this section" or "I think we need more work on this").
   - Tell the students questions that everyone got right, and concentrate on exploring questions that were frequently missed.
3. Explain that you need them to check the points per item and the point totals to make sure their score is accurate. Tell the students you'll walk around the room to look at any answers they wish to discuss, that this is the time to argue with you, and that you are having them review their tests to encourage them to speak up.
4. Walk around the room and discuss items that the students bring up. As you review alternative answers, require good explanations of the students' thinking processes. For example, if a student is thinking correctly with regard to an answer but can't provide a logical explanation, ask that student to prepare a better explanation in order

to gain the points. With a very reluctant group, award a point just because a student was brave enough to argue.

5. Ask the students to revise their point totals, if necessary, on the Test Self-Evaluation Sheet.

6. Also on the Test Self-Evaluation Sheet, tell the students to summarize their performance, indicate whether they are satisfied with it, assess the test itself, identify skills they need to work on, tell how they would like you to help, and indicate what they will do to improve for the next test. (See the questions at the end of the sample in the Appendix.)

7. Have the students staple their Test Self-Evaluation Sheet to the front of the test, putting the sections in order. Collect the tests, and tell the students that the tests will be in your office if they want to talk with you privately about them.

8. Follow up by confirming the final test scores, and arrange individual conferences if necessary. Revise your homework and lesson plans to respond to the students' expressed needs.

Caveats and Options

1. This assessment activity is an excellent way to get the students to attend class the day after a test, when attendance sometimes drops.

2. Some students from cultures with authoritarian classrooms may perceive this grading system as unfair. Spend time talking with the students about your rationale for allowing them to argue about their test grades. Reinforce the notion that doing so is an academic survival skill.

Appendix: Sample Test Self-Evaluation Sheet

Name _____   EAP2, Test 2

Directions: Look through your test and note the number correct in each section. Then describe what you did wrong or how you can improve next time. Add up the total points and the 3 points of extra credit possible to make sure your score is correct.

A. Focused Film Viewing: Fate of the Earth fill-in-the-blank

Why missed?   Points out of 12 possible _____

B. Topic Scramble: Save the Earth, Feed the World
Why missed?   Points out of 5 possible _____

C. Speed Read/Skim/Scan for details
Why missed?   Points out of 7 possible _____

D. Speed Read/Skim/Scan for main ideas
Why missed?   Points out of 9 possible _____

E. Sentence Analysis (relationship/referents)
Why missed?   Points out of 17 possible _____

F. Matching
Why missed?   Points out of 11 possible _____

G. Multiple Choice
Why missed?   Points out of 10 possible (2 each) _____

H. True-False
Why missed?   Points out of 10 possible _____

I. Essay Questions
Required: Points out of 4/4 possible _____ / _____

Option: ___   Points out of 6 possible _____

Option: ___   Points out of 6 possible _____

+ 3 points if typed   _____

– 2 points if directions were not followed   _____

          Total   _____

(Check one.)

___ 85 or above? ___ 75 or above? ___ 80 or above? ___ 70 or above?

Are you satisfied with your performance on this test?   Yes ___ No ___

Were there any problems with the test itself (e.g., confusing questions, confusing or unclear directions)? Please explain.

What do you think you need to work on? Which skills do you need to practice?

How can the teacher help you?

Would you like an appointment with the teacher?

What will you do to improve your performance on the next test?

Contributor

Kim Hughes Wilhelm has taught ESL in Hong Kong and Malaysia. She is currently the curriculum coordinator for the Intensive English Program and an assistant professor of linguistics at Southern Illinois University at Carbondale, in the United States.

◆ Creating Assessment Procedures

U Test U

Levels
Beginning–intermediate

Aims
Assess question formation, reading comprehension, and writing skills

Class Time
2 hours

Preparation Time
None

Resources
Content reading used in a study unit
Rating scale

This activity checks what the students have really understood from a text and what they consider the most important information in it. It also serves as a sample of the students' reading comprehension and writing abilities in a portfolio. Teachers may use the information derived from this activity to reteach or promote practice in weak areas.

Procedure

1. Locate a source text on the topic being studied.
2. Tell the students to read over the text as homework.
3. In class, give each student three sheets of paper (A, B, and C).
4. Ask the students to
   - write their names on the top of each sheet
   - on Sheet A, write four questions that can be answered from the reading and that represent the most important information contained in the text
   - on Sheet B, write the answers to the questions
5. Have the students exchange their Sheet A for a classmate's. Ask each student to
   - write their name at the bottom of the classmate's Sheet A
   - rewrite any questions they consider to have mistakes
   - answer the questions on the partner's Sheet A
6. Tell the students who exchanged papers to work as a pair to check their questions and answers against Sheet B and write a revised version on Sheet C.

7. Collect Sheets C. Take notes on each student's reading comprehension and writing skills (including question formation) and on the content points brought up in the questions.

Feedback and Scoring

1. Use the information on Sheet C for a qualitative assessment.
2. Establish a scoring procedure for each answer (see the Appendix for one possibility).
3. Discuss all the questions and answers with the whole class, and reteach weak points.

Caveats and Options

1. Before using this activity for assessment, have the students do it in groups in class to practice question formation and writing. In this case, the questions asked by one group are answered by another.
2. I have used this activity in an English for science and technology class, focusing the assessment strictly on reading comprehension and having the students write the questions and answers in Spanish, their L1.
3. In a content-based class, use the content of the questions asked by the students as part of later progress or achievement tests. In this way, you take into account what the students have learned and involve the students in the test-making process (Murphey, 1994/1995).

References and Further Reading

Brown, J. D. (1995). *Testing in language programs*. Englewood Cliffs, NJ: Prentice Hall Regents.

Murphey, T. (1994/1995). Tests: Learning through negotiated interaction. *TESOL Journal, 4*(2), 12–16.

Appendix: Suggested Rating Scale

Scoring Guidelines

1. Either have one rater read each answer on two separate occasions, or have two raters read each answer. The total points for each answer will be the average of the two scores.
2. Adjust the scores to fit the grading system.
3. Give more weight to language use and mechanics if the class focuses strongly on the form of the language. The example below reflects a concern with content.

4. Give 0–5 points for each correct answer based on the criteria indicated.

Content

3.0 points	Answer is correct, based on text.
1.5 points	Answer contains only 50% of the required information.
0.5 point	Answer contains almost none of the required information.
0.0 points	Answer contains none of the required information.

Language use

1.0 point	No errors in agreement, prepositions, pronouns, articles, verb tenses
0.5 point	Message conveyed, but some grammar mistakes
0.0 points	Grammar interferes with message getting across at all

Mechanics

1.0 point	Good use of writing conventions: capitals, punctuation, and spelling
0.5 point	Spelling or punctuation mistakes distract from message
0.0 points	Spelling or punctuation mistakes interfere with message getting across at all

Maximum points possible =
5 points/question $\times$ 4 questions = 20 points

Contributor

Dafne Gonzalez has coordinated an EFL program for elementary and high school students. She teaches English for science and technology at Universidad Simon Bolívar in Caracas, Venezuela.

Let Them Make Quizzes: Student-Created Reading Quizzes

Levels
Low intermediate +

Aims
Keep an ongoing
assessment log
Discuss texts in a
focused way
Bridge the gap between
what teachers and
students think should be
learned

Class Time
15–45 minutes (write
items)
15 minutes (administer
and grade quiz)
About 10 minutes
(discuss)

Preparation Time
10–30 minutes

Resources
Class textbook
Quiz Score Sheet
Folders

After years of giving students weekly quizzes, I began to feel that the 2-week cycle required to make quizzes, give them, and grade them was taking too much of my time and that quizzes were really more for me than for the students. Once the students found out their scores, they simply tucked the quizzes away somewhere. Not surprisingly, at the end of the term the students didn't have any idea of what progress they had made— something their cumulative quiz scores could have told them. After reading Murphey (1994/1995) on student-created tests, I devised a basic framework, added structures to ensure that the students kept ongoing records of their own quiz scores, and found a way to use the quizzes to discuss aspects of the texts that students were reading.

Procedure

Preparation

1. Prepare a series of quiz items based on the chapter of the text that the students are reading. They can be questions about the plot or about a particular character in the text. Make sure the questions require a definite answer (i.e., they shouldn't be opinion questions).
2. After the students have read the chapter, divide them into groups of three. Ask the students to write down words or expressions from the text that they had trouble with or are interested in.
3. Elicit the words and expressions from the students, writing them on the blackboard. Get the students to tell you what they think the words mean, and add your own information.
4. Tell the students to choose six words (or another appropriate number) for their next quiz. Write the words in your own notebook, and make sure the students understand that the material will be on the next quiz. Give the students at least a minute to ask questions.

5. Keep the students in their groups. Introduce the questions you prepared in Step 1 by writing them on the blackboard and having the students read them silently. Allow ample time for questions.
6. Ask the students to write two questions about the text that are not vocabulary questions. Either tell them to use your questions as models, or have them write questions that seem different.
7. Circulate as the students talk and write. Allow at least 15 minutes for this step.
8. Elicit the questions from the students, and write them on the blackboard. After at least six are on the blackboard, briefly and objectively explain any grammar or spelling changes you want to make. Praise the questions as creative artifacts of the students. For example, say, "I really like the question, but change this word and put that word there, and the question will be more clear . . . . Do you see?"
9. Choose what you think are the clearest four questions. Tell the students that, in addition to the six vocabulary questions, those four will be on the quiz.

Quiz 1

1. Type the questions up, and make sufficient copies for the students.
2. Administer the quiz.
3. When the quiz is over, either give the answers yourself or have the students give theirs. Have the students grade their own papers.
4. Ask the students if they have other answers that they are not sure about, and write alternative answers that the students suggest on the blackboard. Get the students to refer back to the text itself to form their opinions about the answers. If you have to make a judgment call, explain clearly your reasons for accepting or rejecting the answer, based on the text. Let the students know what page and passage in the text you are basing your judgment on.
5. Hand out copies of the Quiz Score Sheet (see the Appendix), and have the students glue them into the inside front over of their textbook or notebook. Then have the students record their percent-age scores for Quiz 1. (If future quizzes contain 10 items, it will be easy for the students to record their percentage scores and keep track of their progress.)

Subsequent Quizzes

1. Begin the next cycle of student-created quizzes. If you keep the cycle going, the students shouldn't need nearly as much time to write their questions. From time to time, provide models of different types of questions, such as multiple choice or fill-in-the-blank.
2. Have the students keep their quizzes in a special folder and bring it to every class.
3. At frequent intervals, set tasks that will require the students to look back through previous quizzes. For instance,
   - Ask the students to locate a question type they'd like to use on a new quiz.
   - Have the students read the quizzes to review the plot quickly or to review an aspect of a character the students are currently reading about.

Feedback and Scoring

See Quiz 1, Steps 3–5, and Subsequent Quizzes, Step 3.

Caveats and Options

1. Be sure to give the students plenty of time to respond to your questions in classroom discussions. In Japan, students really get going after a minute of silence—it's worth the wait!
2. Be patient as the students learn how to write quiz questions. Their ability will increase quickly as time passes.
3. Consider allowing open-book quizzes (i.e., letting the students look at the books as they take quizzes).

References and Further Reading

Murphey, T. (1994/1995). Tests: Learning through negotiated interaction. *TESOL Journal, 4*(2), 12–16.

Appendix: Quiz Score Sheet

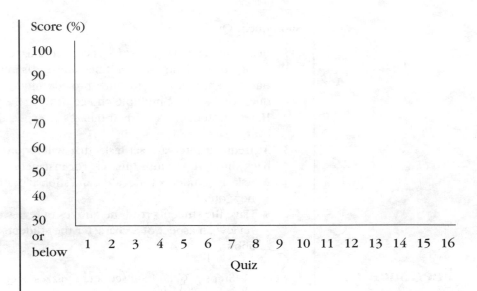

Score (%)

100
90
80
70
60
50
40
30
or
below

1 2 3 4 5 6 7 8 9 10 11 12 13 14 15 16

Quiz

Contributor

Greta J. Gorsuch teaches full time at Mejiro University, Japan, and is a former editor of The Language Teacher.

Developing a Student-Centered Scoring Rubric

Levels
Any

Aims
Understand assessment
through rubrics

Class Time
15-30 minutes

Preparation Time
None

Resources
Overhead projector
(optional)
Chart paper
Marker pens

Rubrics are elaborated scoring guides that clearly delineate the levels of students' performance at points on a scale, typically 1–4 or 1–5 (see the Appendix for an example). Scoring students' performance with a rubric has many advantages, including the ability to set clear performance targets, show growth qualitatively, and discuss students' work with them (as well as with other teachers and parents) based on a common understanding of expectations. One difficulty faced by second and foreign language teachers, however, is that often the language of the rubric is beyond the comprehension level of the students. Additionally, few students are familiar with rubrics, and it is difficult to explain their use and value (even in the students' native language) . This activity models the construction of a rubric with the students, basing it not on an academic abstraction but on a concrete object familiar to them all.

Procedure

Introduction/Warm-up

1. Ask the class, "Who likes hamburgers? Where do you buy them? How much do you pay? Where can you get the best hamburgers?" and so forth. Continue until the students are all comfortable talking about the topic. (If hamburgers are not familiar to your students, use some other familiar food, either simple or deluxe.)
2. Tell the class, "Today we're going to think about what a hamburger is, what a simple hamburger is, and what a great hamburger is."

Building the Rubric

1. Write the numbers 1–5 on a piece of chart paper, leaving enough space to draw a picture and write a description after each number.

2. Ask the class, "What is a hamburger? What does it have to have?" A likely student response is "Bread, meat, lettuce, [etc.]." Then ask the class, "If I have only bread, is that a hamburger?"

3. Draw one half of a hamburger bun on the blackboard. Ask, "How many pieces of bread do I need?" Through questions like these, get the students to describe a simple hamburger: two pieces of bread and a piece of beef. Draw this on the blackboard, or have a student draw it next to the number 1 on the rubric. Next to the drawing, write the key words to describe this level of quality.

4. Again through questions and answers, develop what the students agree is a Level 2 hamburger: two pieces of bread, a piece of beef, lettuce, and ketchup, perhaps. Draw this on the blackboard along with the key words differentiating this level from the previous one.

5. Work through the other levels on the scale in this way. A Level 5 hamburger may be a double or triple with a special sauce, bacon, and cheese—the works!

6. Once the students have developed their rubric, have them work in small groups either to draw their own version of the hamburger rubric on chart paper or to think of their own example (e.g., a movie, a friend) and develop the descriptions for each quality level with words or pictures, depending on their language ability.

Developing the Concept

1. Make the connection between building the rubric for hamburgers and building and using scales to show students how well they are doing their work, whether in writing, speaking, or content mastery.

2. Hang the students' rubrics in the room, and refer to them whenever you want the students to think about levels of quality in their work.

Developing the Rubric

1. Decide with the students what aspect of language learning to develop a rubric for (e.g., class speeches, compositions, test essays).

2. Have the students work in groups to develop such a rubric on chart paper.

3. When the groups have finished, put the sheets of chart paper containing all their results up around the room.
4. Work as a class to develop a single agreed-upon rubric based on the efforts of all the groups.

Feedback and Scoring

See the Procedure.

Caveats and Options

1. As much as possible, involve the students in the creation of the rubrics you use for day-to-day assessment of their progress. Naturally, if you use a rubric for a high-stakes assessment, such as end-of-term grades or reports to parents, you will want to exercise a lot of control over the criteria for performance at each level. Remember, however, that the more students are involved in creating the rubric, the more they will internalize the standards and become proficient at assessing themselves and demonstrating the desired skills and knowledge.
2. Have parents make hamburger rubrics on parents' night or at parent-teacher meetings, and explain to them the actual rubrics you use for scoring. This activity gives the parents insight into how their children are being assessed and makes it much easier to discuss rubric-based assessment data with them throughout the year.
3. With young or low-level language learners, use a 3-point scale instead of a 5-point scale at first. Increase the number of levels in a subsequent lesson.

References and Further Reading

Herman, J., Aschbacher, P., & Winters, L. (1992). *A practical guide to alternative assessment*. Alexandria, VA: Association for Supervision and Curriculum Development.

Popham, W. (1995). *Classroom assessment: What teachers need to know*. Needham Heights, MA: Allyn & Bacon.

Stiggins, R. (1994). *Student-centered classroom assessment*. Upper Saddle River, NJ: Prentice Hall.

Appendix: Sample Holistic Rubric

A simple holistic rubric for L2 learners showing their mastery of writing a story might look like this. Naturally the rubric will vary depending on the features of story writing on which you wish to focus. Note that some rubrics do not define all the levels. Performance at these levels is considered to contain some features of the higher level and some features of the lower.

LEVEL 5: Strong theme. The story is exceptionally clear and engaging. Few grammatical or spelling errors of any kind.

LEVEL 4: Clear theme. The story is elaborated with examples and explanations. Few grammatical or spelling errors; handwriting clear.

LEVEL 3: Clear theme but not elaborated. The basic story line tells only what happened or goes off on unrelated tangents. Few grammatical and spelling errors that interfere with comprehensibility; handwriting adequate.

LEVEL 2: Some evidence of theme, not clearly organized, minimal story line. Grammatical and spelling errors limit comprehensibility; handwriting hard to decipher.

LEVEL 1: No clear theme or organization. Many grammatical and spelling errors that interfere with comprehensibility; handwriting very hard to decipher.

Contributor

Michael A. Power is an evaluation and research specialist for the Everett, Washington, school district, in the United States. He has taught ESL and done extensive ESL teacher training in Asia and the Pacific.

A Continuous Assessment Framework

Levels
Any

Aims
Teachers: Develop criteria and standards for assessing features rarely evaluated in the language classroom

Class Time
A few minutes/class

Preparation Time
1 hour

Resources
None

Do you think the grades you give students are an accurate record of their true abilities? If not, perhaps it is time to ask yourself what you use to measure students' abilities and how you use it. The continuous assessment framework developed in this activity makes clear to both the students and the teacher the method of evaluating features that are rarely assessed in the language classroom (e.g., natural English use, effort, participation, volunteering). It keeps the teaching agenda open for scrutiny, reminding the teacher to be fair and ethical. It provides the students with lifelong learning strategies and encourages the teacher to have a clear set of objectives in the classroom.

Procedure

Thinking About the Framework

1. Before class, think about devising your assessment framework. Answering the questions below will clear up much of the mystery surrounding assessment:
   - What do you look for when you assess your students (e.g., participation, attendance, effort, homework, fluency/accuracy, pronunciation, meeting deadlines)?
   - How much value do you place on the above attributes (e.g., 20% for effort)?
   - What methods (e.g., tests, notes) will you use to measure those attributes?
   - How will you justify your assessments to your students and other concerned parties (i.e., what are your criteria or standards for a good participation grade)?

Involving the Students

1. At the earliest opportunity, broach the subject of assessment with your students. Explain that you are planning an assessment framework and that you'd like some information on how they were assessed in other classes.
2. Prepare an information-gap activity about past testing experiences by creating two different question sheets (see Appendix A).
3. Have the students get into pairs, ask their partner the questions on the sheet, and write down their partner's answers.

Designing the Assessment Framework

1. Ask the students what components (e.g., participation, homework, effort, volunteering) they think they should be assessed on. List them on the blackboard.
2. Ask the students how they should be evaluated on each component (e.g., tests, projects, journals). List their ideas on the blackboard.
3. Tell the students how you feel they should be assessed. Put your list on the blackboard. Explain that by working together, you and the students can make an assessment framework that will be best for everyone.
4. To determine the criteria for assessment, have the students in groups think about what makes a good student. Have them come up with a list while you do the same. Elicit the students' views, and write both lists on the blackboard.
5. Have the students imagine they are the teacher. Write the numbers 5, 4, 3, 2, and 1 vertically on the blackboard. Ask the students to describe a perfect student, and write their ideas beside Number 5 on the blackboard. Do the same for Number 1, the worst student.
6. Distribute one piece of paper to each group. Have the groups complete the criteria for the students represented by the Numbers 4, 3, and 2.
7. Collect the papers from each group. For the next class, collate the information, and make up a table of standards and criteria for your class (see Appendix B).

Feedback and Scoring

1. To make the framework immediately relevant, use it with a class activity at once.
2. Decide before class to observe three or four students only, without their knowledge. Take notes while they are on task.
3. Periodically discuss the assessment framework, as things may have changed and an adjustment may be in order.

Caveats and Options

1. The framework should help the students, not inhibit them, by telling them what they are to be praised on. Do not use it as an overt formal instrument, as it may hinder the students' performance.
2. If you and the students disagree on a particular area of assessment, or if you would like to include something they did not mention or exclude something they suggested, be sure to explain your reasons. The purpose of involving your students in assessment is to develop an open, nonthreatening approach to classroom assessment. Keep your agenda open and honest!

Appendix A: What Do You Think About Tests?

Student's name_____ Partner's name_____

With your partner, ask and answer the following questions about tests and grades. Write down what your partner says. Later, your teacher will collect your papers and share your ideas with the class. Note: There are no correct answers!

1. Last year, in what subjects did you get the highest grades? The lowest grades?
2. How do you feel about tests?
3. Do you think tests describe your true English abilities?
4. What kind of tests do you prefer (e.g., speaking/listening tests, reading/writing tests)? Why?
5. If you were an English teacher, how would you grade the students?

Appendix B: Sample Framework

Continuous Assessment: Effort

5 Consistent and thorough in all class and homework assignments. Genuinely interested and eager to do well.

4 Usually works well, fairly eager, completes most of the homework. Occasionally leads but is inconsistent.

3 Not too persistent but tries. Does average class work, but rarely does more than asked directly. Is interested but not eager.

2 Soon loses interest. Sometimes tries but does not concentrate for long. Completes homework minimally or forgets altogether. Needs prompts to engage in activities.

1 Lacks interest. Dislikes learning and speaking English. Fails to do homework; loses concentration or interrupts others.

Class Assessment

Here are some suggestions you gave me for assessment in English class.

Partici-pation (40%)	Journal (10%; teacher judges quality)	Volun-teering (20%)	Tests (20%; teacher judges quality)	Remem-bering books (10%)	Total (100%)
A = Always comes to class (40%)	A =	A =	A =	A =	A =
B = Usually comes to class (30%)	B =	B =	B =	B =	B =
C = Often comes to class (20%)	C =	C =	C =	C =	C =
D = Sometimes comes to class (10%)	D =	D =	D =	D =	D =
F = Never comes to class (0%)	F =	F =	F =	F =	F =

Acknowledgments

The author thanks Paul Gruba and Sally Cavanough, who inspired this continuous assessment framework.

Contributor

David Progosh studied curriculum and assessment issues at the Modern Language Centre of the Ontario Institute for Studies in Education/University of Toronto. He writes and edits ESL materials and tests.

◆ Making Grading Easier
Raise Your Hand and Be Counted

Levels
High beginning–low
advanced

Aims
Demonstrate ability to
understand and answer
orally questions based
on assigned reading

Class Time
About 1 hour

Preparation Time
15 minutes

Resources
Copies of an article
Handouts
Slips of paper

This enjoyable and competitive assessment activity involves reading, writing, listening, and speaking. It makes the grading of students' oral participation very easy and unbiased.

Procedure

Session 1

1. Before class, choose and read an article appropriate to the class's level. Prepare and copy a list of 10-15 questions based on the information in the article.
2. In class, assign the reading of the article to the class. After the students have finished the reading, distribute the prepared handout of questions, and tell the students to write the answers on the sheet for homework.

Session 2

1. Tell the students to review the article for 5 minutes or so.
2. Give the students the following information:
   - After you ask a question on the handout, the first student to raise a hand will be given the chance to answer.
   - The students cannot read their answers from their handout. The handout is to be used only as a guide.
   - When they answer a question correctly, ask a question, or make a comment about the article, they will be given a slip of paper that is worth 1 point.
3. Ask the questions on the handout.

4. Award each student with a slip of paper for a correct answer or for asking a question. Have the students write their names on the slips of paper.
5. After all the questions have been asked, collect all the slips.

Feedback and Scoring

1. Assess the students' ability to answer questions by counting the points as represented by the slips of paper.
2. Emphasize participation to the students. Participation translates into points received for a correct answer, and points received translate into a better grade.

Caveats and Options

1. To keep the students from guessing what the next question will be, do not ask the questions in the same order as they appear on the handout.
2. Use this assessment activity as a backdrop for a variety of reading materials, such as magazine articles, chapters from a novel, newspapers, and poetry.

Contributor

Juergen J. Bulach has taught ESL in Germany, the United States, and Japan. He is currently an ESL instructor for Japanese students at Seattle International College Japan in Tokyo.

Course of Events

Levels
Beginning +

Aims
Demonstrate integration
of information

Class Time
10 minutes

Preparation Time
30 minutes

Resources
Story, process, or
phenomenon
Handout
Vertical and horizontal
scoring aids

Feedback and Scoring

This variation on a guided writing task encourages even beginning-level students to develop their overall understanding of a story, process, or phenomenon by requiring them to examine the relationships between individual events. A novel scoring system is used to grade the activity.

Procedure

1. Analyze the story, process, or phenomenon your class is about to study, and make a list of the 11 most significant events.
2. Type up your list with a blank to the left of each item.
3. Scramble the items by cutting them up and pasting them onto another piece of paper. (To reduce unconscious bias, I arrange them from the shortest to the longest utterance.)
4. At the top of the paper, add a set of directions (e.g., *Put the following events in order from first to last by numbering them from 1 to 11*; see Appendix A).
5. Teach the story, process, or phenomenon.
6. Hand out the assessment activity, and have the students complete it.

1. Create a scoring key (using the templates in Appendix B) and a scoring method such as the following to determine how well your students have synthesized the information.
   - In the column marked *Key* in the vertical scoring aid, list the numbers of the events in the correct sequence. (Item 1, "The War of 1812 ends," comes fifth in the sequence, so the number 5 appears at the top of this column in the vertical scoring aid in Appendix C.)
   - In the column marked *S1*, list the responses of the first student (or group of students) in the order in which they appear on the

exercise. (My first student put "The War of 1812 ends" seventh, so the number 7 appears at the top of this column in the vertical scoring aid in Appendix C.) Continue for subsequent students (or groups of students).

- Transfer the information from the vertical scoring aid to the horizontal scoring aid. Make sure the students' answers still correspond as they do in the vertical scoring aid. (In the horizontal scoring aid in Appendix C, my first student's No. 7 still corresponds to No. 5 in the *Key* row, as it does in the vertical scoring aid.) The purpose of this transfer is to reconstruct the student's time line and discover the pattern. (My first student's pattern goes as follows: $2 < 3 < 4 < 6 < 7 > 1 < 8 < 10 > 9 > 5 < 11$; the pattern of the key, of course, is $1 < 2 < 3 < 4 < 5 < 6 < 7 < 8 < 9 < 10 < 11$.)
- Count every < as 2 points of raw score, for a maximum of 20 points. (The order ascends seven times in the row marked *S1* in the horizontal scoring aid, for a raw score of 14.)

2. If you wish, use the following conversion scale: 20 = A, 18 = B, 16 = C, 14 = D, below 14 = F. (My first student would receive a grade of D.)

Caveats and Options

1. Because this instrument indicates which way a student's chronology flows and not the proximity of the responses to the actual positions of the events on the correct time line, you may not want to use it when the exercise involves absolute, direct cause-and-effect relationships (e.g., the functioning of an internal combustion engine).

2. This exercise is well suited to a variety of applications, including language arts, science, and history. However, its purpose is to promote synthesis of information; thus do not give your students a list of events merely to memorize (e.g., the steps of photosynthesis). If the subject is history, deemphasize dates and stress context.

3. This exercise was originally designed as an individual checkup or as part of a larger test. However, it can be used as a cooperative learning tool in a modified jigsaw approach:
   - Prepare in advance 11 index cards, each listing an event from the exercise.

- During the last 15 minutes of class, assign each student to a group and administer the exercise as a test, making sure to collect all materials and scratch paper at the end.
- During the first 15 minutes of the next day's class, assign each student to a different group, making sure that no two students who worked together the previous day work together again, and readminister the exercise.
- Once all the papers have been turned in, give immediate feedback using the following method:
  ○ Give 11 students each an index card. Ask them to put the cards in sequence by forming a line at the front of the room.
  ○ Have the whole class participate by negotiating the place of each event in the sequence.
  ○ Verify the order of the cards.

References and Further Reading

Good, T. L., & Brophy, J. E. (1994). *Looking in classrooms* (6th ed.). New York: HarperCollins College.

Madsen, H. S. (1983). *Techniques in testing*. New York: Oxford University Press.

Appendix A: Sample Assessment Handout

Name_____

Course of Events (20 points)

Directions: Put the following events in order from first to last by numbering them from 1 to 11.

_____ The War of 1812 ends.

_____ Mexico becomes a free country.

_____ Thomas Jefferson becomes president.

_____ The United States buys Louisiana from France.

_____ British soldiers burn Washington, DC.

_____ The United States wins the Battle of New Orleans.

_____ Cherokee Indians begin the Trail of Tears.

_____ James Monroe issues the Monroe Doctrine.

_____ American soldiers return from World War II.

_____ Lewis and Clark explore the Louisiana Territory.

_____ The American public elects its first Western president.

Appendix B: Scoring Aid Templates

Vertical Scoring Aid for Course of Events

Student responses										Key
S1	S2	S3	S4	S5	S6	S7	S8	S9	S10	

Horizontal Scoring Aid for Course of Events

	Key											Score
	1	2	3	4	5	6	7	8	9	10	11	20
S1												
S2												
S3												
S4												
S5												
S6												
S7												
S8												
S9												
S10												

Appendix C: Scoring Aids for Sample Assessment Handout

Vertical Scoring Aid

Student responses			
S1	S2	S3	Key
7	6	10	5
8	7	11	7
2	1	7	1
3	2	5	2
6	5	4	4
1	4	3	6
5	10	2	10
10	8	8	8
11	11	1	11
4	3	6	3
9	9	9	9

Horizontal Scoring Aid

Key												Score
	1	2	3	4	5	6	7	8	9	10	11	20
S1	2	3	4	6	7	1	8	10	9	5	11	14
S2	1	2	3	5	6	4	7	8	9	10	11	18
S3	7	5	6	4	10	3	11	8	9	2	1	8

Contributor

Paul Lyddon teaches content-based ESL in Grades 6–8 at Piedmont Open Middle School, Charlotte, North Carolina, in the United States.

Getting the Point(s): An Adaptable Evaluation System

Levels
Any

Aims
Understand, control, and
predict class grade
Be evaluated
appropriately and
individually
Be recognized for effort

Class Time
One or more class
sessions

Preparation Time
Variable

Resources
Grading system handout

Feedback and Scoring

Caveats and Options

This assessment activity helps students understand, control, and predict their grade in a class or their progress through a program. The students are evaluated appropriately and individually, regardless of class or program size, and they are recognized for the effort spent, regardless of their level relative to other students. The point system provides a range of different but equivalent ways to earn points, allowing the students to choose those they find most congenial without increasing the teacher's record-keeping burden, and allows students in multilevel classes (from true beginning- through advanced-level students) to work at a level appropriate for them.

Procedure

1. List and prioritize, or have the students list and prioritize, what they should do to succeed in a class or program.
2. Assign points to each item on the list such that students must meet absolute requirements in order to acquire sufficient points to pass, options of equal importance receive equal points, greater effort or better performance receives more points, and so on (see the Appendix for an example).
3. Explain the system to the students.

1. Monitor the students' accumulation of points.
2. For the final evaluation, simply add up the points accumulated.

1. The amount of time needed for this assessment activity varies. If the students tailor their own system, allow one class period or more for setup plus 10–15 minutes periodically for fine-tuning. If you use a

prepared system, allow 10–15 minutes to explain initially plus time for later clarification as needed. You may collect data for the awarding of points during or outside class.

2. The preparation time needed depends on the complexity of the class or the program. To devise a system for one Japanese university class takes me about an hour, mostly spent on prioritizing factors and playing with numbers. The time required to add the number of points naturally depends on how often you do it and how many students you have.

3. The students should be able to keep track of their own points and know exactly how they are doing at any time, but remind them periodically of how many points they have.

4. Adapt the system for more complex or intensive learning contexts (e.g., full-time intensive ESL programs).

5. Periodically, award points for various activities in the form of merit badges or other tangible tokens of accomplishment. Devise a system whereby the acquisition of certain badges or a certain number of badges indicates progress through a program.

6. Award points for work in self-access centers or off-campus tasks. One possibility is to issue passports that are stamped or signed by persons with whom the students have interacted in English. Or, in a scavenger hunt approach, convert into points tangible evidence of tasks done in English.

7. Factor test scores into the evaluation by assigning points that clearly indicate the importance of those scores relative to other factors.

8. Adapt the information in the evaluation system for progress report forms. For example, the arrangement of attendance points in the Appendix resulted in much less tardiness. Use similar provisions to encourage or discourage other behavior.

References and Further Reading

Ando, S., & Sell, D. (1989). *Reading better and faster*. Ashiya, Japan: Seido Language Institute.

Davis, R., & Armstrong, H. (1995). Using English beyond the classroom. *The Language Teacher*, *19*, 52–53, 55.

Fuji, T. (1993). Classroom management: Creating motivation by use of a clear grading system. *The Language Teacher*, *17*, 37, 39.

Gorsuch, G. J. (1991). Helping students create their own learning goals. *The Language Teacher*, *15*, 3, 9.

Stoda, K. (1994). An aggressive "AET Money Contest": Ask me three questions, please! *The Language Teacher*, *18*, 7-9.

Appendix: Sample Grading System

Below is the point system from a first-year English reading class at a Japanese university. Most students assume that they will pass if they are physically present in around half the classes, even if they do nothing else. The system was designed to discourage chronic tardiness and to convey the message that students must do something to earn points and that using a language is a better way to learn it than talking about it in another language. Points were assigned based on the following assumptions: 25 class sessions with about 10 spot-checks and about 10 quizzes, resulting in an ideal total of around 600 points. In the Japanese system, an A is considered to be above 79%; a B, 70-79%; a C, 60-69%; and a D (no credit), below 60%.

Evaluation

Grades at the end of the year will be based on the points earned by each student. The points needed for each grade follow:

A: ≥ 480   B: 420-479   C: 360-419   D: ≤ 359

Below are the ways to earn points.

Item		Points
Attendance (each class):	On time (seated and ready before the chime finishes)	10
	Late (up to 15 minutes)	5
	Very late (more than 15 minutes)	2
Working seriously in class (unannounced spot-checks):	No problem during the spot-check	2
	Working but not well	1

Surprise quizzes:	All answers correct	6
	Some answers correct, some not	3
Homework:		
SRA rate builders	Well done	1
(per card, up to five/week)	Poorly done	$\frac{1}{2}$
SRA power builders	Well done	2
(per card, up to five/week)	Poorly done	1
SRA skills development cards (per card, if needed)	Done	1
Reading reports (up to 1/week, including summer vacation)	Well done Poorly done	10
Language journals (per entry, up to five/week, including summer vacation)	Well done Poorly done	1 $\frac{1}{2}$

Contributor

Ron Grove is an associate professor of area studies at Mejiro University in Iwatsuki, Japan, where he uses this assessment activity in his English classes.

◆ Evaluating Curricula Thermometer

Levels
Any

Aims
Demonstrate comfort
level and involvement
with classroom activities

Class Time
Less than 5 minutes

Preparation Time
None

Resources
None

This activity represents a whole-class assessment technique that allows students to react immediately to a certain classroom activity. It can also be used to assess their reactions to a particular topic or issue discussed in class or covered in reading material. The Thermometer is a feedback device that indicates trends within the group of students, enables students to influence the continuum of the class, and serves as a tool for starting a dialogue between the instructor and the students. For instance, a teacher who finds out via the Thermometer that most students do not feel comfortable with a certain activity or topic could explain that activity more carefully or provide more background information on the topic. Students like this activity because they value the fact that the instructor cares about what they think of a classroom activity or assignment.

Procedure

1. After a classroom activity or reading assignment, draw three thermometers on the blackboard, one showing a temperature associated with a day at the beach, another reflecting the temperature on a mild rainy day, and the third reflecting the temperature on a chilly day.
2. Ask each student to reflect on the classroom activity or the reading assignment for a short while.
3. Ask the students to select the thermometer that best reflects their comfort level or degree of involvement with the classroom activity or reading assignment. Allow each student only one choice, and have the students indicate that choice by standing by whichever thermometer best matches their opinion.

Feedback and Scoring

1. The feedback on the teaching activities or reading topics goes to the teacher. Quickly count the students standing near each of the three thermometers, and jot down the count next to each thermometer.
2. Afterwards, ask the students why they felt a certain way by having them jot down next to "their" thermometer reasons for their ideas, thoughts on the assignment, and so on.

Caveats and Options

1. Allow a maximum of 3 minutes on the first occasion to explain the concept of the Thermometer. Usually, the students quickly learn how to respond to this classroom assessment technique.
2. Leave the room while the students are responding to this classroom assessment technique so that their responses will be anonymous and more reliable.

Contributor

Claudia A. Becker is an assistant professor at the University of Illinois, Chicago, in the United States, where she is also the director of the basic German language program.

Multiple Assessment Action Logging

Levels
Any

Aims
Demonstrate
understanding of
classroom activities
Be involved in
evaluating classroom
activities

Class Time
0–5 minutes

Preparation Time
30 minutes

Resources
Action Log
Requirements handout

Feedback and Scoring

In an action log, students evaluate classroom activities after each class by writing in a notebook that teachers read weekly. Teachers can then assess students' understanding of and success with the activities and make appropriate adjustments. The logs are not diaries in that the students write only about things related to class; thus they are of high interest for teachers and encourage continual teacher development (Murphey, 1992, 1993).

Procedure

1. Prepare an Action Log Requirements handout like the one in Appendix A or B.
2. In class, ask the students to write in their notebooks outside class either freely about what happened in class or explicitly about matters that you are eager to get reactions to. For the latter option, list the activities or points on the same part of the blackboard each day to remind the students to comment on them.
3. Set a time for collecting the logs or having students drop the logs off (e.g., have different classes drop their logs off on different days of the week).

1. Read the logs, writing comments where appropriate.
2. Keep your responses short except when individuals show a special need, but make your responses longer at the beginning of the term to let the students know you appreciate their help. After using the logs for more than 150 students a week for 2 years, it usually takes me about a minute per log to read and comment. Ninety percent of the comments are short phrases like *Thanks for the feedback, you're doing great!* with perhaps a smiling face and my initials.

3. Tag certain pages, and make photocopies of them to keep in your files. Return the logs in the next class, or have the students pick them up at a designated time.

Caveats and Options

1. Give beginning-level students certain formulas for reacting to classroom activities (e.g., *Today we did . . . . I liked . . . . I didn't like . . . . I want to do . . . more*)
2. Have a beginning-level class give grades or number ratings to classroom activities (see Appendix B).
3. Give the students the last 5 minutes of class to write in the logs, and collect them in class.

References and Further Reading

Murphey, T. (1992). Letting the students in on teacher reflection processes. *The Teacher Trainer, 6,* 20–21.

Murphey, T. (1993, January). Why don't teachers learn what learners learn? Taking the guesswork out with action logging. *English Teaching Forum,* 6–10.

Appendix A: Action Log Requirements for Higher Level Students

As soon as possible after every class (so you remember well what happens), write a short description of the class in a notebook. (1) Say briefly what we DID and (2) COMMENT about what you learned and what you liked. List the different activities and segments. You may want to take short notes in class to remind you. Comment on those activities you especially liked and could learn from, and on those you didn't like and think could be improved. I need your feedback so that I can teach you better. I read your Action Logs. I like your suggestions and will try to use them if possible.

If there is anything else (e.g., outside problems) that you think I should know (and that influences your learning), please tell me.

An example of an entry:

Written April 8, 21:00*

1. DID: Today we listened to a story, did shadowing, retelling, speed reading and sang a song.
2. COMMENT: Shadowing seems especially interesting. I'm going to try it in my other classes. I didn't understand some of the points in speed reading: What is chunking? Sometimes you spoke too fast. Please speak slower. My partners were Yuki and Hiroko** and I enjoyed getting to know them. We got a lot of homework, but it looks like fun. I'm looking forward to the rest of the classes. Oh, and I like singing.

*Always put the date of the class and the time you write. **Always use people's names when you refer to partners.

Appendix B: Action Log Requirements for Lower Level Students

Your Action Log

After every class, write in a notebook a grade for each activity that we did in class. I will list the activities in the upper left-hand corner of the blackboard in each class. You are also free to comment on the class if you want to. I read your Action Logs. I like your suggestions and will try to use them if possible.

An example of an entry:

Written April 9, 20:00*

DID	Grade on interest	Grade on usefulness
story	A	A
shadowing	B	A
retelling	B	A
speed reading	B	C?
song	A+	B

*Always put the date of the class and the time you write.

Contributor

Tim Murphey teaches and learns at Nanzan University in Nagoya, Japan, and does research into alternative learning forms.

Wow! Marvelous Task

Levels
Any

Aims
Try out suggested
behaviors in class
Tell teachers which
tasks work
Identify barriers to
following teachers'
suggestions

Class Time
5–10 minutes

Preparation Time
Variable

Resources
Students' environment

Feedback and Scoring

Caveats and Options

This assessment activity aims to get students to try out suggested behaviors that will help them develop skills and change limiting beliefs. The teacher learns from students what tasks work and what the barriers are to following the teacher's suggestions. The task test is used to assess classroom activities and plausible or possible student behavior with a view toward constructing a richer acquisition environment. The activity reflects a trying-is-succeeding philosophy: If the students do the task and report what happens, they earn a high grade (and the teacher finds out whether the tasks work as they were intended to).

Procedure

1. List learning concepts from your class and behaviors you would like the students to try out.
2. Make a list of tasks around these concepts (see the Appendix for a sample list). Copy the list.
3. In class, pass out the task list, and explain the tasks if necessary. Give the students a deadline (e.g., a week or two) for completing the tasks and writing a short paragraph about each.

1. Tell the students that their grade depends only on whether they do the tasks and write about them, not on whether they are particularly successful at the tasks.
2. If the students do the task and report what happens, give them a high grade.

1. After doing such tests several times, adapt the tasks to make them more performative. For example, when I learned that some of my

students were approaching foreigners in groups of three to ask the time, in later assessments, I told the students to do this individually.

2. Tell the students about past students' successes at doing the tests, previous students' courage to try new things, and the rewards of trying new things.

3. In an ESL environment, have the students perform other real-world tasks in English (e.g., ask for directions and information from local people, call numbers for recorded information).

References and Further Reading

Murphey, T. (forthcoming). *Language hungry: A guide for proactive language learners.* Manuscript in preparation.

Appendix: Sample Task List

The following task test was given in a large-city EFL setting. Tasks correspond to individual learning strategies (1-9), interactive learning outside class (10-12), and collaborative learning (13-17) that the teacher suggested or gave lessons on.

Directions: Wow! Marvelous! Test due December 21, 1996. Do the following tasks within the next 2 weeks and write a short report (a short paragraph) about each one. Write in dark ink. You are not allowed to show your answers to anyone, but you can talk to them and tell them your answers (in English only).

Scoring: All tasks done and commented upon = A+; one grade lower for each task not done or not completely done; one grade lower for every day late.

1. Talk to yourself in English every morning when you wake up. Tell yourself what you are going to do that day (e.g., "First I'm going to eat, then brush my teeth, then ... go to school, eat lunch with friends").

2. Listen to bilingual ZIP FM radio when you get up in the morning (at least five mornings for the next 2 weeks), and write down at least

three expressions you hear disk jockey James Haven say that you might use (e.g., "Wow, what a marvelous day!").

3. Notice and write down at least five words or phrases in English from advertising that you see around you every day on your way to and from school. The words and phrases should be interesting things that you could use (e.g., "Just do it!" in the Nike advertisement with Michael Jordan).

4. Sing the song "Twelve Ways to Blissness" to yourself every morning while you are coming to school for at least a week. Did you memorize it easily? Write about it.

5. Wear your watch upside down for 2 weeks. Ask two different classmates each day for 10 days (20 different people) "What time is it?" (a) If they answer "Now is the best time to be happy!" say, "Yes, and smiling makes you beautiful." (b) If they tell you the time, say, "Thanks, and what a great time it is to be happy, too!"

6. Silently shadow or echo another professor in one of your classes, then reformulate what the professor said to someone right after class (as soon as possible). Could you remember more? What was the experience like?

7. Shadow or echo an easy radio or TV program for 15 minutes (e.g., *Sesame Street,* an English lesson). How did it go?

8. SPURR (Specifically Personal Use Repeat and Recycle) three words or expressions from your language lab class that you want to learn. Write the SPURR sentences here and say how you practiced them meaningfully.

9. (alone, not with friends) Ask at least three different foreigners, "Excuse me, what time is it please?" What did they say? How did you feel?

10. Greet (say *hello* or *good morning*) to your Japanese English teachers in English at least three times in the next 2 weeks (and longer if you like).

11. Teach a friend or member of your family the 10 gesture-idioms. Write about it. Retell two of Murphey's stories to friends or family, using as much English as possible so that they understand.

12. Think of a mistake you made. Tell three different classmates about it in English. Make it funny when you tell it. How did it feel?

13. Find a special partner in your regular oral communication class, and agree to speak mostly English with that partner for 2 whole weeks, in and out of class. Support each other. Remind each other. Write your partner's name and describe what happened, when you started, and when you finished. When you speak, it's OK to use some Japanese when you don't know the English. Maybe your partner can translate it for you. Shadow your partner!

14. Find another friend (different from the one in No. 13) who is willing to talk to you in English, and telephone each other four nights straight (in a row). Tell each other what you did that day. Prepare what you want to say during the day. How did it work? Was it useful? Would you like to continue?

15. In English, write one note of encouragement and friendship a day for 5 days to your friends in your English classes. Ask a question or two also. Give the notes to them outside class (e.g., "Yuki, I really like the way you speak English. Your pronunciation is very clear. Thank you for talking to me so much in English. I can learn a lot from you. Your Friend Yuko. P.S.: Can I borrow your notes for the day I was absent? Don't you think [name] is handsome?"). When you get a note, respond to the question, and ask another if you'd like.

16. Ask your friends if they know the word *tickle* in English. If not, show them what it means by tickling them. (Blame it on your homework if they get angry.)

17. Give an unexpected compliment a day to someone in English (e.g., "I like your hairstyle!").

18. Loan the person you sit with in the fourth class an audiotape of one of your favorite songs in English with a lyric sheet and a note telling why you chose that song. Listen to the song you get (shadow it), and read the lyrics and note. Write your partner about the song, and return the tape in the fifth class.

19. Find at least two friends in this class, and talk about your answers to each of these tasks only in English. Write the friends' names and what you learned.

Daily in English reminder: Talk to myself when I wake up, listen to Zip FM, notice English advertising going to school, sing "Twelve Ways . . ." in my head, give a compliment to someone, speak English mostly to my 2-week partner, give a note to a friend, ask a few classmates "What time is it?", say hello to my JTEs, shadow my teachers, ask friends if they know the word *tickle* (tickle them!), at-home telephone partner, write and answer notes.

Occasional: SPURR LL words, loan favorite song in Class 4, teach 10 gesture-idioms, ask three foreigners the time, tell three friends a mistake, shadow TV English and songs, retell stories, talk about tasks with two friends.

Contributor

   Tim Murphey teaches and learns at Nanzan University in Nagoya, Japan, and does research into alternative learning forms.

Part V: Alternative Ways of Assessing Written Skills

Editor's Note

Traditionally, language tests were designed to test the four language skills as separately as possible. For instance, an overall English language proficiency test battery might be made up of five separate skills tests: four multiple-choice tests (grammar, listening comprehension, reading comprehension, and vocabulary) and a composition test.

A quick look at the skills from the point of view of channels and modes will indicate that it is not always possible, or indeed desirable, to separate the skills when doing assessment, especially classroom assessment. Each skill can be described in terms of its channel and its mode. *Channel* refers to the means used to communicate. The two possible channels are the written and the oral. In other words, the message is conveyed by either light waves or sound waves. The two skills involved in the written channel are reading and writing. The two skills involved in the oral channel are listening and speaking.

Mode refers to the direction of communication involved. The two possible modes are the *receptive* and the *productive*. In other words, the message is either received (receptive) or sent (productive). The two skills involved in the receptive mode are reading and listening. The two skills involved in the productive mode are writing and speaking. The following diagram (adapted from Brown, 1996, p. 28) shows how the modes and channels are related. Notice that reading is the receptive written skill, writing is the productive written skill, listening is the receptive oral skill, and speaking is the productive oral skill.

	Channels	
	Written	Oral
Receptive	Reading	Listening
Productive	Writing	Speaking

Modes

Modes and channels help us separate the characteristics of the four skills in our minds, and such a separation is sometimes useful. Indeed, I have used the written channel to describe the assessment activities found in this part of the book and the oral channel to describe the activities in the Part VI.

The moment you start thinking about real language production or about language assessment, however, it becomes almost impossible to keep the skills separate. Consider what testers do when they assess reading comprehension ability. Typically, they ask the students to read a passage and answer multiple-choice questions. The students read the passage. They read the questions. Then they select the correct answer by circling it or filling in a little dot on an answer sheet. All of that is at least a little like what people experience in real-life reading, and, at least, no other language skills are involved.

However, what about listening comprehension? Traditionally, testers have presented aural passages to the students via a tape recorder and asked the students to read the responses and select the correct answer. That is, the task mixes listening and reading and does so in a way that is not very similar to any real-life task. How often do you listen to something in real life, then select a written answer? I suppose it happens sometimes, but not often.

Similar problems arise in trying to test writing and speaking. How can you give students a writing prompt without requiring them to read or listen? The answer is that you can't. And how do you get students to speak without giving them some instructions that require them to listen or read in some way (as in an interview)? Again, the answer is that you don't. And how authentic are writing and speaking tests devised with written prompts or with interview procedures, anyway?

Of course, using L1 prompts or pictures can circumvent some of these problems, but those strategies aren't really like real-life language activities either, all of which suggests that the quest to test pure language skills may have always been a bit quixotic, if not completely impossible.

Given recent trends in language teaching toward more authentic communication in the learning process, it is no surprise that the majority of contributions in this part of the book and in Part VI (indeed, throughout the book) propose assessment activities that combine two or more skills. Apparently, teachers have recognized the futility of separating the skill areas in the teaching processes as well as in the related classroom assessment processes.

This part of the book, on written-channel skills, includes those contributions that deal primarily with reading, reading and vocabulary combined, vocabulary, and writing and grammar.

The five contributions that focus primarily on reading do so with different purposes: to encourage active reading of longer and more substantial resource material (Taking the Speed out of Reading Tests); to keep track of students' progress in reading while motivating them (Keeping Track With Free Readin'); to assess reading comprehension and critical thinking abilities (The Reading Beat: Investigative Questioning and Reading Comprehension); to help students read material above their level intensively for an extended period of time (A Window on the Reading Process); and to practice reading by figuring out a text's organization (Sort It Out).

The contributions that primarily combine reading and vocabulary do so with the following purposes: to assess students' comprehension of written descriptions (Have You Seen My Brother?); to assess students' newspaper-reading skills (Extra! Extra! Read All About It!); to assess students' vocabulary development and reading comprehension (On the Spot!); and to read with a specific purpose while inferring words from definitions and context (Definition-Resource Cloze).

The six contributions that deal primarily with vocabulary are all included here, even though some of them use the oral channel, because vocabulary is their focus. They are designed for the following purposes: helping learners be aware of their knowledge of vocabulary by examining everyday objects in stores (Going to the Supermarket); helping students demonstrate process organization and activate vocabulary related to food and cooking

(Party or Test: Who Cares? Let's Eat!); assessing students' knowledge of numbers (The Price Is Right); assessing students' knowledge of color vocabulary (Color-Coordinated Quiz); building vocabulary in real-time, on-line computer discussions (Vocabulary Information-Gap Electronic Discussion); and reinforcing the relationship between a word and its various meanings (A Vocabulary Quiz Given by Students to Themselves).

The contributions that concentrate on writing and grammar involve these purposes: to help students understand the qualities of an acceptable library research paper and help teachers evaluate such papers (Check It Out: A Library Research Checklist); to assess students' production of the three spoken versions of the past tense ending *-ed* (Tense Excitement Throwing a Die); and to help students understand and practice the comparative form (Who Is He?).

References and Further Reading

Brown, J. D. (1996). *Testing in language programs*. Upper Saddle River, NJ: Prentice Hall.

◆ Reading
Taking the Speed out of Reading Tests

Levels
Intermediate +

Aims
Gain credit for active
reading tasks
Use longer, more
substantial resource
material

Class Time
Variable

Preparation Time
Minimal

Resources
Texts
Reading task

This assessment activity creates a situation in which students get credit in a course for doing active reading tasks (tasks in which they read and do something with the reading). Such activities encourage students to take on much longer and much more substantial reading materials than they may have tackled previously.

Procedure

1. Before class,
   - Choose resource texts that are stimulating and challenging to your students and that allow for active reading tasks.
   - Prepare an active reading activity for the assessment (see the Appendix). Skills to assess might include the standard range of analysis or application skills that require students to construct from the text or to reconstruct modified text. Tasks might include completing or constructing texts or diagrams, matching, generating questions or answers, creating or filling in tables, and marking the text in specified ways. Avoid tasks such as summarizing, for which the students can prepare a written draft.
2. A reasonable amount of time in advance, for example the evening before the assessment,
   - Distribute the text to the students so that they can read through it for homework and remove any obstacles caused by time constraints.
   - Make it clear that the students will be required to do something with the text, but do not indicate what that will be.
   - Tell the students to bring the text to the assessment activity.

3. On the assessment day, give the students the active reading task. Have spare copies of the text available. Do not allow time for the process of getting to know the text, but do allow time to use the material.

Feedback and Scoring

1. Score tasks like those in the Appendix by counting the number of correct responses.

Caveats and Options

1. Colleagues may oppose the idea of allowing the students to see the text in advance, particularly in more formal examinations in which they feel that it amounts to cheating or giving an unfair advantage. Make it clear that the assessment is not being compromised or revealed in advance, and take great care to ensure that this is so.

References and Further Reading

Hughes, A. (1989). *Testing for language teachers*. Cambridge: Cambridge University Press.

Lunzer, E., & Gardner, K. (1984). *Learning from the written word*. Edinburgh, Scotland: Oliver & Boyd.

Nunan, D. (1989). *Designing tasks for the communicative classroom*. Cambridge: Cambridge University Press.

Appendix: Sample Active Reading Tasks

Trainee teachers were asked to read a magazine article on land degradation. To demonstrate their ability to use text and to plan for using texts in the classroom, they were then asked to carry out tasks such as the following.

1. Complete the table showing the causes of deforestation.

	Wildlife	Commercial felling	Population expansion	Agriculture
Causes				
Solutions				

2. One group of students: Underline the main points in the passage. Use these to prepare a set of 10 questions to ask other students as an assessment of their understanding of this passage.

3. Describe the process of soil erosion by filling in the flowchart.

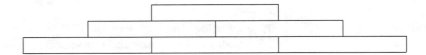

4. Draw pictures to illustrate six factors that contribute to land degradation.

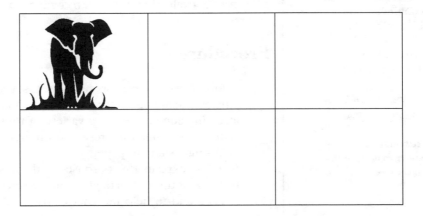

Contributors

Rex Berridge, a teacher educator and formerly an English language adviser with the British Council, is now director of the Language and Learning Centre, University of Wales Aberystwyth, in the United Kingdom. Jenny Muzambindo, a teacher educator and expert in English teaching and the methodology of teaching across the curriculum, is senior lecturer in English at Belvedere Technical Teachers' College, Zimbabwe.

Keeping Track With Free Readin'

Levels
Any

Aims
Provide formative
evaluation of reading
comprehension
Be motivated to read

Class Time
20–25 minutes

Preparation Time
15–30 minutes

Resources
Short magazine or
newspaper articles

Motivating large classes of EFL students who are accustomed to traditional grammar and translation instruction to take charge of their reading can be a major task. Plotting their improvement during a short school term may also be difficult. This assessment activity gives students a chance to read and respond to a text of their choice and gives the teacher a formative evaluation tool with which to regularly spot-check their progress.

Procedure

1. Before class, choose six or seven short magazine or newspaper articles (including pictures if possible) appropriate to the students' level. Include articles on a variety of topics, such as sports, politics, economics, human interest, and entertainment. Arrange the articles on a single sheet of paper.
2. In class, explain the purpose of the task. For example, say, "The purpose of this task is to give you a chance to read interesting articles in class and to help me check how well you understand what you read."
3. Give each student a copy of the sheet of paper containing the articles. Instruct them to
   - scan the headlines and pictures, choose one article, and read it as quickly as possible, avoiding the use of dictionaries if they can
   - write down what they feel about the article and indicate whether they learned anything new
4. Allow the students a short amount of time to read and respond. About 20–25 minutes works well for articles of as many as 250 words. Make sure the students devote most of the time to responding to the article.

Feedback and Scoring

1. Collect the students' responses and rate them. Do not be tempted to correct writing errors. Use a simple three-level rating scale, such as the following, or a similar scale:
   - ✓– Brief response with no direct reference to the contents of the article
   - ✓ Brief response but some direct reference to the contents of the article
   - ✓+ Lengthy response including direct reference to the article, feelings about the topic, and the relationship of new knowledge to previous knowledge
2. Read some of the responses aloud at the next class. Edit the writing before reading so that the class hears an error-free form of the original. Be sure to read one or two of the shorter responses to encourage the class to do a good job.

Caveats and Options

1. Repeat this activity at regular intervals throughout the term. Adjust the difficulty of the reading according to the ratings.
2. Avoid stressing the evaluation side of the activity to the students. This activity is supposed to be a low-pressure, motivating experience.
3. Either keep the written responses yourself, or have the students keep them in folders. Use them in a portfolio assessment scheme.
4. If you wish, use numbered ratings that can be averaged or added up, but doing so is not recommended because it defeats the basic aim of the task as a formative evaluation.
5. Alternate this activity with written responses to articles that the students choose from newspapers and magazines found in the library. Respond in the same way as for the in-class activity described here.
6. Report to the class how many students read each article as a survey of their interests and to encourage the students to read texts on a variety of topics.

Contributor

Nicholas O. Jungheim is an associate professor at Ryutsu Keizai University in Ibaraki, Japan. His interests include language testing, intercultural communication, and nonverbal communication.

The Reading Beat: Investigative Questioning and Reading Comprehension

Levels
Advanced

Aims
Develop effective
questioning strategies
Demonstrate
comprehension of a text
and critical thinking
ability

Class Time
50 minutes

Preparation Time
30–60 minutes

Resources
Narrative reading
passage

I came up with this assessment activity as a way to simultaneously enhance students' involvement with a text and provide a rough-and-ready estimate of their comprehension of a text. My advanced-level ESL reading students had responded enthusiastically to investigative reporting read in class, so I thought they would enjoy and benefit from trying their hands at the process. By suspending the classroom reality, the activity allowed my students to picture themselves as investigative reporters following up a lead. The interview prompts written by the students gave me an idea of their ability to ask in-depth questions and to approach a text with a critical eye. The students had an opportunity to ask more questions than they would in a full-class discussion, and they asked questions that they might not otherwise have asked (e.g., due to inhibitions). Assuming the roles of the characters in the story caused them to analyze the text from a different perspective and told me how well they understood the relationships between particular characters and the overall text. The students enjoyed this activity, and its repetition over the course of a semester left me with strong impressions of their capacity to get to the bottom of a reading assignment.

Procedure

1. Identify a reading of appropriate length for your students. The most effective reading for this activity will include a narrative story line. Assign the reading for homework.
2. Write up a brief article assignment from the editor of a magazine or newspaper, explaining that the students will have to create an interview schedule that probes for the truth behind the reading.

3. Have the students bring the completed reading assignment to class. Explain to the students that they are now investigative reporters who must dig up the truth by interviewing a particular character from the story.

4. Give the students the editor's article assignment. Have the students choose a character whom they would like to interview. Encourage the students to develop questions that probe a character's motivation, an interpretation of the character's actions, and a rationale for actions and events in the story. Stress that the questions should not be of the *yes-no* variety. If you wish, provide model questions (e.g., "What did you mean by . . .?" or "What did you hope to accomplish in . . .?").

5. Tell the students that there is a deadline for their story. Give them 15 minutes to come up with 10–12 questions before the interview.

6. After 15 minutes, assign partners to the students. Have one partner assume the role of the character that the other partner wants to interview. Tell the students to take notes on the answers to their questions during real-time conversation, just as an actual reporter would have to do.

7. Give each student 15 minutes to conduct the interview. After the first interview, have the students switch roles, and give the second student 15 minutes to conduct an interview.

8. Collect the interview schedules and notes.

Feedback and Scoring

Follow up the activity with a writing session:

1. Look over the notes from the interviews, and return them to the students as approved stories that will run in the next edition.

2. Have the students write up their interviews in a newspaper or magazine format (with a byline and boldfaced interviewee and interviewer dialogue).

3. Publish the stories in a collection, and give a copy to each students.

Caveats and Options

1. At first, the students may rely heavily on questions of the type *What did you mean when you said . . .?*, which does not provide much information on their critical relationship with the text. Before the next session, discuss methods of question formation that (a) give a

context to the question being asked and (b) attempt to relate events in the text to other text-internal or text-external events (e.g., *Given this situation, how is it that you said* X, *but did* Y?). Such questions are much more revealing of the students' comprehension and questioning ability.

Contributor

John M. Norris is an ESL teacher at the University of Hawai'i at Manoa, in the United States, where he is also a doctoral student and conducts research on L2 assessment.

A Window on the Reading Process

Levels
Any

Aims
Read intensively and for global meaning
Comprehend difficult reading passages
Demonstrate understanding without traditional comprehension questions

Class Time
20 + minutes/session

Preparation Time
Variable

Resources
Complete text of several pages

This activity helps students read intensively for an extended period of time. It is especially useful in situations that require students to understand language that is above their level. The second purpose is to assess which students can cope with the reading demands of the activity and which students need additional work on reading skills. This method assists students enrolled in adjunct courses in any content discipline and encourages them to do the large volume of complex reading that is assigned.

Procedure

1. Select a reading passage consisting of at least several dozen paragraphs. The passage should be a little above the level that the students can comfortably handle.
2. Number each paragraph of the reading.
3. Select one third to one half of the paragraphs for paraphrasing. Rewrite the selected paragraphs, being careful to retain the propositional content and focus of the original. However, be sure that the rewritten paragraphs are syntactically and lexically different from the originals.
4. Type up the rewritten paragraphs in random order. Place a blank for an answer before each paragraph.
5. Give each student a copy of the original reading passage (with paragraphs numbered) and a copy of the paraphrased paragraphs.
6. Have the students read the original passage and the rewritten paragraphs, determine which original paragraphs match the rewritten paragraphs in meaning, and write the original paragraph number in the blank space in front of the rewritten paragraph.
7. Assign the unfinished portion of the matching as homework.

Feedback and Scoring

1. Give the students feedback on their answers while they work (e.g., O = right; X = wrong).
2. Note how many correct matches the students make in the time allowed in order to identify students who are having problems with reading (as well as those who are reading fluently).

Caveats and Options

1. Be sure that the rewritten paragraphs cannot be matched with the originals simply by scanning for lexical similarities. Part of the purpose is to induce the students to process text at a deeper level of meaning.
2. This activity is limited only by the amount of time you have for preparation and by your skill at paraphrasing. The time the students spend on the activity can vary, too, but allow a minimum of 20 minutes per session so that they can experience sustained intensive reading.
3. Precede the activity by a schema-setting introduction, or use the activity itself as the introduction to further activities.

References and Further Reading

Craik, F. I. M., & Lockhart, R. S. (1972). Levels of processing: A framework for memory record. *Journal of Verbal Learning and Verbal Behavior, 11*, 67–84.

Widdowson, H. G. (1992). *Practical stylistics* (pp. 108–144). Oxford: Oxford University Press.

Contributor

Patrick A. Rosenkjar holds an EdD in second language acquisition from Temple University Japan (TUJ). He designs and teaches content-based adjunct courses in TUJ's undergraduate school.

Sort It Out

Levels
Intermediate

Aims
Practice intensive
reading
Learn how texts are
organized

Class Time
30 minutes

Preparation Time
1 hour

Resources
Course text
Handout and answer
key

Reading is fundamental in the process of language learning because it (a) fosters cultural growth, (b) gets students in contact with English-speaking cultures, (c) encourages vocabulary building in meaningful contexts, and (d) promotes thinking in order to draw conclusions.

Procedure

1. Choose two or three short passages from your course text or any other source. Mix up the sentences in each text. With these, develop a passages handout and answer key (see the examples in Appendixes A and B). Make a copy of the handout for each student.
2. Give the students the passages handout and explain the directions. Allow the students 10 minutes to read the texts.
3. When the time is up, ask the students yes-no or short-answer questions about each of the texts. Have them number and write their answers below the sentences for each text.

Feedback and Scoring

1. Use the answer key to score the handouts.
2. If you wish, give 6 points for sorting each text out and 2 points for each of the short-answer responses.

Caveats and Options

1. Instead of mixing up the sentences in the texts, put three or four nonsense sentences into a text and ask the students to find them.
2. Use only one text. Create different versions by varying the details within it, and ask the students to spot the mistakes.

3. Mix the sentences from all the texts together, and have the students separate them into passages before ordering the sentences within each passage.
4. To make the activity easier, type out each sentence on a different line, stick the sentences onto a card, and cut the card into sentence strips. Then have the students move the sentences around as they sort them out.

References and Further Reading

Phillips, S. (1993). *Young learners.* Oxford: Oxford University Press.

Appendix A: Sample Passages Handout

Directions: Number the sentences in logical order from 1 to 6.

A. Devi and the Tree
____ Sometimes she also liked to climb the trees and sit there in her secret place.
____ One of the trees was Devi's special reading tree.
____ Five hundred years ago, a young girl called Devi lived in a town in the mountains in India.
____ Her family's house had a big garden.
____ In later life, Devi liked to sit under the beautiful trees in the garden and read a book.
____ Sometimes Devi and her friends had picnics or played games together there.

B. The Thieves
____ "Good idea!" said Taffy. "We are going to be rich."
____ "Let's go to the house tomorrow night. Let's steal the diamonds!"
____ "There are some diamonds in one of the rooms of the big house on the hill," Jack said.
____ Jack was a thief, too.
____ One day Jack saw some pictures in the newspaper.
____ Taffy was a thief.

Appendix B: Sample Answer Key

A. Devi and the Tree
1. Five hundred years ago, a young girl called Devi lived in a town in the mountains in India.
2. Her family's house had a big garden.
3. Sometimes Devi and her friends had picnics or played games together there.
4. Sometimes she also liked to climb the trees and sit there in her secret place.
5. In later life, Devi liked to sit under the beautiful trees in the garden and read a book.
6. One of the trees was Devi's special reading tree.

B. The Thieves
1. Taffy was a thief.
2. Jack was a thief, too.
3. One day Jack saw some pictures in the newspaper.
4. "There are some diamonds in one of the rooms of the big house on the hill," Jack said.
5. "Let's go to the house tomorrow night. Let's steal the diamonds!"
6. "Good idea!" said Taffy. "We are going to be rich."

Questions:
1. Where did Devi live?
2. Where did she read the book?
3. Who were Taffy and Jack?
4. What did they find?
5. Where is the big house?

Scoring: 6 points for sorting each text out and 2 points for each correct short answer.

Contributor

Zully G. Tondolo holds a bachelor's degree in modern language education from the Universidad de Carabobo in Valencia, Venezuela. She has worked as an English teacher for 8 years at the elementary, high school, and adult levels.

◆ Reading and Vocabulary
Have You Seen My Brother?

Levels
Any

Aims
Demonstrate
comprehension of
written descriptions

Class Time
10-15 minutes

Preparation Time
5-10 minutes

Resources
Handout
Sets of eight colored
pencils
Cassette player and
audiotape (optional)

This activity assesses students' comprehension of written descriptions of people. In a situation similar to real life, students draw and color the person described.

Procedure

1. Seat the students in a row, allowing ample space between individual students.
2. Give each student a set of eight colored pencils: black, white, blue, red, green, orange, brown, and yellow.
3. Give oral instructions for the activity (see the Appendix), and answer the students' questions about the procedure.
4. Give each student a handout containing the written instructions and dialogue (see the Appendix). Allow the students 3-5 minutes to read the instructions, and answer any remaining questions.
5. Give the students 15 minutes to finish the task. Monitor them as they work.
6. Collect the students' work when the time is up.

Feedback and Scoring

1. Give 1 point for each correct item. In the example in the Appendix, scoring would be as follows:
   ● Genre: 1 point
   ● Descriptive adjectives: 1 point for *short* and 1 point for *heavy*: subtotal of 2 points
   ● Hair: 1 point for color, 1 point for length: subtotal of 2 points
   ● Clothing: 1 point for each correct item of clothing: subtotal of 4 points

- Color: 1 point for correct color of each item of clothing: subtotal of 4 points
- Maximum possible: 13 points

2. Transform the scores into your grading system (e.g., a percentage).

Caveats and Options

1. Be sure the students have already been introduced to and have thoroughly practiced the vocabulary and expressions needed for describing people (e.g., simple, short descriptive adjectives; body parts; clothing and colors; the present tense of *to be* and *to have* and the present continuous of *to wear* in their affirmative, negative, and interrogative forms), both in the oral and written forms and in the receptive and productive modes.
2. Prepare several similar dialogues, changing the person's gender, characteristics, and clothes.
3. Ask the students to bring their own colored pencils (and have a few sets as backup) as a way of minimizing cost and effort.
4. To use the activity to assess oral comprehension, give the students a handout with the instructions and a space for drawing. Either read the dialogue aloud, or audiotape it with two native speakers and play it back to the students. In either case, make the dialogue realistic, or play it back three times. Use the same scoring procedure.

Appendix: Sample Handout

Name _____ Grade _____ Date _____

Have You Seen My Brother?

Instructions: Read the following dialogue. Draw a picture of the person described in the dialogue, and color your drawing according to the information given.

Setting: A dentist's office. A is a young girl, around 18 years old. B is the dentist's secretary.

A: Good afternoon.
B: Good afternoon. May I help you?
A: Sure. Did Arthur leave already?
B: Arthur?

A: My brother. He had an appointment at three. I came to pick him up.

B: Is he tall and thin?

A: No, he's short and heavy.

B: Does he have long brown hair?

A: Yes, he does.

B: Is he wearing blue jeans and a yellow T-shirt?

A: Yeah, he's also wearing a green jacket and black shoes.

B: Oh, I think he just went to the restroom.

A: What a relief! Can I wait for him here?

B: Certainly.

Contributor

Beatriz de Aguerrevere holds a BA in EFL and an MEd in adult education and has 27 years' experience as an EFL teacher at the high school, college, and graduate levels.

Extra! Extra!
Read All About It!

Levels
Intermediate +

Aims
Understand the layout
of a newspaper
Develop skimming,
scanning, and
vocabulary skills
See the value of
newspapers for
developing English and
getting information and
opinions

Class Time
1½ hours

Preparation Time
1 hour

Resources
Daily newspaper,
preferably short

This activity allows teachers to assess students' reading skills in class with the morning newspaper. Thus it deals with current information that is likely to be relatively interesting to the students.

Procedure

1. Buy copies of a daily newspaper for yourself and the students in your class.
2. Write questions about the newspaper on a sheet of paper or on the blackboard in class. (See the Appendix for sample questions.)
3. Hand out the newspapers and questions in class, and have the students answer the questions.
4. Have the students write their names on their answer sheets and newspapers, and collect them.

Feedback and Scoring

1. Correct the answer sheets.
2. Bring them to class, and go over the answers.

Caveats and Options

Use the newspaper as the basis of a 1-month course of study:

1. Focus each class on a different aspect of the newspaper, for example, features of the newspaper (e.g., headlines, articles, captions, standings, graphs) or sections of the newspaper (e.g., the front page; the business, sports, entertainment, national, local, international, science, nature, and children's sections).

Appendix: Sample Questions for Newspaper Assessment

2. Once the class has looked at the various sections, bring a newspaper into the last class and assess the students with questions based on that day's entire newspaper.

General

1. How much does the newspaper cost?
2. What is the weather for today?
3. How many sections are there in the newspaper?
4. On what pages are the sports articles?
5. What is the exchange rate for the dollar and the yen today?
6. What movie [compact disc, play, actor, musician] is featured in the Entertainment section?
7. What is the theme for today's editorial?

Skimming and Scanning

Look at the advertisements and answer the following questions.

1. How much does the [item] cost?
2. How many cans of [item] can I get for $2.00?
3. Where is the store located?
4. How much does it cost to travel to [place]?
5. What's the telephone number of the agency that offers trips to [place]?

Vocabulary

1. Look at the headline [. . .] on page [number]. [Note: Give the page numbers sometimes to help the students find the article. For some of the scanning and skimming questions, do not give the page numbers.] The word [. . .] probably means
    a. [Add meaning and distractors.]
    b.
    c.
    d.
2. [synonym study] Read the article entitled [. . .]. Look for words that mean the same as the following words.

Advice Column

1. Read the advice column. Explain why you agree or disagree with the advice.
2. Read the first letter in the advice column. Write a letter of advice to the author.

Entertainment Section

1. How many movies [compact discs, plays] are reviewed?
2. Write the names of the movies [compact discs, plays] that are reviewed today. Scan the reviews and check whether each is ___ positive, ___ negative, or ___ mixed.
3. When does [name of event] start? When does it end? Where can I get tickets?

Sports Page

1. Look at the sports standings and answer the following questions. Who's in first place in [. . .]? What player has the most [. . .]? Who has the most wins in the [. . .]? Who won the baseball game in [. . .] last night? What was the score of the basketball game in [. . .] last night?
2. I'm interested in football. Write the headlines of the article(s) in the sports sections will I read.

Specific Articles

Read the article entitled [. . .] and answer the following questions.

1. Whom is the article about?
2. What happened?
3. Where does the story take place?
4. When does the story take place?

Letters Section

Read the letters section.

1. Which letter talks about [. . .]?
2. In which letter is the writer most angry? least angry? commenting on a previous letter? commenting on a previous article? complaining?
3. Write a letter to the editor based on a topic that you feel strongly about.
4. Write a letter to the newspaper based on one of the letters.

Editorial

1. What is the editorial theme for today?
2. Read the editorial and write whether you agree or disagree with the writer.

Imagination

1. Write a different headline for any article in the newspaper. Also write the original title and page of the article.
2. Look at the picture on page [. . .]. Write your own caption for the picture.
3. Look at the picture on page [. . .]. Write a completely different story for the picture.

Comics

1. Read the "Peanuts" cartoon. Why is Lucy sad?
2. Read the "Blondie" cartoon. What is relationship between the two people?

Contributor

Herman Bartelen teaches at Kanda Institute of Foreign Languages in Tokyo, Japan.

On the Spot!

Levels
Beginning +; elementary

Aims
Demonstrate vocabulary
development and
reading comprehension

Class Time
Variable

Preparation Time
Variable

Resources
Objects
Pictures

For every new word children are required to learn, they have to master a rather large number of interrelated elements of information. Teachers need to be able to make formative assessments of students' ongoing learning on the spot. This activity gives teachers immediate information about each student's vocabulary development and reading comprehension at any moment without using a paper-and-pencil test.

Procedure

1. To check the ability to match a target object with the appropriate sound symbols,
   - Show the class the target object (e g , a pencil).
   - Ask a student, "What is this?" If the student can provide the correct answer, you know that the student can match the object with the correct sound symbols.
2. To check the ability to match a picture of the target object with the appropriate sound symbols,
   - Show the class a picture of the target object (e.g., a horse).
   - Ask a student, "What is this?" If the student can provide the correct answer, you know that the student can match a picture prompt with the correct sound symbols.
3. To check the ability to match the target print symbols with the appropriate sound symbols,
   - Write the target object's print symbols (e.g., the word *book*) on the black- or white board. Point to them.
   - Ask a student, "What is this word?"

4. To check the ability to match the target object with the appropriate print symbols,
   - Write sets of print symbols (e.g., *engine, elephant, eraser, erase, error, ear, answer, anger*) on the black- or white board. Show the class the target object (e.g., an eraser).
   - Point to the black- or white board and ask a student, for example, "Which word is *eraser*?" Have a student select a word by pointing to it.

Feedback and Scoring

1. Count and record the number of correct responses.
2. Keep track of which responses were correct in order to give students diagnostic feedback. In this way this assessment activity has positive backwash effects because it encourages students to focus on aspects of the target language in which they are weak.

Caveats and Options

1. Assess the vocabulary development and concept learning of students at other levels of proficiency by changing the content and readjusting the focus appropriately. With more advanced-level classes, assume that the students are already familiar with the concepts involved in the teaching of the target language. However, if you select content at the appropriate level of difficulty, the above procedures can provide a useful means of assessing the current language proficiency of individual group members.
2. Clearly, assessing whether students can match sounds with print is not the same as asking them to match print with sounds. You need to know if students have mastered both these skills as well as many other skills involved in learning a concept. The skills assessed in the Procedure are the key elements that you will probably want to assess.
3. If you wish, assess the students' ability to match an object with a picture and a picture with an object, either at an earlier stage in the reading process or when pictures are stylized in some way.
4. Show the students different examples or categories of the target object. To learn how well students' concept of *dog*, for example, is established, offer pictures of several different kinds of dogs, and ask the students to provide the print and sound symbols that match the pictures. Or offer pictures of various breeds of dog mixed up with

examples of cats, horses, or other four-footed animals to determine if the students have learned category inclusion and exclusion.

5. The table below contains a matrix of the various combinations of matching procedures for assessing students.

	Object	Picture	Sound	Print	Concept
Object	—	✓	✓	✓	✓
Picture	✓	—	✓	✓	✓
Sound	✓	✓	—	✓	✓
Print	✓	✓	✓	—	✓
Concept	✓	✓	✓	✓	—

Contributor

Carol MacLennan is a senior lecturer at the Hong Kong Institute of Education.

Definition-Resource Cloze

Levels
Advanced; postgraduate
EFL teachers-in-training

Aims
Read with a specific
purpose
Infer words from
definitions
Use context to
determine suffixes and
inflections of words
Understand the purpose
of a text

Class Time
1 hour

Preparation Time
3 hours

Resources
Definition-Resource
Cloze Test
Answer key

This activity assesses the students' ability to ascertain missing words using the context itself and the definition provided for each word. Students also use their background knowledge on the topic as a resource.

Procedure

1. Pass out the Definition-Resource Cloze Test (see Appendix A) to each of the students.
2. Have the students read the passage quickly to get the general meaning.
3. Ask the students to fill in the missing words by looking at the definitions provided for each of the blanks and to decide on the specific morphology of the word according to the context.
4. Ask the students to create a title for the text.

Feedback and Scoring

1. Using an answer key like the one shown in Appendix B, score the test as follows: 22 total points—1 point for each of the blanks and 2 points for the title.

Caveats and Options

1. For very advanced-level students, leave blanks in the definitions, resulting in another cloze test.

References and Further Reading

Foundation in education: Dictionary of education (2nd ed.). (1959). New York: McGraw-Hill.

Hulse, S. H., Deese, J., & Egeth, H. (1975). *The psychology of learning*. New York: McGraw-Hill.

Webster's new world dictionary of the American language (2nd ed.). (1978). New York: Collins.

Appendix A: Definition-Resource Cloze Test

This assessment activity is designed for teachers learning the English of psychology. Thus the criterion for leaving a word out was that it be a noun related to the field.

Name: _____

1. Read the passage quickly to get the general meaning.
2. Fill in the missing words using the definition given for each of the blanks as a resource.
3. Check your answers.
4. Give a title to the text.

Note: This is a 22-point test: 1 point for each blank and 2 points for the title.

Title: _____

Extinction produces the most dramatic _(1)_ of patterns of reinforcement upon behavior. All _(2)_ affect resistance to extinction somewhat differently, but it is an important general _(3)_ that a pattern that involves some _(4)_ in the nature of reinforcement _(5)_ from response to response will produce greater _(6)_ to extinction than a condition where all _(7)_ are reinforced immediately, 100 percent of the time, in just the same way.

Results obtained by many, many _(8)_ show that a pattern of partial reinforcement greatly increases resistance to extinction. Skinner (1938) and Humphreys (1939) demonstrated this in some of the earliest _(9)_ on the problem, and since that time, literally hundreds of experiments have

1._____
2._____
3._____
4._____
5._____
6._____
7._____
8._____
9._____

repeated these results with a wide variety of __(10)__, apparatuses, and experimental __(11)__ (Jenkins & Stanley, 1950; Lewis, 1960; and Robbins, 1971, provide extensive reviews of the literature concerned with this __(12)__).

Resistance to extinction following __(13)__ with a pattern of variable amounts of __(14)__ increases as the range, or variability, of the amounts increases. Greatest resistance to extinction was obtained following __(15)__ with 10 units on half the __(16)__ and 0 units on the other half (partial reinforcement), and resistance to extinction was least if all trials had been reinforced with the mean __(17)__ of 5 units (continuous reinforcement). The important point, however, is that intermediate resistance to __(18)__ was obtained when the __(19)__ in amounts given from trial to trial lay between the __(20)__ of continuous and partial reinforcement.

10._____
11._____
12._____
13._____
14._____
15._____
16._____
17._____
18._____
19._____
20._____

Definition Resource

(1) anything brought about by a cause or agent
(2) a reliable sample of traits, acts, tendencies, or other observable characteristics of a person
(3) an established practice that serves as a guide
(4) the complete or partial alteration of an item in form, quality, or relationship
(5) attendant circumstances
(6) the tendency to respond in an opposite direction from that of an applied force
(7) any implicit or overt change in an effector organ, substance, or item consequent to stimulation
(8) someone who searches into; inquires into systematically
(9) any action or process undertaken to discover something not yet known or to demonstrate or test something known
(10) someone or something undergoing a treatment, experiment, or other procedure
(11) a particular course or method of action
(12) a fact, occurrence, or circumstance that is open to observation

(13) modification so that an act or response previously associated with one stimulus becomes associated with another

(14) strengthening of a conditioned response by reintroducing the original unconditioned stimulus

(15) a process of helping others acquire skills and knowledge

(16) an act of testing something to see if it works

(17) a collection or mass considered as a unit in terms of its size, number, etc.

(18) the process by which the repeated response to a conditioning stimulus reduces the response to a minimum

(19) the limits within which variable amounts or qualities are included

(20) either of two things that are as different or as far as possible from each other

Appendix B: Answer Key

Title: Patterns of Reinforcement and Extinction

(1) effect

(2) patterns

(3) rule

(4) change

(5) conditions

(6) resistance

(7) responses

(8) investigators

(9) experiments

(10) subjects

(11) procedures

(12) phenomenon

(13) conditioning

(14) reinforcement

(15) training

(16) trials

(17) amount

(18) extinction

(19) range

(20) extremes

Contributor

Edith Malagarriga is aggregate professor of TESOL at the Universidad de Carabobo in Valencia, Venezuela. She teaches English literature and didactics and is involved in teacher training programs.

◆ Vocabulary
Going to the Supermarket

Levels
Any

Aims
Be aware of own
knowledge of English
vocabulary

Class Time
Variable

Preparation Time
None

Resources
None

Many learners think they don't know any English vocabulary because they aren't aware of the large amounts found on packages, bottles, bags, and canned goods in supermarkets and in different departments in stores, even in EFL situations. This activity helps students understand these resources and helps the teacher better understand the problems some students have, for example, in understanding simple instructions or producing certain sounds.

Procedure

1. Tell the students to go to a supermarket, look for five items in each department with brands or components (e.g., nutritional information, chemical elements) in English, and write down the information about the products.
2. Have the students bring their lists to class and read them to their classmates.
3. Make a chart like the following on the blackboard, and have the students organize the items into groups to assess their knowledge of the different groups of words.

Food	Cleaning products	Beauty aids	Gardening products
cornflakes	Bold 3 mildew remover	shampoo	

Feedback and Scoring

1. Use the lists to assess the students' performance in a role play in which one student is the customer and a second one, the clerk.
2. Prepare a checklist of factors that you want to give feedback on, or use the checklist in the Appendix to give the students feedback.

3. Consider having the students evaluate each other using some variant of the checklist.

Caveats and Options

1. Ask the students to look for English words on appliances, manuals for appliances, or other items they have at home.
2. Instead of having the students read their lists to the whole class, have the students gather in groups of three or four to check their own lists, produce a new list, and read it to the class.

Appendix: Language Skills Checklist

Listening
____ 1. Understands simple directions
____ 2. Understands simple yes-no questions
____ 3. Understands simple *wh-* questions
____ 4. Understands vocabulary related to the activity
____ 5. Understands contractions and common shortened forms
____ 6. Understands language of peers

Speaking
____ 1. Pronounces vowel sounds correctly
____ 2. Pronounces consonant sounds well
____ 3. Pronounces blends correctly
____ 4. Uses word stress correctly
____ 5. Produces simple yes-no questions
____ 6. Produces simple *wh-* questions
____ 7. Produces vocabulary related to the activity
____ 8. Uses peer-group language properly

Contributor

Maria Irene Albers de Urriola is an instructor in the Faculty of Economic and Social Sciences and in the Department of Modern Languages, Faculty of Education, at the Universidad de Carabobo, in Valencia, Venezuela.

Party or Test: Who Cares? Let's Eat!

Levels
Intermediate +

Aims
Demonstrate ability to
organize a process
Activate vocabulary
Talk about food in an
informed way in a
nonthreatening
atmosphere

Class Time
3 hours

Preparation Time
1 hour

Resources
Dictionaries
Handout
Scoring grid

Students usually talk about both their native country's and U.S. food in very general terms (e.g., *it's good, it's OK*). This activity introduces the vocabulary of preparing foods and describing their various tastes. As an assessment, students prepare a dish from their own country for a lunch or dinner party, describe how to prepare their dish, and describe the flavors of the many dishes they taste.

Procedure

Day 1

1. Ask the students to divide into groups of two or three, preferably with each of the students coming from a different language background.
2. Have the students use dictionaries (electronic or paper) to negotiate the meanings of the Terms Used for Food Preparation in the handout (see Appendix A). Add any other necessary vocabulary. Go from group to group and facilitate.
3. Tell the students to discuss the words on the handout and describe a food from their country that each word applies to.

Day 2

1. Have the students decide on a dish to prepare for a class lunch or dinner.
2. Ask the students to divide into groups of two or three. Tell them to practice vocabulary germane to their dish and practice telling how to prepare the dish. Circulate from group to group, and facilitate questioning about the tastes of the various dishes.
3. Ask the students to bring the dish to the next class meeting.

Day 3

1. Have the students taste the foods that their classmates have prepared.
2. Have the students describe the preparation and taste of their dish and the taste of two or three other students' dishes.

Feedback and Scoring

1. Use the scoring grid shown in Appendix B to assign and compute scores.

Caveats and Options

1. Use the party format to practice or assess the ability to introduce others, engage in small talk, talk about past experiences, practice formal or informal language, and use other conversational strategies.
2. This assessment activity works best at the end of a term or in the middle of a semester as a way of breaking the monotony.
3. Instead of preparing the food, the students can bring food picked up from a restaurant, but they should be able to describe how the food is prepared.
4. Hold several parties. Have part of the class prcparc food for the first one, and rotate that duty for the next one.

Appendix A: Terms Used in Food Preparation

Adjectives Used to Describe Food

sweet	sour	delicious
gross	disgusting	nasty
tasty	thick	hot
spicy	bitter	salty

Phrases and Sentences Used to Describe Food

It tastes:

good	unusual	different	excellent	like X

Verbs Used in Preparing Food

Cutting	*Cooking*
slice	steam
dice	boil
quarter	simmer
	fry
	bake

Ingredients

Spices	*Main ingredients*
curry powder	cabbage, leeks, carrots, onions
soy sauce	tofu, rice, noodles
ginger	meat (e.g., beef, shrimp, chicken, pork)
salt	peanuts
pepper	tomatoes
red pepper (cayenne)	
garlic	
oregano	

Measurements

a pinch	a teaspoon
a tablespoon	a cupful
a package	a head [of cabbage]

Process Description

First	Then	After that
After cutting [cooking, mixing],		Finally

Appendix B: Scoring Grid

Maximum points possible = 40.

Category	Score
Use of appropriate phrases	0 1 2 3 4
Comprehensibility	0 1 2 3 4
Grammar (doesn't interfere with the meaning)	0 1 2 3 4
Natural speech (isn't scripted)	0 1 2 3 4
Pronunciation (doesn't interfere with meaning)	0 1 2 3 4
Sufficient description	0 1 2 3 4
Description of own food's taste	0 1 2 3 4
Description of method of preparation	0 1 2 3 4
Description of ingredients	0 1 2 3 4
Description of two dishes' tastes	0 1 2 3 4

Contributor

Jim Bame is a lecturer at Utah State University, in the United States. His interests are interactional and transactional conversation analysis, task-based language learning, and discourse analysis.

The Price Is Right

Levels
Beginning–low
intermediate

Aims
Demonstrate knowledge
of numbers

Class Time
5–10 minutes

Preparation Time
45–75 minutes

Resources
Sunday newspaper
advertising inserts
Large sheets of paper
Glue

This activity livens up assessment activities by including a price compo-nent. The students give the teacher the prices of household items as they practice small and large numbers in context.

Procedure

1. From the multicolored Sunday newspaper advertising inserts (e.g., from big electronics and department stores), cut out 10–20 pictures of different sale items (e.g., televisions, computers, cameras, articles of clothing) along with their prices. Choose items in various price ranges ($1–$20, $21–$99, $100–$999, and $1,000 +).
2. Glue four or five items in different price ranges on each of several large sheets of paper.
3. Give the students, or have them select, one sheet of pictures.
4. Ask the students to tell you orally the price of each item on the sheet.

Feedback and Scoring

1. Grade the responses based on accuracy, pronunciation, or both.

Caveats and Options

1. This activity is best done one-on-one while a test is being adminis-tered. Have one student meet with you at your desk while the others are writing.
2. Include vocabulary (*The video cassette player costs $275*), adjective order (*I paid $25 for the dark blue blouse*), or functions (*I'd like to buy the TV for $499*) as part of the test. With more advanced-level classes, include fractions and percentages.

Contributor

Dennis Bricault is the director of ESL programs and an instructor in Spanish at North Park College, Chicago, in the United States. He is pursuing a PhD in higher education administration.

Color-Coordinated Quiz

Levels
Beginning–low
intermediate

Aims
Demonstrate knowledge
of color vocabulary

Class Time
5–10 minutes

Preparation Time
30–60 minutes

Resources
Full-color Sunday
newspaper advertising
inserts or catalogues
Large sheets of paper
Glue

This activity adds a dimension to a unit test by including a color component that helps students demonstrate their knowledge of vocabulary and word order. This component is based on readily available material taken from the newspaper or catalogues.

Procedure

1. From multicolored department store advertising inserts in the Sunday newspaper or from catalogues, cut out 10 pictures of different items (e.g., articles of clothing). Choose items in a wide selection of colors that the students have studied.
2. Glue the items onto a large sheet of paper. Number the items from 1 to 10.
3. Give one student the sheet, and ask the student to write a description of each item (e.g., *A woman is wearing blue jeans and a red t-shirt*) on a separate sheet of paper. Tell the student to pass the sheet of pictures on to the next person in class after finishing the descriptions.
4. Continue until everybody has had a chance to respond, and collect the students' descriptions.

Feedback and Scoring

1. Grade each response on accuracy of vocabulary, spelling, word order, content, or all of these features.

Caveats and Options

1. Try not to choose articles of clothing with unusual colors or hard-to-describe designs (e.g., a paisley tie).
2. Do the activity orally.

3. For large classes, prepare several sheets, or use fewer items on each sheet.
4. Add language functions (*I'd like to buy a pair of black shoes*) or longer sentences (*He's wearing a blue and red tie*) to the required response.
5. Put each sheet in a plastic cover to protect it as the students pass it around the class.

Contributor

Dennis Bricault is the director of ESL programs at North Park College, Chicago, in the United States. He has 15 years' experience as a teacher and administrator in Spain, Hungary, and the United States.

Vocabulary Information-Gap Electronic Discussion

Levels
Intermediate

Aims
Build and contextualize
vocabulary
Develop grammar
Participate in real-time,
on-line discussion

Class Time
Two class meetings (or
regularly during the
term)

Preparation Time
1–2 hours

Resources
Computer lab
Local area network
(optional)
Internet access
(optional)

This assessment activity helps students contextualize vocabulary through an authentic exchange of new information and participate in a real-time, on-line discussion without the hassles of interruption, racism, genderism, social status, or accent (Warschauer, 1995, p. 44).

Procedure

1. To set up the activity, do one of the following:
   - If your school has access to a computer lab but is not hooked up to a local area network (LAN) (or if you would rather split your class in half and have the students "chat" within the class), go to Step 4.
   - If your school district has a LAN but does not have access to the Internet, contact another teacher within the school district who has students at the same L2 proficiency level.
   - If your school has access to the Internet, contact another teacher with students at the same L2 proficiency level by e-mailing Tom Robb, a Student List Manager, at trobb@cc.kyoto-su.ac.jp or by posting a notice on *TESLCA-L* (the computer-assisted language learning branch of *TESL-L*, an e-mail discussion list).
2. With the other ESL teacher, create a long list of vocabulary from an agreed-upon lexicon or topic (e.g., animals and words describing how and where they live). Divide the vocabulary list into two parts, one for each class.
3. Construct a worksheet with the vocabulary words that the other class (or group) will be explaining to your students. Be sure to provide ample room to take notes directly on the sheet.

4. With the other teacher, match the students up with electronic discussion pals (or pal groups), keeping in mind that two or three students can use a single computer.

5. Decide on a date and time for the discussions. Reserve the computer lab for that time.

6. The day before the electronic discussion is to take place, distribute the vocabulary that your students will explain to the students in the other class along with related information on the topic.

7. Teach the vocabulary to the students in whatever way you prefer, giving them time to look up vocabulary words and ask questions, if you wish. Alternatively, assign the students homework about the vocabulary as preparation for the electronic discussion the next day.

8. Explain how to do the activity and how to use the computer for an electronic discussion.

9. Have the students conduct an electronic discussion with their partners in the other class. Encourage the students to use their notes to relay information to their electronic pals and to ask clarification questions about the new vocabulary that they are learning from the other students. Provide help when needed.

10. Ask the students to complete their worksheets.

11. When the task is completed, have the students print out a hard copy of their discussion.

Feedback and Scoring

1. Gather and analyze the students' worksheets and hard copies.

2. Determine if the focus of the activity was to learn vocabulary, chat communicatively, implement discrete grammar points, or a combination thereof.

3. Construct a grading scale that reflects the activity's focus (e.g., recognition of target vocabulary, 40%; correct use of verb tenses, 20%; clear instructions given to the other student, 40%).

4. Count the number of vocabulary words that the student filled out in the worksheet, and give points accordingly.

5. On the hard copy of the discussion, highlight all of the points that will be graded. Divide the number of correct attempts by the total number of attempts.

6. Highlight and count the number of unresolved miscommunications between the students that result from poor explanations of vocabulary. Or count the number of successful attempts at informing the other student about a vocabulary word.

7. Adjust each set of scores to its percentage value in the final grade. For example, if a student writes down 18 vocabulary words and leaves 2 blank, and vocabulary accounts for 40% of the grade, the student would score 36%. Add the percentages together for a final grade.

Caveats and Options

1. Be sure to allocate enough time to prepare this assessment activity. You will need at least 30 minutes to connect to and discuss the activity with the other teacher, 30 minutes in the computer lab, and 1 hour to get the students ready for the activity.

2. To circumvent off-topic responses by electronic pals, advise your students that they may chat about tangential topics only after they have exchanged all of the information.

3. Advise your students never to give any personal information, such as their home telephone number or address, over the Internet.

4. Encourage an e-mail exchange if the partners want to stay in touch.

5. If you are unable to arrange a meeting time with another class (because of time zone differences), set up an e-mail discussion. E-mail changes the nature of real-time discussion but opens the door to process writing tasks.

6. Create an information-gap task that focuses on explicit grammar points (e.g., the past tense, English subject-verb agreement strings, adjective or adverb placement, relative clauses) or on process writing through an overall analysis of semester-long electronic discussions.

7. Instead of highlighting the points to be assessed yourself, have the students do so before they hand in their hard copies.

References and Further Reading

The Internet handbook for school users. (Available from Educational Research Service, 2000 Clarendon Boulevard, Arlington, VA 22201 USA; telephone (703) 243-2100; Stock No. B1084)

The Internet manual for classroom use. (Available from Educational Research Service, 2000 Clarendon Boulevard, Arlington, VA 22201 USA; telephone (703) 243-2100; Stock No. B0187)

Warschauer, M. (1995). *E-mail for English teaching: Bringing the Internet and computer learning networks into the language classroom.* Alexandria, VA: TESOL. (Also see http://www.lll.hawaii.edu/~ markw)

Contributor

Rebecca Fisher did her master's degree in ESL at the University of Hawai'i, in the United States. Her special interests include computer-assisted language learning and ESL software programming.

A Vocabulary Quiz Given by Students to Themselves

Levels
High beginning +

Aims
Demonstrate acquisition
of new vocabulary
Reinforce the
relationship between
words and various
meanings
Speak and listen in class
Practice synonyms,
circumlocution, and
public speaking
techniques

Class Time
Variable

Preparation Time
Minimal

Resources
Vocabulary handout
Master spelling list

This quiz harnesses apprehension about quiz taking and fear of public speaking to motivate students to absorb a word's definition so that they can describe the word—without using it—in front of class. In studying for the quiz and taking it, the students must access more than one possible definition for each word. In taking the quiz, students learn new angles on the meanings of words or, at least, are mildly amused when their fellow students give their uniquely worded definitions.

Procedure

Preparation

1. In class, explain the concept of synonyms as a way to infuse variety into language use. Explain *circumlocution* (describing a word in other terms when you don't know what the word is) as a communication strategy.
2. Also in class, introduce public speaking techniques (e.g., volume of voice, the need to face listeners, strategies for dealing with the stress of public speaking, eye contact).
3. Outside class, prepare a vocabulary handout:
   - Include two vocabulary words for each student in the class plus three or four more words in case a student disqualifies a word (e.g., for 20 students, 2 × 20 = 40, and 40 + 4 = 44 words).
   - Include some words that are very easy to define.

Several Days Before the Quiz

1. Hand out the vocabulary list. Go over the particular definitions of the words that you want the students to focus on. If possible, say the definitions in a variety of ways. The more ways you explain the words, the better.

297

2. Encourage the students to practice saying the definitions aloud.
3. Explain the rules of the quiz:
   - The definer must define the word for the rest of the class but cannot use the word or any word containing it in their definition. If they do, that word is disqualified, and you will give the definer another one.
   - The rest of the students must listen to the definition and write the word being defined. They receive 1 point for each correctly defined word they write.
   - The definer receives 3 points for each word that three fourths or more of the students guesses correctly.
   - The definer has 2 minutes to define the word. If the definer cannot do so in that time, 2 points are deducted from the score, and the definer's turn is finished.
4. Ask class members at random to repeat the rules as a means of assessing their comprehension. Encourage clarification questions.

The Day of the Quiz

1. Have the students arrange their chairs in a circle, if possible.
2. Ask the students to clear their desks except for one sheet of paper and a writing tool.
3. Repeat the rules of the quiz.
4. Show a student a word chosen randomly from the master list. Mark that word in some way on the list. Roll or fold the master list so that the definers cannot see words defined previously.
5. Have the student define the word for the class. Keep track of the time. If the student has not defined the word within 2 minutes, note that and move on to the next student, who must try to define the same word.
6. After a student successfully defines a word, ask if there are any questions or comments. Have the rest of the students write down the word on their quiz papers.
7. Repeat Steps 4-6 with the next student (move clockwise or to the first student's left). Continue until all the words have been defined.
8. Collect the students' papers.

Feedback and Scoring

Score the papers as follows:

1. Give 1 point for each correct word on the quiz paper.
2. Give 3 points to the definer for each word that three fourths or more of the class guessed correctly.
3. Deduct 2 points from the definer's score for any definitions that took more than 2 minutes.

Caveats and Options

1. Allow more time for the first administration of a quiz of this type than for subsequent ones because you will need to explain the rules and ensure that the students understand them.
2. The lessons contained within this type of quiz are most effective if the quiz is administered repeatedly throughout the semester.
3. Require the students to give their definitions in sentence form. For example, in defining the word *computer*, the student must say something like, "This is a machine that you write into and play video games on."
4. Encourage the class to ask questions of the definers while adhering to the same rules about using the word.
5. Using previously studied words, give a review quiz by following the same procedure, but require class members to call out the definitions. Award 1 point to the first correct response heard. (Note that this version of the quiz could be biased toward or against certain personality types.)

Contributor

Jeffrey A. Uhr, originally from Cleveland, in the United States, obtained a bachelor's degree in TESL at the University of Hawai'i, in the United States, in 1996. He teaches English part time and is seeking a master's in creative writing.

◆ Writing and Grammar
Check It Out: A Library
Research Checklist

Levels
Advanced

Aims
Understand the qualities
of an acceptable library
research paper in the
U.S.
Teachers: Evaluate
research papers
objectively and
consistently

Class Time
20 minutes

Preparation Time
30 minutes

Resources
Library Research Paper
Checklist
Manila envelopes

Here's a way to facilitate the process of researching and writing a paper for students and teachers alike. Students use the checklist to guide, record, and revise their research, teachers use it to evaluate both the process and the product of the students' work, and everybody's job becomes clearer and simpler.

Procedure

1. When you introduce the research paper, distribute a copy of the checklist (see the Appendix) to each student. Go over it carefully, explaining each of the steps and criteria. Explain how the students should use the checklist and how you will use it in evaluating their papers (see Feedback and Scoring below).
2. Tell the students to use the checklist as a guide and record while carrying out their research by checking off (in the spaces on the left) each step in Part A as they complete it and each requirement for the paper in Part B as they meet it.

Feedback and Scoring

1. Use the checklist in the Appendix to evaluate the students' papers by writing (in the spaces on the right) the number of points awarded to the student for each step of the process and for each criterion.
2. The number of points assigned will vary from teacher to teacher. If you wish, share the point values with the students.
3. To give feedback, pass back the filled-out checklists to the students, and explain the scoring system.

Caveats and Options

1. The checklist reflects my own requirements and criteria for library research papers; naturally, adjust it to reflect yours.
2. Note that the checklist does not specify how the students are to carry out the steps and meet the criteria for the finished paper; be sure to give the students this information.
3. The checklist is not intended to substitute for other types of responses to the students' work. For example, when either the process or the product is faulty, give specific instructions for revision.
4. Use Part B of the checklist to evaluate either the first or the final draft of the research paper. I use it for both: I return it with the first draft accompanied by instructions for revision, and when it is returned with the final draft, I revise the evaluation to reflect any improvement.

References and Further Reading

Moulton, M., & Holmes, V. (1994). Discovery writing: ESL student research with a purpose. *TESL Reporter, 27*, 15–20.

Reid, J. (1993). *Teaching ESL writing*. Englewood Cliffs, NJ: Prentice-Hall Regents.

Appendix: Library Research Paper Checklist

Name _____

Check off each requirement in the space at left when you complete it. When I evaluate your paper, I will write in the number of points you receive for each requirement. Put this paper in your manila envelope (on top of all your other papers) and turn it in each time.

A. Steps to be turned in: You must meet all the requirements described in the other handouts. Turn in your manila envelope with *all* research paper materials in it each time.	Date due		
	Sect. 01	Sect. 04	Points
____ 1. Topic and research question	9/25	9/26	1.____
____ 2. Source cards and photocopies of sources	10/11	10/10	2.____
____ 3. Stack of note cards and copies of highlighted sources	10/23	10/24	3.____

___ 4.	Title, thesis statement, and outline	11/6	11/7	4.___
___ 5.	First draft, (revised) outline, and reference list	11/15	11/21	5.___
___ 6.	Final draft, title page, outline, and (revised) reference list	12/6	12/5	6.___

B. Requirements for the library research paper

___ 1.	You have used from five to eight sources of sufficient variety and quality.	1. _____
___ 2.	There is a fair match between the content of your sources, note cards, outline, and paper.	2. _____
___ 3.	You have presented at least four pages of evidence that supports your final thesis; your paper is at least six pages long.	3. _____
___ 4.	You have written your paper according to the principles of formal academic writing; you have written in a plain style.	4. _____
___ 5.	You have used direct quotation only for a good reason; you have used quotation marks; you have quoted exactly.	5. _____
___ 6.	You have smoothly integrated material taken from your sources into your own writing.	6. _____
___ 7.	You have given credit where credit is due in parenthetical textual citations and in the correct form.	7. _____
___ 8.	You have listed *all* of your sources in the correct form in the list of references.	8. _____
___ 9.	You have produced your paper according to the guidelines in chapter 10.	9. _____

___10.	You have carefully read your paper aloud to yourself and have corrected as many language and mechanical (spelling, punctuation, capitalization, form) errors as possible. If necessary, you have enlisted the help of a tutor in editing your paper.	10. _____
___11.	You have carefully proofread your typed paper before turning it in.	11. _____

Contributor

Sylvia Mulling teaches at Kean College of New Jersey, in the United States, and is a TESOL liaison to the United Nations.

Tense Excitement
Throwing a Die

Levels
Beginning

Aims
Demonstrate ability to
distinguish spoken past
tense *-ed* forms

Class Time
10–15 minutes

Preparation Time
5–20 minutes

Resources
Handout
Die

In this activity, students try to fill in 12 spaces on their sheet with words that have the appropriate spoken past tense endings. To do the activity, the students must be familiar with the regular past tense endings of /t/, /d/, and /Id/. By introducing a chance element, the teacher can make the assessment competitive and exciting for the students, easily assess the students' understanding of the different pronunciations involved, and test words relevant to the needs and abilities of the class.

Procedure

1. Give the students each a copy of the handout (see the Appendix). Explain that they will choose words from the six columns below the squares and write one word in each of Squares A–L according to the pronunciation of its past tense ending. They can fill in the squares in any order.
2. Roll the die and call out the number. Tell the students to look in the appropriate column, choose one word, and write it in one of the squares that matches the pronunciation of *-ed* as marked in the bottom right-hand corner of each square. For example, if you roll the number 1, the students choose among *laughed*, *cried*, *cleaned*, and *wanted*. If they choose the word *laughed*, they have the option of writing the word in Square A, D, G, or K.
3. After the students have chosen a word and written it in a square, tell them to check off (or cross out) the word from the column so that they do not use it a second time. As the options decrease, the students may find that on some occasions they are not able to fill in a square. Most students, however, should complete the sheet at about the same time.

Feedback and Scoring

1. Collect the students' sheets, and simply check that the word written in each square matches the phonetic past tense ending in the bottom right-hand corner.
2. Identify any problem areas to focus on in future sessions.

Caveats and Options

1. Play the game in groups of three to six students. Have the students take turns rolling the die one at a time. In each case, the number rolled applies only to their own sheet. The students attempt to be the first to complete the sheet.

Appendix: Sample Handout

A	B	C	D
/t/	/Id/	/d/	/t/
E	F	G	H
/Id/	/d/	/t/	/Id/
I	J	K	L
/d/	/Id/	/t/	/d/

1	2	3	4	5	6
laughed	listened	opened	danced	robbed	played
cried	departed	walked	studied	played	carried
cleaned	brushed	shopped	closed	washed	splashed
wanted	climbed	emptied	called	mounted	shampooed

Name _____

Contributor

Trevor Ballance teaches EFL at Kings English School in Tokyo, Japan.

Who Is He?

Levels
Beginning

Aims
Comprehend, practice,
and demonstrate
learning of the
comparative form

Class Time
15 minutes

Preparation Time
5 minutes

Resources
Six pictures of men
Magnets
Cards

This assessment activity focuses on the comparative form in English. The students learn to understand and practice it, and the teacher monitors the students' learning of comparatives.

Procedure

1. Make or find six pictures of men with different physical characteristics, each with a dog having different physical characteristics. Label each picture with the man's name; call one of them *John*. Write one of the other names on each card. With the magnets, arrange the pictures on the blackboard so that John is at the upper left (see Appendix A) to make it easier for the students to compare the other men with John.

2. Have the students each pick a card. Ask them not to show it to the other students.

3. Show the students how to describe the men by using John and Mark as examples. Make sure to use the third-person singular pronoun *he*, not the name *Mark*, so that you don't give away the answer (e.g., say, "He has a smaller dog than John does," not "Mark has a smaller dog than John does").

4. Have one student describe the person on his or her card by comparing him to John. Remind the student to use the pronoun *he* in the description.

5. Have the other students raise their hands to answer when they know which person is being described.

Feedback and Scoring

1. Rate the students' ability to use the comparative by using the checklist in Appendix C.

Caveats and Options

1. Make sure the students know that the pictures on the blackboard are all men with dogs. To make the task easier, list the characteristics to compare (see Appendix B).
2. Make sure the students use the third-person singular pronoun *he* when making a comparison.
3. Have the students do this activity in small groups, preferably with no more than five students.
4. Give each student a sheet of paper with John's picture on the left and a blank space on the right. Describe the missing person by comparing him to John, and have the students listen to your description and draw a picture.

Appendix A: Pictures

John   Mark

Dave

Kevin

Craig

Tom

Appendix B: Characteristics to Compare

face	length of hair	height
legs	shoes	size of dog
clothes	body size	age

Appendix C: Checklist for Student Performance

Circle one score for each criterion.

	Poor ↔ Good
Uses regular comparison -er correctly	0 1 2 3 4 5
Smoothly uses regular comparative with *more/less*	0 1 2 3 4 5
Uses irregular comparatives such as *better*	0 1 2 3 4 5
Uses correct nouns for comparison	0 1 2 3 4 5
Uses ... *is* ... *than* ... format	0 1 2 3 4 5
Makes comparison points clearly	0 1 2 3 4 5
Total score	_____ /30

Contributor

Mika Kirimura is a student in the Department of ESL at the University of Hawai'i at Manoa, in the United States.

Part VI: Alternative Ways of Assessing Oral Skills

Left to right: Arthur Perlstein, Yoon O Chang, and Robert Shepherd at English for Success, Annandale, Virginia, USA.

Editor's Note

In the Editor's Note to Part V, I discussed how the written and oral channels of communication and the modes of producing or receiving a message are related to each of the four language skills. Naturally, those distinctions are as related to this part of the book, on oral-channel skills, as they are to Part V, on written-channel skills.

Here, I would like to take up an issue that is also related to both Part V and Part VI: performance assessment. As mentioned in Part V, language tests were traditionally designed to measure the four language skills separately. Language tests were also designed to be taken with paper and pencil insofar as that was possible. The present TOEFL test battery, wherein listening comprehension, writing and analysis, and reading are all tested using multiple-choice, paper-and-pencil items, is a good example.

Given recent trends in language teaching toward notional-functional or task-based syllabuses and toward more practice with authentic communication and language use, it is no surprise that the majority of contributions in this part of the book and in Part V (as well as elsewhere in the book) propose assessment activities that require students to actually do something with the language. Such assessment activities are often called *performance assessments*.

Performance assessments should meet four conditions: (a) The students should be asked to do something with the language; (b) in the process they should be performing some sort of meaningful task; (c) the tasks should be as authentic as possible; and (d) the tasks must typically be rated and scored by qualified judges. Those four characteristics can serve as a working definition for performance assessments, and a quick look through this book will convince you that many of the contributions are performance assessments according to that definition. But why would teachers go to all the trouble of doing performance assessments?

In brief, performance assessments allow teachers to (a) assess the students in contexts that simulate authentic language use, (b) compensate for the negative effects of traditional paper-and-pencil tests, and (c) promote positive washback by assessing the same language points and activities that students are learning in the everyday classroom.

Unfortunately, several disadvantages of performance assessments must also be overcome, including the facts that performance assessments can (a) take considerable time to administer, (b) cause reliability and validity problems, and (c) increase the risk of test security breaches. With a little attention, teachers can minimize all of these problems. For instance, the *administration time problem* can be solved in part by integrating the performance assessment activities right into the class time, just as any other activities are. That is the strategy advocated by many of the contributions to this book. The *problems of reliability* that are inherent in the use of raters can be mitigated by selecting only qualified raters, using two or more raters, giving the raters clear guidelines, training the raters, retraining them from time to time during the rating process, carefully monitoring the ratings as the raters produce them, and revising all of these steps before doing the ratings in other classes or during other terms. The *validity problem* can be at least partially overcome by carefully matching the assessment tasks to the sorts of teaching points and learning activities that are going on in the particular course and by assessing the students a number of times throughout the term. Finally, the *security problem* can be minimized by creating a variety of tasks, with different students performing different tasks, and by setting up conditions so that students who have already performed are unable or, at least, unlikely to communicate the nature or content of the task involved to students who have not yet performed theirs.

The majority of the assessment activities in this part of the book are performance assessments, and they are all focused on the oral channel. That is not to say that the written channel is not used at all, but the oral channel is the main one used in these activities. Naturally, many of the assessment activities elsewhere in this book also involve the oral-channel skills, but in those cases oral skills are not the primary focus. The first section in this part of the book includes assessment activities focused on listening and note-taking; the second section contains activities focused on speaking and pronunciation.

The 10 assessment activities in the listening and note-taking section are designed for a number of different purposes: helping students feel more comfortable and confident when speaking with native speakers (We Are Here to Communicate!); helping students adjust to different gestures, body language signals, and dialects in English (The Traveling Teacher Listening Assessment Tour); assessing students' aural comprehension through visuals (Get the Picture); assessing the students' comprehension of reduced forms in spoken American English (Reduced-Forms Dictations); assessing students' bottom-up listening skills (Watch Your Listening); helping students recognize key words and pertinent details, find main ideas and supporting details, and make inferences from the language contained on videotapes (The Couch-Potato Diagnostic Listening Test); monitoring listening comprehension of a laser disc movie segment at the discourse, sentence, or word level (The Laser's Edge: Assessing Listening With Laser Disc Video); developing students' awareness of their listening strategies, abilities, and needs for improvement as well as helping them capture more details and larger chunks each time they hear a speech sample (Colors Galore!); encouraging note-taking and assessing students' abilities to quickly locate main ideas and details in a written text and follow aural directions (LSS: Listen and Skim/Scan); and assessing students' academic listening and note-taking abilities (Welcome to English 101).

The seven assessment activities in the speaking and pronunciation section are designed to develop students' oral fluency and presentation skills, improve their listening skills, and work on listening comprehension strategies (What Can You Do?); to provide criteria for students to use in rating their class presentations and those of their peers (Presentation Check); to assess students' communicative speaking abilities (Guess What My Favorite Animal Is); to help students plan a skit project and assess their own performance (Skit Assessment); to assess students' proficiency in speaking (Assessing Spoken Language Proficiency); to motivate students and assess their linguistic and pragmatic skills (Karaoke-Dokey); and to help instructors rapidly evaluate pronunciation in class (Assessing Production and Reception of Minimal Pairs).

References and Further Reading

Allaei, S. K., & Connor, U. (1991). Using performative assessment instruments with ESL student writers. In L. Hamp-Lyons (Ed.), *Assessing second language writing in academic contexts* (pp. 227–240). Norwood, NJ: Ablex.

Gottlieb, M. (1995). Nurturing student learning through portfolios. *TESOL Journal, 5*(1), 12–14.

Hauptman, P. C., LeBlanc, R., & Wesche, M. B. (Eds.). (1985). *Second language performance testing*. Ottawa, Canada: University of Ottawa Press.

McNamara, T. F. (1995). Modelling performance: Opening Pandora's box. *Applied Linguistics, 16,* 159–179.

Shohamy, E. (1995). Performance assessment in language testing. *Annual Review of Applied Linguistics, 15*, 188–211.

◆ Listening and Note-Taking
We Are Here to Communicate!

Levels
Intermediate +

Aims
Become comfortable
speaking with native
speakers

Class Time
30 minutes–3 hours

Preparation Time
0–30 minutes

Resources
Audiotapes
Cassette recorders

Many language students around the world study English for years in high school and college, but they feel uncomfortable speaking it when confronted with a native speaker. This discomfort is often due to a lack of confidence. The assessment activity described here enables students to practice speaking to native speakers and build up their confidence so they can feel proud of their language ability. Furthermore, teachers can use this assessment activity to check that the students have grasped lessons taught in the classroom, from syntax and semantic knowledge, to politeness and turn-taking skills, to the ability to maneuver the topic smoothly (Fraser, 1990; Gumperz, 1992; Janney & Arndt, 1992).

Procedure

1. Decide on the topic and the main points to be assessed (e.g., grammatical structure, specific vocabulary, turn-taking skills).
2. Tell the students on how the assessment activity works:
   - what they will need (an audiotape and a cassette recorder each)
   - how to conduct the interview
   - when the audiotape is due
   - what points they will be graded on (see the Appendix for an example).
3. Have the students conduct and audiotape interviews with native speakers outside class.

Feedback and Scoring

1. Collect the audiotapes from the students on the due date.
2. Grade the audiotapes according to the criteria decided on, or use the chart in the Appendix.

Caveats and Options

1. Summarize clear questions or discussion points to use in the interviews so that the students have an outline to follow.
2. Let the students know what you are grading them on, or some students may give you material that cannot serve as the basis of a reliable grade.
3. For greater reliability in grading, enlist another person or several other people to listen to the audiotapes and grade them.
4. In addition to the communicative assessment discussed above, take a whole language approach and develop other tests and activities (Rigg, 1991). For example,
   - Have the students write journals or papers about their discussion with the native speaker or their feelings about doing the assessment activity.
   - Before the activity, have the students brainstorm questions and role-play how they think the discussion will go.
   - For a bigger project, group the assessment activities and lessons around one subject, such as foreigners' ideas about a country or a guide to a country (or, in the case of ESL students, a guide to the United States) for foreigners. Then have the students publish within their school a book on the subject based on what they find out from their interviews (Fried-Booth, 1982).
5. Adapt the activity for beginning-level students by simplifying the topic and task.

References and Further Reading

Brown, J. D. (1996). *Testing in language programs.* Upper Saddle River, NJ: Prentice Hall.

Fraser, B. (1990). Perspectives on politeness. *Journal of Pragmatics, 14*, 219–236.

Fried-Booth, D. (1982). Project work with advanced classes. *ELT Journal, 36*, 98–103.

Gumperz, J. (1992). Contextualization and understanding. In A. Duranti & C. Goodwin (Eds.), *Rethinking context* (pp. 230–252). Cambridge: Cambridge University Press.

Janney, R. W., & Arndt, H. (1992). Intracultural tact versus intercultural tact. In R. J. Watts, S. Ide, & K. Ehrlich (Eds.), *Politeness in language* (pp. 21–41). Berlin: Mouton de Gruyter.

Rigg, P. (1991). Whole language in TESOL. *TESOL Quarterly, 25*, 521–542.

Appendix: Scoring Card

Circle the appropriate number: 1 = no competency;
2 = some competency; 3 = competency;
4 = above-average competency

Fluency (smoothness of speech, lack of significant pauses)	1 2 3 4
Grammar (accuracy of grammar, especially the structures taught in class)	1 2 3 4
Vocabulary (use of varying vocabulary, especially words taught in class)	1 2 3 4
Pragmatics (e.g., appropriate levels of politeness, turn-taking skills)	1 2 3 4
Comprehensibility (ability to make self understood despite other problems)	1 2 3 4

Total _____

A = 16–20; B = 11–15; C = 6–10; Fail = 5

Contributor

Shanti L. Arnold is a master's degree candidate in ESL at the University of Hawai'i, in the United States.

The Traveling Teacher Listening Assessment Tour

Levels
Beginning +

Aims
Develop listening skills
Understand various
registers of spoken
English
Understand kinds of
body language used in
speaking
Adjust to varied accents
of English

Class Time
30–45 minutes

Preparation Time
30 minutes/teacher

Resources
At least two teachers
Video camera and
videotapes (optional)

In this activity, visiting teachers each give a short talk of a predetermined length to another teacher's class. They can tell a short story (funny, sad, or strange); relate a personal experience; or give a talk about a country, a formal lecture, a self-introduction, or an informal lecture on any topic. The activity presents students with an authentic approach to listening: a real teacher in a real classroom in a real mode.

Procedure

1. Set up a group of teachers (a minimum of two, the more the better), including yourself, who will give talks in each other's classes. The relative levels of the classes are not so important, but the teachers should be aware of the level of the students in the other classes so that they can gear their talk toward that level.
2. Decide on the length of time for each talk.
3. Ask each teacher to prepare a talk to give in a classroom.
4. Ask each teacher to prepare five questions (fill-in, multiple-choice, or true-false) based on the talk. For example,
   - The speaker talked about _____.
   - What is the main idea of the talk?
   - The teacher used the word [. . .] several times in the talk. What do you think this word means?
     a. [. . .]   b. [. . .]   c. [. . .]   d. [. . .]
   - The speaker [. . . .]   True ____ False ____
   - The teacher used one gesture several times. She [describe the gesture]. What do you think this gesture means?
     a. [. . .]   b. [. . .]   c. [. . .]   d. [. . .]
   - The teacher said, "[exact phrase]." By this, she meant
     a. [. . .]   b. [. . .]   c. [. . .]   d. [. . .]

5. Prepare the students for the exercise by informing them how the visiting teacher program works.
6. On the day of the talk, give the students the questions written by the teacher who will speak to them, and have them read the questions over.
7. Exchange classes with the other teacher(s).
8. Write your name on the blackboard in the classroom you are visiting. Give your talk, keeping in mind the questions you wrote.
9. When the talk is finished, have the students answer the questions. Collect the answer sheets.
10. Go over the answers with the students, and then return to your home class. Be sure to give the students' answer sheets to the teacher of the class you visited.
11. In your own class, take up any outstanding questions or comments. Discuss the experience with your students. Ask them what it felt like to listen to another speaker and whether the visiting teacher was easier or more difficult to understand than you are.

Feedback and Scoring

1. Correct your students' answer sheets outside class.
2. In the next class, go over the answers with the students.

Caveats and Options

1. A school can develop an extensive and invaluable database of video listening exercises by videotaping the teachers' talks. After the talks are videotaped, have another teacher check and review the questions written for the talks. Label the videos according to topic and difficulty level, and store them systematically with the question sheets.

Contributor

Herman Bartelen teaches at Kanda Institute of Foreign Languages in Tokyo, Japan.

Get the Picture

Levels
Beginning–low
intermediate

Aims
Assess aural
comprehension through
visuals

Class Time
5–10 minutes

Preparation Time
30–60 minutes (find
materials)
10–20 minutes (cut,
paste, photocopy)
10–20 minutes (develop
listening passages)

Resources
Visuals
3-in. × 5-in. cards

Including visuals on exams and quizzes may reduce test anxiety. For example, teachers can check students' listening comprehension by asking them to put a sequence of pictures in order or to circle a picture, a number, or both. This activity concerns two types of recognition. *Simple* recognition requires students to listen to a passage and circle each vocabulary item mentioned. *Sequential* recognition asks the students to listen to a passage and put picture cues in order. The Procedure offers four options for assessing these two types of recognition.

Procedure

1. Decide on the task to assess, and choose one of Steps 2–5 as appropriate.
2. Listen and recognize (simple recognition)
   - Choose a series of vocabulary items (e.g., fruits and vegetables). Copy 10–15 visuals (e.g., from a basal text), or make simple line drawings. Cut and paste the visuals onto the assessment sheet.
   - Write a short narrative that uses some (but not all) of the vocabulary in context (e.g., describe a shopping trip).
   - To perform the assessment, read the passage through twice. Have the students circle the vocabulary items mentioned.
3. Listen and recognize (simple recognition)
   - Prepare the visuals and narrative as in Step 2, but include prices, quantities, or both in the narrative.
   - To perform the assessment, read the narrative and have the students circle the items purchased, the number bought, and the price of each. Either give the students a choice of numbers (e.g., 3, 13, 30), or have the students write them next to the pictures.
4. Listen and recognize (sequential recognition)
   - Prepare the visuals and narrative as in Step 2, but use a picture

story (e.g., a cartoon story, a series of commands, or a process) instead of pictures of objects.

- To perform the assessment, read the narrative and have the students listen and put the pictures in order. Include a few extraneous pictures to make the activity more challenging and to prevent students from guessing the answers through the process of elimination.

5. Listen and select (simple recognition)
   - Mount pictures of 10–15 vocabulary items on 3-in. × 5-in. cards. Color the pictures with pencils or markers.
   - Write short descriptions for some (but not all) of the pictures, using colors, shapes, and categories.
   - To perform the assessment, read the description. Have the students pick up the card that refers to the item described. For example, if you say, "This is a fruit. It's usually red but can also be green or yellow. It's round [etc.]. What is it?", the student should pick up the card with an apple on it.

Feedback and Scoring

See Steps 2-5 of the Procedure.

Caveats and Options

1. This assessment activity works best in small groups. I use it with pairs of students as part of the oral component of Spanish tests.
2. To use the activity in larger groups, prepare more cards.

References and Further Reading

Any text on Total Physical Response, the St. Cloud method, or the Winitz-Reed method is useful. I recommend the following:

Stevick, E. (1982). *Teaching and learning languages.* Cambridge: Cambridge University Press.

Winitz, H. (1981). *The communicative approach to foreign language instruction.* Rowley, MA: Newbury House.

Contributor

Dennis Bricault is the director of ESL programs and an instructor in Spanish at North Park College in Chicago, in the United States. He has taught in Spain, Hungary, and the United States.

Reduced-Forms Dictations

Levels
Any

Aims
Demonstrate
comprehension of
reduced forms in
spoken American
English

Class Time
10–15 minutes

Preparation Time
2 hours

Resources
Reduced-Forms
Dictation Handout
Reduced-Forms Scoring
Handout
Cassette player
Audiotape

Years ago, one of the authors was asked by a student, "Please to speak more slowly." The author had heard that request so many times that it irritated him, and without thinking, he fired back, "No! You listen more quickly!" That was the beginning of the development of a series of lessons that were reasonably successful (see Brown & Hilferty, 1989, 1995, for more information on what reduced forms to teach and how to teach them; see Brown & Hilferty, 1986, 1987, for evaluations of this project). One important aspect of the project was the development of the reduced-forms dictation described here, which we used in our speaking classes as weekly quizzes and as part of the final exam.

Procedure

Create the Dictation

1. Write a dialogue between two people that includes all of the reduced forms that you want to assess. Make it as natural sounding as possible. For instance,

   David: Whenerya goin' ta Tokyo, Janice?
   Janice: I'm gonna go on Saturday, David.
   David: Boy! I wish I were gettin' ouda here fer awhile. Ya gotcher plane ticket?
   Janice: Na. I gotta gedit tamara.
   David: Whaddaya hafta do in Tokyo?
   Janice: I gotta giv'em some drawings, but I also wanna do some sightseeing.
   David: Where'll ya go?
   Janice: I wanna gedouda Tokyo 'n see Nikko.
   David: 'kay, ava good time.
   Janice: 'kay, g'bye.

2. Locate two native speakers who have very different voices (perhaps a male and a female) and who can read such a dialogue naturally.
3. Have the native speakers audiotape the dialogue three times, each time at a fast but natural rate of speech. The first time, have them read fast and straight through the dialogue. The second time, have them read fast but stop after each turn and give the students ample time to write out the full forms. The last time, have them read fast and straight through to give the students a chance to review their work.
4. Prepare a reduced-forms dictation sheet with the speakers' names on it (see Appendix A). Include directions such as the ones in Appendix A. Also prepare a scoring sheet with directions (see Appendix B).

Administer the Dictation

1. Hand out the Reduced-Forms Dictation.
2. Read the directions to the students. Ask the students if there are any questions. If so, answer them.
3. Play the recording. Walk around the classroom to double-check that the students are writing the full forms of the words they are hearing.

Feedback and Scoring

1. Have the students exchange papers.
2. Pass out the Reduced-Forms Scoring Handout (Appendix B). Read the scoring directions to the students.
3. Have the students correct each other's dictations.
4. Collect all the dictations. Check the corrections, compile and record the scores, and give the students feedback in the next class on how they did as a group and individually.

Caveats and Options

1. The students may find this novel form of assessment difficult at first, but our experience is that they quickly come to understand the value of such assessment activities.
2. Administer reduced-forms dictations periodically so that you and the students can monitor their progress. With low-level students, start with dialogues that are read more slowly but with all the appropriate reduced forms, and gradually administer faster and faster dictations.

References and Further Reading

Brown, J. D., & Hilferty, A. (1986). Listening for reduced forms. *TESOL Quarterly, 20*, 759-763.

Brown, J. D., & Hilferty, A. (1987). The effectiveness of teaching reduced forms for listening comprehension. *RELC Journal, 17*, 59-70.

Brown, J. D., & Hilferty, A. G. (1989, January). Teaching reduced forms. *Modern English Teaching*, 26-28.

Brown, J. D., & Hilferty, A. G. (1995). Understanding reduced forms. In D. Nunan & L. Miller (Eds.), *New ways in teaching listening* (pp. 124-127). Alexandria, VA: TESOL.

Appendix A: Reduced-Forms Dictation Handout

Dictation directions: This is a reduced-forms dictation. That means you will hear natural English with all its reductions. Your job is to write down the full forms of all of the words to show that you understand what the speakers are saying. Do *not* write contractions like *can't* or *don't*. You will hear the dictation three times: once read straight through, then again with pauses to give you time to write, then one last time straight through so that you can check your work. Do your best.

David:

Janice:

David:

Janice:

David:

Janice:

David:

Janice:

David:

Janice:

Appendix B: Reduced-Forms Scoring Handout

Scoring directions: Score only the full forms of words that are underlined in the dialogue below. It is not necessary for the words to be spelled 100% correctly, but they must be readable and have the correct grammatical endings. Circle each word that is correct on your colleague's dictation. Then count up the total number of circled words. The maximum score possible is 50.

David: When are you going to Tokyo, Janice?
Janice: I am going to go on Saturday, David.
David: Boy! I wish I were getting out of here for a while. You got your plane ticket?
Janice: No. I have got to get it tomorrow.
David: What do you have to do in Tokyo?
Janice: I have got to give them some drawings, but I also want to do some sightseeing.
David: Where will you go?
Janice: I want to get out of Tokyo and see Nikko.
David: Okay, have a good time.
Janice: Okay, goodbye.

Contributors

James Dean Brown (ESL Department, University of Hawai'i at Manoa, in the United States) has published numerous articles on language testing and curriculum development, and three books on reading statistical studies, language curriculum development, and language testing. Ann Hilferty is currently a doctoral student at Harvard University, in the United States. She has published numerous articles in TESOL Quarterly, Foreign Language Annals, RELC Journal, *and* TESOL Newsletter, *and is the coauthor of* TESOL: Techniques and Procedures *(Heinle & Heinle).*

Watch Your Listening

Levels
Low intermediate +

Aims
Demonstrate bottom-up
listening skills

Class Time
10–15 minutes

Preparation Time
20 minutes

Resources
Video clip with 15- to
20-line two-person
dialogue
Video cassette player

One of the keys to using video successfully in the ESL classroom is to carefully add relevant previewing, viewing, and postviewing activities. Cloze-type activities such as this one can both motivate students and help develop their listening skills. Because the students know they will be receiving a grade, they are usually very motivated to work together and listen carefully. As a result, the quiz functions as both an effective learning activity and an assessment device.

Procedure

1. Locate an appropriate dialogue on a videotape. Dialogues from movies or TV dramas are preferable to those from commercially produced ESL videos.
2. Type up the dialogue, leaving blanks for three or four turns of one of the speakers in the middle of the dialogue. Each blank should be one sentence long. If one speaker's turn is several sentences long, leave one of the middle sentences blank to give the students more context to work with.
3. In class, instruct the students to fill in the blanks with the exact words the speaker is saying. If you wish, tell the students that you will not deduct for spelling mistakes but that you will take a point off for each word that is missing or wrong (see Feedback and Scoring, Step 2).
4. Several (at least four) times, play the videotape to the end without pausing.
5. Collect the papers.

Feedback and Scoring

1. Develop an answer key for the words that the speaker said in each blank, and correct the students' answers.
2. Because the focus is on listening and meaning, you may decide not to count misspellings as incorrect.

Caveats and Options

1. This quiz works best as a semiregular classroom activity. A good balance seems to be two intensive listening activities followed by a quiz. Over time, this sequence significantly improves the students' ability to follow natural-speed dialogues without the use of subtitles.
2. If you have a small class, give the students the remote control for the video player, and let them play the clip as many times as they want within a given time period. I usually set a limit of about 15 minutes.

Contributor

Charles Browne teaches EFL at Aoyama Gakuin University in Tokyo, Japan. He is hoping to survive the hectic pace of Temple University Japan's EdD program.

The Couch-Potato Diagnostic Listening Assessment

Levels
Intermediate

Aims
Demonstrate strengths
and weaknesses in:
Recognizing key words
and pertinent details
Finding main ideas and
supporting details
Making inferences

Class Time
1¼ hours

Preparation Time
3 hours

Resources
Video cassette player
Two videotaped clips
Listening assessment

Students worldwide are watching more hours of video per week than any other group at any other time in the history of the human race. If these students truly are the video generation, then using video as a means of language instruction and assessment is clearly the way to win students' interest and increase their motivation. This diagnostic assessment capitalizes on their interest in video for the purpose of analyzing and surveying the students' mastery of several bottom-up and top-down listening microskills, including recognizing key words and pertinent details as they are linked in the speech stream (bottom-up), finding main ideas and supporting details (top-down), and making inferences from the information provided (top-down).

Procedure

Preparation

1. Locate two appropriate video clips, each 30–60 seconds long, from authentic sources (i.e., materials originally made for native speakers of English). Choose video clips that are short and focused rather than feature-length films designed to burn class time. For example,
   - Special television news reports or programs such as *20/20* are excellent, as the visuals set the context of the topic within seconds. Note that special reports often contain vocabulary specific to a given topic or field. Try to choose video clips that are on a subject the students have had exposure to in class.
   - Movies or scenes from television programs can work well, especially in a functional curriculum. Choose specific scenes for the contexts the students are studying (e.g., how to greet friends, how to say goodbye).

- Commercials are short and must use language and visuals to create a scene or context within seconds. Commercials can be purchased in "greatest-hits" compilations that you are permitted by law to use for educational purposes.
2. Prepare a listening assessment (see Appendix A for an example) such that each video clip and the accompanying subpart corresponds to the microskills listed in the Aims.

Part 1 (23–25 minutes)

1. Ask the students to sit where they can see the monitor and hear well and to clear their desks.
2. Play the first video clip. Have the students watch and listen without taking notes.
3. Hand out Part 1 of the listening assessment (see Appendix A, Part 1). Read the instructions for Part 1 to the students.
4. Play video clip once again. Have the students take notes on their listening assessment handouts.
5. Ask the students to complete Part 1 of the handout, and collect it when they have finished. Allow 8–10 minutes to complete the exercise.

Part 2 (23 minutes)

1. Repeat Steps 1–5 above using Part 2 of the listening assessment (see Appendix A, Part 2) and the second video clip. Allow 10–12 minutes to complete the exercise.

Part 3 (23 minutes)

1. Play the second video clip again. Have the students watch without taking notes.
2. Hand out Part 3 of the listening assessment (see Appendix A, Part 3). Read the instructions to the students
3. Allow the students 15 minutes to complete Part 3, and collect it.

Feedback and Scoring

1. Score Parts 1–3 separately, and put all three scores and comments on a scoring sheet (see Appendix B).
2. Although the activity is designed to assess listening skills, you do not have score it as you would a discrete-point test. If you wish, break down the students' proficiency assessment by microskill, score each skill separately, and add up the scores to arrive at one integrated listening score.
3. Hand back the sheet to the students with the listening assessment.

Caveats and Options

1. Although it is natural for the students to feel that video clips played at natural speed are far too fast, once they are taught listening skills and strategies, they will be able to listen both for the gist and for key information, thereby enabling them to communicate better with native speakers in real situations.
2. Rather than rewinding the videotape during the administration of the assessment, record each video segment for as many consecutive viewings as required. For example, record the first video clip two times in a row.
3. Be sure to check the video equipment before you use it.
4. If you wish, make helpful suggestions, such as good-language-learner strategies, available in the students' L1, thereby encouraging autonomous language learning (Wenden, 1991). Similarly, if it will benefit the learners' understanding and if the situation permits, have the scoring sheet translated into the learners' L1.

References and Further Reading

Brown, H. D. (1994). *Teaching by principles.* Englewood Cliffs, NJ: Prentice Hall Regents.

Richards, J. (1989). *The language teaching matrix*. Cambridge: Cambridge University Press.

Stempleski, S., & Tomalin, B. (1990). *Video in action*. Hemel Hempstead, England: Prentice Hall International.

Wenden, A. (1991). *Learner strategies for learner autonomy.* Hemel Hempstead, England: Prentice Hall International.

Appendix A: Sample Listening Assessment

Part 1

The students watch a video clip featuring a woman and a travel agent discussing the woman's itinerary.

Instructions: Watch the video clip. Fill in the chart.

Day	Time	Place	Action
Thursday			
			visit the Great Wall
		Hong Kong	
	7:30 a.m.		

Part 2

The students watch a video clip from a news story called "Sneaker Wars."

Instructions: Watch the video. Circle the main ideas in Column A. Then draw lines from those main ideas to the supporting information in Column B.

A	B
Sneakers are popular with trendy teenagers.	The colors and styles change every season.
Sneakers appeal to many different types of people for different reasons.	Nike and Reebok both have design teams.
Nike and Reebok like to compete with one another.	Women wear them to work, kids love to play in them, and athletes wear them to compete.
Nike is more serious about sports than Reebok.	Both Nike and Reebok have testing centers to keep up with the latest technology.
Fashion is a key element of sneaker sales.	The presidents of Nike and Reebok refuse to meet.

Part 3

The students watch a video clip of a man on the telephone with another man, named Bob (not pictured). They cannot hear Bob's end of the conversation.

Instructions: Watch the video. Answer the following questions in one or two words.

1. What is the topic of conversation?
2. Is Bob indoors or outside?
3. Is Bob the boss or the caller?

Appendix B: Scoring Sheet

Part	Score
1. Recognizing key words	____ / ____
2. Finding main ideas	____ / ____
3. Making inferences	____ / ____
Total	____ / ____

Contributor

Steve Golden has conducted teacher training workshops and presentations from Hokkaido to Okinawa, Japan. He is currently Japan English language teaching marketing manager for Prentice Hall Japan.

The Laser's Edge: Assessing Listening With Laser Disc Video

Levels
Intermediate +

Aims
Demonstrate
comprehension of a
movie segment at
discourse, sentence, or
word level

Class Time
10 minutes

Preparation Time
30 minutes

Resources
Movie on laser disc
Laser disc players
(ideally one/student)
Question handout

Laser discs in constant angular velocity (CAV) format permit frame-by-frame access to and numeric labeling of motion video segments of any length. The teacher can not only direct the learner's attention to specific scenes, sentences, or words but also ask the learner to isolate the location of speech acts, sentences, and words. This technology permits the teacher and learners to focus on comprehension at the global and local levels.

Procedure

1. Select a scene from the movie, and note the numbers of the beginning and ending frames.
2. Identify the words, phrases, or discourse structures that you predict will be difficult for the learners to comprehend, and note the frame numbers.
3. Prepare a question handout (see the sample in Appendix A) based on the items you have identified.
4. Have the students watch the movie and answer the questions on the handouts.
5. Collect the handouts.

Feedback and Scoring

1. Prepare an answer key (see the example in Appendix B), and use it to score the activity.
2. Because the frames change quickly (approximately 33 frames/second), it will be impossible to specify one frame number as the answer. Rather, specify a frame number plus or minus 50 frames. This will give you a pretty close match.

Caveats and Options

1. This kind of assessment is adaptable to computer-based, self-access learning modules using either laser discs or digital video CD-ROMs. However, the preparation and courseware development time required is understandably much longer than for a paper-and-pencil version.

Appendix A: Sample Question Handout

Raiders of the Lost Ark: Scene 1 (02127–20330)

Discourse Level
- Indy orders his guide, Satipo, to avoid the beam of light in the cave. What are the frame numbers for this order?
  Frame numbers _____ – _____

Sentence Level
- Indy and Belloq are old rivals. Belloq says something to tell us this. What are the frame numbers for this one *sentence*?
  Frame numbers _____ – _____

Word Level
- Indy mentions the name of another archaeologist who also looked for the golden idol in the cave. He later finds this man's dead body. He says the man's name *twice.* What are the frame numbers for each time he says the name?
  First time: Frame numbers _____ – _____
  Second time: Frame numbers _____ – _____
- What was the name? _____

Appendix B: Sample Answer Key

Note that frame numbers are all plus or minus 50.

Raiders of the Lost Ark: Scene 1 (02127–20330)

Discourse Level
Frame numbers 09680–09710 ("Stop! Stay out of the light.")

Sentence Level
Frame numbers 16500–16650 ("Dr. Jones, again we see that there is nothing you can possess which I cannot take away.")

Word Level
First time: Frame numbers 07662–07721 ("Forrestal")
Second time: Frame numbers 10110–10300 ("Forrestal")
Name: Forrestal

Contributor

Donna Tatsuki is a former national chair for the Video Special Interest Group, Japan Association for Language Teaching.

Colors Galore!

Levels
Beginning

Aims
Become aware of
listening strategies
Build listening mastery
through repetition
Capture more details
and bigger chunks
Decide strategies for
future listening activities

Class Time
One class period weekly

Preparation Time
30–45 minutes

Resources
Colored pencils or pens
Audio-based materials
Cassette player

This assessment activity primarily develops students' awareness of their listening strategies, abilities, and areas to improve. The activity should also build the students' listening mastery through repetition and encourage them to capture more details and larger chunks with each repetition. Moreover, the activity guides students in deciding what to do differently and what to attend to the next time they are listening.

Procedure

1. Choose one set of audio-based materials suitable for short (30- to 90-second), focused listening activities (see References and Further Reading). Prepare fill-in-the-blank charts or comprehension activities that correspond to the audio materials (e.g., for low-proficiency students, focus on listening for prices, occupations, times, dates, addresses, phone numbers, locations, directions, and so on).
2. Pass out, for example, a blue, a red, and a green pen to each student, or have them take out their own. Colored pencils and pens in other colors are fine as long as all the students have the same three colors. Also hand out the comprehension activities.
3. Introduce the students to the main topic of the text they will hear. Explain that they will listen to the text many times and that the main purpose is to improve their listening comprehension and see what new information they can learn each time they listen.
4. Cover new or difficult vocabulary using the chalkboard and vocabulary-building techniques (e.g., categorizing vocabulary by concept).
5. Ask the students to use the blue pen. Introduce the activity and directions, and guide the students through the first answer to make sure they are comfortable and oriented to the task.

6. Play the audiotape, and have the students fill in their answers, using only the blue pen. Do not allow the students to erase any of their answers.

7. Play the audiotape a second time, and ask the students to use the red pen to add missing information to their answers. If the students wish to change an answer, ask them to cross out the previous answer rather than erase it.

8. Circulate and check the students' answers to see if a third repetition is required. If so, ask the students to use the green pen as they finish their work.

9. Elicit students' comments on what information they were able to get the first, second, and third times through the activity. Discuss any trends and any progress the students made. Write successful strategies on the chalkboard to draw the students' attention to them.

10. Ask each student to write at the bottom of the page (a) strategies they felt they were good at (that they used successfully), (b) strategies they felt they could improve (what they will do differently next time), and (c) questions or concerns they have about the task.

Feedback and Scoring

1. Collect the students' papers, and analyze them item by item and student by student to determine (a) items that were problematic and require further work as a group and (b) individual learners' needs.

2. Record the scores, and provide regular practice (once or twice a week) in this technique.

3. As the students become comfortable with the process, you may wish to have them note the number of items they were able to get right the first time through, the second time through, and so on to make them more aware of their listening progress.

Caveats and Options

1. The first time you do this assessment activity, you may need 45–60 minutes of planning time to become familiar with the materials and 10–15 minutes to introduce the students to the task.

2. With more proficient learners, use this procedure with cloze listening and listening dictation tasks.

3. Use this activity as an assessment or diagnostic procedure at the beginning of the term to identify weak competencies of individual learners and target areas for future instruction.
4. Consider addressing individual learners' needs by providing targeted homework, individualized learning centers or activities for specific skills, or computer-based work on appropriate software.

References and Further Reading

Helgesen, M., & Brown, S. (1994). *Active listening: Building skills for understanding*. Cambridge: Cambridge University Press.

Richards, J. C., Gordon, D., & Harper, A. (1995). *Listen for it: A task-based listening course* (Rev. ed.). Oxford: Oxford University Press.

Rost, M. (1986). *Strategies in listening: Tasks for listening development*. White Plains, NY: Longman.

Rost, M., & Munetsugu, U. (1995). *Basics in listening: Short tasks for listening development* (Rev. ed.). Hong Kong: Longman/Lingual House.

Contributor

Kim Hughes Wilhelm is an assistant professor of linguistics and the curriculum coordinator at the Center for English as a Second Language (CESL) at Southern Illinois University, Carbondale, in the United States. Catherine Caldwell is a general and advanced-level English instructor specializing in listening skill building at CESL.

LSS: Listen and Skim/Scan

Levels
High beginning +

Aims
Use note-taking
strategies
Demonstrate ability to
quickly locate main
ideas and details in
written text
Follow aural directions

Class Time
10–20 minutes

Preparation Time
10–20 minutes

Resources
Two one-page texts
Index cards (optional)
Highlighting pens
(optional)

This assessment activity primarily measures students' abilities to quickly and successfully locate main ideas and details in a written text and to listen and follow directions in an integrated listening and reading task. The students also learn to read quickly under pressure, use reading skills and strategies, and listen and respond to the teacher's directions. Students employ note-taking strategies when they attend to the next bit of aural information before finishing with the first. With LSS, students feel that they are able to make progress in both listening and reading, and they see its application, particularly when they are studying English for academic purposes.

Procedure

1. Prepare questions on the details or main ideas in one of the texts (see Appendixes A and B). The first time you do this activity, prepare a maximum of 10 questions. Also prepare directions that encourage the students to interact with the reading as they respond (see the examples in Appendixes A and B).
2. Teach the students how to speed-read. For example, give them the following instructions:
   - Use an index card to move at a steady pace through the passage. Do not backtrack.
   - Allow your eyes to hit each line only two or three times. Focus on the subject, the verb, the direct object of the main clause, and noun clauses.
   - Use a "typewriter return" to quickly jerk your eyes to the beginning of the next line.
   - Remember that the power positions of a reading are the beginning and the end (the first and last paragraphs).

3. Tell the students that you are going to give them 2–4 minutes to speed-read a text and that they will need to listen to directions and follow them to show that they can find main ideas and details in the text. (Decide on a length of time based on how long the reading is and how quickly the good readers in the class finish.)

4. Hand out the second text. Time the students as they speed-read it.

5. Give the students the directions.. Move fairly quickly through the items (i.e., move on when the fastest three or four students seem to have found the answer). Encourage the students to jot down notes to help them remember the directions for answers they can't find quickly enough.

6. Collect the papers promptly so that the students don't have much time to go back over their answers. Remember that you are assessing listening and reading ability under timed circumstances, wherein the pressure should encourage improvement in speed, reading skills, and focused listening.

Feedback and Scoring

1. Identify the frequency of correct and incorrect answers for each question. Discuss with the students the questions they most frequently missed. Try to identify why the students missed them and which questions may have been confusing or appropriately answered with an answer different from the one you selected.

2. Help the students be aware of the following strategies and assess their own ability to use them:

● speed-reading: Review the techniques, and ask the students to assess their abilities in each as well as their overall reading speed. Ask if they need more guidance or practice.

● focused listening to directions: Give the directions orally again, and ask the students to list (verbally or on paper) key words for the task as they listen. Do it a second time and, if needed, write the key words you would choose on the chalkboard. Discuss any directions that the students found confusing or difficult.

● skimming/scanning to locate answers or key words in text: Note that the order in which you ask the questions may differ from the order in which the answers appear in the text.

3. Ask the students to figure their scores. You may wish to ask for a hand count (e.g., ask "Who got more than eight correct? fewer than five?") to note who is most and least successful with this activity. The hand count also helps less proficient students be more aware of their need to improve.

Caveats and Options

1. Do LSS regularly (at least twice a week).
2. Do LSS very quickly (for 5 minutes at end of the period or as a transition from one activity to another) after the students are familiar with the format.
3. Consider using LSS as a warm-up or extension activity for other content-based materials.
4. Progress from reading for details and literal information to reading for main ideas (see Appendixes A and B).
5. Consider using two or three LSS activities in Weeks 1 and 2 as diagnostic assessments to quickly identify students who need practice in listening, skimming, and scanning.

Appendix A: Sample LSS (Details)

EAP2 Core   Unit 2: Laws of Ecology

"Nutrient Cycles." In G. Tyler Miller, Jr. (1994), *Living in the Environment* (8th ed., pp. 78–79). Belmont, CA: Wadsworth.

Directions: Speed-read for 45 seconds to become familiar with the main structure of the reading "Nutrient Cycles." Listen and follow directions as you then locate details. (7 points possible)

Teacher's Questions

1. What percent of organism mass is made up of macronutrients? Circle.
2. How many micronutrients are there? Circle.
3. What's another word for nutrient cycles? Circle.
4. What "drives" nutrient cycles? Circle two answers.
5. What's an example of a nutrient that cycles quickly? Circle. One that cycles slowly? Circle.

Appendix B: Sample LSS (Main Ideas)

EAP2 Core   Unit 3: Biodiversity

"Protecting Coastal Zones." In G. Tyler Miller, Jr. (1994), *Living in the Environment* (8th ed., p. 139). Belmont, CA: Wadsworth.

Directions: Speed-read for 2 minutes to become familiar with the main structure of the reading "Protecting Coastal Zones." Listen and follow directions as you then locate answers. (13 points possible)

Teacher's Questions

1. Is the purpose of this article to persuade or to inform? Circle *persuade* or *inform* on Line 1 below the reading. (persuade)
2. Locate the thesis statement. Highlight it and put a star next to it. (last sentence)
3. What is the controlling idea of Paragraph 1? Highlight it. (". . . we are destroying or degrading the very resources that make coastal areas so enjoyable")
4. What is Paragraph 2 about? Write it in one or two words on Line 2 below the reading. (contamination)
5. What kind of structure is used in Paragraph 3 (e.g., example, compare/contrast, amplification)? Write your answer on Line 3 below the reading. (compare/contrast)
6. What is Paragraph 4 about? Write it in one or two words on Line 4 below the reading. (beach erosion) Is this a natural process? Put an *X* next to the line that tells you. (Last line of Paragraph 4)
7. How many solutions to beach erosion are offered by the writer? Circle the solution or solutions offered. (prevent development; allow development only behind protective dunes)

Contributor

Kim Hughes Wilhelm is an assistant professor of linguistics and the curriculum coordinator at the Center for English as a Second Language, Southern Illinois University at Carbondale, in the United States.

Welcome to English 101

Levels
Advanced

Aims
Demonstrate academic
listening and note-taking
abilities

Class Time
20 minutes

Preparation Time
3 hours

Resources
Cassette recorder
Audiotape

This measure assesses students' academic listening with authentic materials and tasks. It can be used in a classroom as a pretest to identify students' problem areas in academic listening and note-taking or as a posttest to determine students' acquisition of academic listening skills. The listening material simulates a first-day-of-class lecture in an academic course at a university. Students listen to a teacher introducing the syllabus for a new semester; as the syllabus lecture is played on the audiotape, students identify what is most important and take appropriate notes, as if they were taking notes in the course.

Procedure

1. Prepare a syllabus for the hypothetical class, including details on office hours, required textbooks, grading policies, and course requirements. Use a variety of items, including numbers (e.g., "office hours every Tuesday from 4:30 to 5:30") and key terms (e.g., the name of the textbook spelled out). Write a script based on the syllabus as it would be presented on the first day of a course. Build in enough repetition to make note-taking possible (e.g., "Good afternoon. I am your teacher, Sara Branch. That's Branch, B-R-A-N-C-H").
2. Record the lecture on audiotape. If appropriate for the level of the students, pause after each piece of information.
3. Review the audiotape. Improve unclear or ambiguous sections.
4. Pilot the activity by having a representative group of students listen to the lecture and take notes.
5. Use the activity by playing the audiotaped lecture while the students take notes.

Feedback and Scoring

1. Use the results from the piloted assessment activity to create a scoring key:
   - Either score each piece of information, or score items representing several levels of difficulty. For example, out of a possible 40 items, choose 20 that include several pieces of information missed by few students on the pilot, several missed by many students, and several in the middle range of difficulty.
   - Choose items to score based on whether they would be essential for the students to understand for success in the course.
   - Use answers from the piloted activity to compile alternative responses to the exact answer (e.g., misspelled textbook name, using *papers* instead of *pages*).
2. Score the activity using the key.

Caveats and Options

1. If resources are available and your classroom dynamics permit, record the lecture on videotape, which would add nonverbal cues to the listening activity and result in an even more authentic classroom simulation.
2. Use the activity to practice certain skills. For example, focus on page numbers, and have the students practice hearing the difference in stress between, for example, the words *fifty* and *fifteen*.
3. Follow the activity with comprehension or vocabulary-in-context questions to assess other listening skills.
4. Include this style of assessment activity in a placement test for a series of academic listening classes.

Contributors

Lia M. Plakans is an MA student in TESL/linguistics and a teaching assistant, and Cynthia L. Myers is the coordinator of ESOL placement testing and an adjunct instructor, both at Iowa State University, in the United States.

◆ Speaking and Pronunciation
What Can You Do?

Levels
Intermediate +

Aims
Develop oral fluency
and presentation skills
Improve listening skills
Practice strategies for
aural comprehension

Class Time
2 class periods

Preparation Time
1–2 hours

Resources
Sample Oral
Presentation Outline
Presentation Critique

This enjoyable activity can be used early in the term to (a) determine students' oral proficiency and (b) function as an icebreaker among the students and between the students and the teacher. Although many ESL classrooms are centered on the teacher-solicit/student-response/teacher-react format, this standard classroom pattern is not always interesting for the students or the teacher. Nor does it challenge students to develop skills other than responding to questions. In this activity, students prepare a short oral presentation on something they are good at doing. Other students listen attentively, ask questions when necessary, and fill out a brief critique.

Procedure

1. Give the students a sample framework (possibly an outline) for organizing their thoughts into an oral presentation (see Appendix A for an example).
2. Assign a short (5- to 10-minute) presentation on the topic "Something I'm Good at Doing." Deliver such a presentation to the class yourself:
   - Provide an outline of key points you will cover in your presentation. Make it clear to the students that they will be doing a similar activity.
   - During your presentation, either give the students an example of the final product (freshly baked cookies) or do a demonstration (juggling). The students will be expected to do the same (provide props) in their presentations.
   - If you wish, allow questioning during or after the presentation. Encourage the students to jot down their questions and to ask for clarification and explanation.

3. Give the students some class time and at least one night to prepare their presentations. If you wish, give them ideas for topics to help them get started.
4. Before their presentations, have the students submit a short outline of their topic to you, but not to the other students.
5. Have the students take turns making their presentations to the class. Ask the rest of the class to listen and ask questions.
6. After each presentation, give the students a few minutes to fill out a simple, brief critique of the presentation (see Appendix B for an example).
7. Congratulate the speakers and collect the critiques. See what each student understood.

Feedback and Scoring

1. As feedback, return all of the critiques to the student presenters, or summarize the critiques and give the presenters the summaries. You may also want to grade their outlines and presentations.

Caveats and Options

1. This assessment activity works best in a small class; 5–15 students is ideal. The activity can work in a larger class, but the presentations should be very brief and perhaps done in pairs or groups.
2. If you wish, spread the presentations out over a period of time (one or two per class over a week) so that each student has more of the spotlight and doesn't need to rush.

Appendix A: Sample Oral Presentation Outline

Topic: How to make great chocolate chip cookies
I. (How did you get interested in this activity?)
My mother wasn't a great cook, but my grandmother was. She loved to bake and so . . . .

II. (How and when do you do this activity?)
I bake cookies every holiday season. I like to send boxes to my sisters each Christmas. Making about 12 dozen cookies takes a whole afternoon, about 5–6 hours . . . .

III. (Give a step-by-step description of your activity.)

First I buy the ingredients, then I get out my old pans and bowls. I mix everything by hand. I put together the dry ingredients first, then add the liquid ones. Mixing them takes about 10–15 minutes. I always add extra chocolate chips, because my family loves chocolate. The baking takes a long time. I grease a baking sheet and put 1-inch balls of dough about 2 inches apart. Each batch makes two dozen and takes about 20 minutes to make.

IV. (Demonstrate your activity or give out a sample product.)

Here are the cookies I made for today. What do you think?

V. (Ask the class if there are questions.)

Appendix B: Presentation Critique

1. Who is the student?
2. What is the topic?
3. When does the student do this activity?
4. Why does the student do this activity?
5. What was good about the presentation?
6. What could the student improve about the presentation?

Other comments:

Contributor

Eddi Mckay is an ESL instructor at the Intercultural Communications College in Honolulu, Hawai'i, in the United States.

Presentation Check

Levels
Intermediate +

Aims
Assess peers and self in
class presentations

Class Time
20 minutes
5 minutes after each
presentation

Preparation Time
1 hour

Resources
Library materials,
magazines, newspapers
Tips for Making a Good
Presentation
Presentation Self-Check
Presentation Peer Check

Feedback and Scoring

This presentation check guides students in the process of researching, organizing, and delivering a class presentation and aids in determining a grade for their work.

Procedure

1. Tell the students that they are to prepare a 3- to 5-minute presentation to the class. A possible topic is travel (e.g., "What country would you like to visit? Find some information about the country you want to visit and tell the class about it.").
2. In class, discuss what makes a good presentation. Start by giving the students your criteria (see Appendix A).
3. Hand out copies of the Presentation Self-Check and Peer Check (see Appendixes B and C) so that the students have a clear set of guidelines on which they will be assessed.
4. Assign a due date and set a schedule for the presentations.
5. In class, assist the students in preparing their presentations so that you can monitor the amount and quality of their research, organization, and preparation.
6. On presentation day, have the students fill in the presentation check forms for themselves and all other students as the presentations proceed. Take notes so that you can compare your grades with the ones they assign later.

1. Collect the self-check and peer check forms, tally the scores, and give each student a grade.
2. Use the forms, and have the students use them, to identify areas that need improvement.

Caveats and Options

1. Always keep in mind that the purpose of the presentation check is to clarify criteria and standards, thereby aiding the students in monitoring their own learning and creating a cooperative classroom environment.
2. In large classes, divide the class into groups on presentation day to speed up the procedure.
3. If you wish, solicit the students' ideas in developing criteria and standards for your own self-check and peer check forms.

Appendix A: Sample Tips for Making a Good Presentation

- Research. Find a book, such as an encyclopedia, and take notes on your topic. Write down important dates, names, events, and vocabulary. Find out interesting or unusual facts to share with others.
- Organization. Organize your presentation. Talk about your subject in a logical progression (e.g., chronologically, thematically, by cause and effect).
- Preparation. Before class, practice delivering your presentation aloud. Work on pronunciation, intonation, fluency, and other aspects of the presentation. Ask a friend to listen to you and make suggestions on how to make your presentation better.
- Presentation. During your presentation, try to be calm and relaxed. Never read your notes! Use the look-up-and-say technique. Make eye contact. Get the audience involved. Invite questions.

Appendix B: Presentation Self-Check

Name_____

Directions: Look at the following questions and rate your presentation. Circle the number that best describes it.

1. Research: I researched my subject using books, magazines, or other sources of information.

1	2	3	4	5
not at all		a little		a lot

2. Organization: I organized my research in a logical way and included interesting facts.

1	2	3	4	5
not at all		a little		a lot

3. Preparation: I practiced my presentation to work on pronunciation, intonation, fluency, and other aspects.

1	2	3	4	5
not at all		a little		a lot

4. Presentation: I was well prepared and got others involved in a discussion on my topic.

1	2	3	4	5
not at all		a little		a lot

5. I helped others learn new information and vocabulary through my presentation.

1	2	3	4	5
not at all		a little		a lot

6. Overall, I think my presentation was

1 = bad   2 = below average   3 = average   4 = good   5 = excellent

Total: ____ /30

Appendix C: Presentation Peer Check

Name of presenter_____

Write down a question you would like to ask the presenter.
Look at the following questions and rate the presenter. Circle the number that best describes the presentation.

1. Research: The presenter researched the subject.

1	2	3	4	5
not at all		a little		a lot

2. Organization: The presenter was well organized.

1	2	3	4	5
not at all		a little		a lot

3. Preparation: The presenter was well prepared.

1	2	3	4	5
not at all		a little		a lot

4. Presentation: The presenter got me involved in a discussion on the topic.

1	2	3	4	5
not at all		a little		a lot

5. The presenter helped me learn new information and vocabulary through the presentation.

1	2	3	4	5
not at all		a little		a lot

6. Overall, I think the presentation was

1	2	3	4	5
not at all		a little		a lot

Total: _____ /30

Contributor

David Progosh studied curriculum and assessment issues at the Modern Language Centre of the Ontario Institute for Studies in Education/University of Toronto. He writes and edits ESL materials and tests.

Guess What My Favorite Animal Is

Levels
Beginning; secondary
school

Aims
Demonstrate ability to
speak communicatively

Class Time
50 minutes

Preparation Time
20 minutes

Resources
Map of a zoo
Rating scale

This assessment activity is designed specifically for students who have mastered a junior high school level of English (that is, 3 years of English) but are not good at speaking. The purpose of the activity is to assess their ability to use language communicatively.

Procedure

1. Ask the students to name animals that they know about.
2. Hand out the map of the zoo. Ask the students which animals are found in a zoo.
3. Ask the students to choose their favorite animals and to think about the animals' features. Write difficult or unfamiliar words on the blackboard, and explain them to the students.
4. Form pairs of students.
5. Have the students guess what their partner's favorite animals are by using *wh-* questions.
6. Have the students change partners and repeat Step 5.

Feedback and Scoring

1. Take each pair aside, and have one of the students interview the other about his or her favorite animal using *wh-* questions.
2. Rate one student's performance according to the scale shown in the Appendix.
3. Have the students reverse roles. Rate the other student's performance.
4. If you wish, assign numbers for the purpose of grading. For instance, with a scheme like *Excellent = 5, Good = 4,* and *Poor = 3* for each of the four rating categories, a maximum score of 20 points (and a minimum of 12) would be possible.

Appendix: Rating Scale

Pronunciation	Excellent	Nativelike
	Good	Accurate enough to understand
	Poor	Hard to understand
Grammar and vocabulary	Excellent	Nativelike fluency in English grammar and precise vocabulary usage
	Good	Some grammar problems and some vocabulary misuse, but they don't interfere with communication
	Poor	Severe grammar problems and inappropriate use of vocabulary
Body language	Excellent	Effective use of body language such as eye contact, hand movements, facial gestures, and loudness of voice
	Good	Inadequate use of body language
	Poor	Lack of body language
Communication	Excellent	Communicates well, understands partners' questions correctly, and answers to the point
	Good	Takes time to communicate, some misunderstanding, but manages to communicate
	Poor	Finds it hard to communicate

Contributor

Rieko Shimazaki is an instructor at Iidabashi Foreign Language Institute in Japan.

Skit Assessment

Levels
Any

Aims
Plan a skit project
Assess own
performance
Teachers: Monitor
participation

Class Time
2–3 hours

Preparation Time
3 hours

Resources
Skit Assessment Sheet
Critical Comments Sheet
Contest Voting Sheets
Video camera
Video cassette player

Performing a drama or skit is one of the language learning activities linked with a communicative syllabus. Students have to take initiative in such an activity, and teachers need to monitor them carefully. One difficulty is how to assess such an activity and produce scores as on a regular language test. The skit project suggested here will help both students and teachers logically assess the project.

Procedure

Introducing the Project

1. Tell the students that they will be putting on a skit for the rest of the class and that they can include anything they like, including artwork, dancing, and music.
2. Explain that the expected time for each skit will be 2 minutes times the number of members in the group. That is, each member of the group should speak for at least 2 minutes in the group's skit. For instance, if a group has four members, the total time for the skit will be approximately 8 minutes (2 minutes × 4 people = 8 minutes).

Planning the Skit

1. (10 minutes) Have the students form skit groups of three to six students.
2. (15 minutes) Tell the students to discuss the theme of their skit and to give their skit group a name related to the theme (e.g., "September Wind," "Tom Sawyer's Adventure").
3. (20–30 minutes, or for homework) Have the students write and submit a 200- to 300-word summary of their skit.

4. For homework, tell the students to make a list of words in their skit (with their definitions) that might be difficult for the other students to understand.
5. (30 minutes, or for homework) Have the students write a scenario.

Monitoring and Commenting on the Skit

1. Pass out the Skit Assessment Sheet (see Appendix A) to each group. Explain to the students that they will fill in each step in the sheet according to the schedule.
2. Make appointments with each group for counseling. Include at least three separate 15-minute appointments to cover (a) a summary, (b) a scenario, and (c) a rehearsal. Once the appointments are made, make a schedule of appointments and give it to each student.
3. Give the students feedback at each step. Be sure to check grammatical accuracy and word choice in the scenario step and to check appropriateness of nonverbal behavior and accuracy of pronunciation in the rehearsal step.
4. Post a checklist of the steps that all of the groups have completed.

Peer Critiquing

1. Pass out the Critical Comments Sheet (see Appendix B) at the time of the final performance.
2. Have the students write comments as the audience on the skit, language use, pronunciation, and general acting.

Feedback and Scoring

Self-Assessment

1. Have the group assess its preparation of the skit (see Planning the Skit above) using the space in the third column of the Skit Assessment Sheet (Appendix A).
2. Have the group assess its final performance (the scenario, grammatical correctness, pronunciation, language use and fluency, nonverbal expressions, and overall performance) using the Critical Comments Sheet (Appendix B).

Scoring and Grading by the Teacher

1. Give feedback to the groups for their rehearsals (in Monitoring and Commenting on the Skit above) using the Skit Assessment Sheet.
2. Grade the final performances using the Skit Assessment Sheet.

Assessment by the Other Students

1. Have the students vote on the best skit, actor, actress, music, and special talent using the Contest Voting Sheet (see Appendix C).
2. Tally the votes and announce the results in class.
3. Give prizes as appropriate.

Caveats and Options

1. Be sure to give each group (not each student) a Skit Assessment Sheet so that the students know what they should do next at all times. In addition, because the activity lasts about a week and has an irregular schedule (i.e., the regular language class might continue along with the skit project), it is crucial for the students to record each step on the Skit Assessment Sheet.
2. Replace scoring or grading by the teacher(s) with a participation grade (i.e., pass or fail).

References and Further Reading

Maley, A., & Duff, A. (1982). *Drama techniques in language learning: A resource book of communication activities for language teachers* (Rev. ed.). Cambridge: Cambridge University Press.

Appendix A: Skit Assessment Sheet

Step			Date	Sign
1	Group			
2	Members			
3	Theme (goal of the project)			
4	Title			
5	Summary			
6	Vocabulary list	Use separate sheet.		
7	Scenario	Use separate sheet.		
8	Rehearsal	Language 1 2 3 4 5 Grammar 1 2 3 4 5 Pronunciation 1 2 3 4 5 Fluency 1 2 3 4 5 Nonverbal 1 2 3 4 5 Overall acting 1 2 3 4 5 / Comments:		
9	Final performance	Overall grade A B C / Comments:		
10	Prizes			

Appendix B: Critical Comments Sheet

Comment on the following.
1. Scenario

2. Pronunciation

3. Language use and fluency

4. Nonverbal expression

5. Overall performance

Appendix C: Contest Voting Sheet

Vote for the following prizes.

Best Skit (Write the group's name.):
Best Actor:
Best Actress:
Best Music (Write the group's name.):
Special Talent:

Contributor

Sayoko Okada Yamashita teaches in the Japanese Language Program at International Christian University, Tokyo, Japan. She has published articles on applied linguistics and Japanese language teaching, books on language testing and pragmatics, and a Japanese language textbook.

Assessing Spoken Language Proficiency

Levels
Any

Aims
Demonstrate oral
productive language
proficiency

Class Time
15 minutes/student

Preparation Time
2–3 hours

Resources
Informational materials
Guidelines for Rating
Speaking Performance
Three teachers

How accurately a speaking performance demonstrates a person's spoken language proficiency is affected greatly by three factors: The speaker (a) has to know something about what he or she is going to say, (b) needs someone who wants to listen, and (c) should not feel too nervous. Interview procedures that are commonly used for assessing spoken language proficiency seem to be weak in terms of all three factors. In addition, the only-one-time performance involved in an interview does not promote the reliability of the measurement. The assessment activity presented here addresses these issues much more effectively.

Procedure

Pretest Preparation

1. Find some material on any interesting topic that is at the appropriate level of difficulty for the students (see the examples in Appendix A).
2. Break up the material into individual pieces of information. Each piece should be long enough that the students cannot easily memorize it in words or sentences. Put these pieces of information on separate slips of paper.
3. Give each of the three teachers one of the slips of paper.

Assessment

1. Ask each student in turn to go to the first teacher to get the first piece of information. Allow the student to ask questions in order to confirm the information and to take simple notes if the information is too long to remember.

2. Ask the same students to go to the second teacher to (a) report the information they got from the first teacher and (b) get the second piece of information.
3. Ask the same students to go to the third teacher to (a) report the information they got from the second teacher and (b) get the third piece of information.
4. Ask the same students to go back to the first teacher to report the information they got from the third teacher.

Feedback and Scoring

1. Have all three teachers use the Guidelines for Rating Speaking Performance (see Appendix B) to rate the students as they perform. Give one score (from 4 to 25) to each student on each of the categories (pronunciation, grammar, fluency, and accuracy) in the guidelines.
2. Collect and sort all the Guidelines for Rating Speaking Performance sheets.
3. Average the scores given by the three teachers in each of the four categories, and put these averages (along with the student's name) on a fourth Guidelines for Rating Speaking Performance sheet.
4. Average the four category scores to get the student's total score, and write it on the new sheet.
5. Report the four separate scores and the total score to the students. Either hold conferences in which you give the students a copy of the Guidelines for Rating Speaking Performance and discuss their scores, or simply give them the fourth Guidelines for Rating Speaking Performance sheet.

References and Further Reading

Brown, J. D. (1996). *Testing in language programs*. Upper Saddle River, NJ: Prentice Hall Regents.

Educational Testing Service. (1992). *SPEAK scoring key*. Princeton, NJ: Author.

Appendix A: Sample Information Materials for Three Different Levels

The samples presented here are intended only to give an idea of what I understand to be appropriate degrees of language difficulty and complexity of information for different levels of learners. They do not reflect any depth of analysis of this complex area.

Low Level

Hong Kong was originally part of China. About 150 years ago, it became a British colony. That is, Great Britain got the right from the Chinese government to rule Hong Kong. On July 1, 1997, after its long colonial period, Hong Kong was returned to China.

Intermediate Level

In 1996, a year before Hong Kong was handed back to China, the many controversial attitudes that existed were very apparent. Pro-China supporters were out by the thousands welcoming the island's return and the end of colonial rule. However, the prodemocracy activists were equally lively in their warnings that, if the current freedoms of Hong Kong were not respected by the Communist government after 1997, the consequences would concern not only individuals but the whole international community.

Advanced Level

As 1997 was the year that Hong Kong reverted to its motherland, those on all sides of the controversial issue were bustling with energy. China supporters were full of anticipation and were out by the thousands to welcome the island's return and the end of colonial rule. There was even a big clock at Tiananmen Square in Beijing counting down the time in seconds to the monumental event. However, the prodemocracy activists were also very energetic, warning that if the human rights, freedom of the press, and democracy that Hong Kong had known all those years were not maintained after 1997, the consequences would be grave not only for individuals but for the whole international community.

Appendix B: Guidelines for Rating Speaking Performance

Skill area	25–22 Excellent	21–16 Good	15–10 Adequate	9–4 Unacceptable
Pronunciation	There are occasional nonnative pronunciation errors, but the information is very well conveyed.	There are some consistent phonemic errors and foreign stress and intonation patterns, but the information is quite clear.	There are frequent phonemic errors and foreign stress and intonation patterns, but the information can still be inferred.	Because of frequent phonemic errors and foreign stress and intonation patterns, the information is totally incomprehensible.
Grammar	There are sporadic minor grammatical errors, but the information is very well conveyed.	There is generally good control of all constructions, though with some grammatical errors, but the information is quite clear.	There is some control of basic grammatical constructions but with major or repeated errors, so that the conveying of meaning is interfered with.	Because there is virtually no grammatical control except in simple stock phrases, the information is totally incomprehensible.

Skill area	25–22 Excellent	21–16 Good	15–10 Adequate	9–4 Unacceptable
Fluency	Speech is smooth and effortless, almost nativelike.	There are some nonnative pauses, but they do not interfere with conveying meaning.	There are numerous nonnative pauses, a nonnative flow, or both, but the meaning can still be inferred.	Speech is so halting and fragmentary or has such a nonnative flow that the meaning is totally incomprehensible.
Accuracy	Appropriate lexicon and syntactic features are chosen, and the information is accurately conveyed.	Where appropriate lexicon and syntactic features are lacking, techniques are employed in order to clearly convey the information.	Inappropriate lexicon and syntactic features are used, but the information can still be inferred.	Because wrong lexicon and syntactic features are used, the information is totally incomprehensible or wrong.

Contributor

Xiao-rui Zhang completed her master of education degree at Temple University Japan. Her focus is TESOL research that will benefit Chinese learners.

Karaoke-Dokey

Levels
Beginning +

Aims
Become interested in a task
Demonstrate linguistic and pragmatic skills

Class Time
10–20 minutes

Preparation Time
Variable

Resources
Satisfactory location
Karaoke sound system, audiotapes, and song handouts
Sign-up sheet

This assessment procedure was used with students in a university-level oral English course. Dictations based on the songs were assigned as homework each week, reviewed in the next class, and then used as the basis of paired conversation and journal writing. For their final assessment, students chose either a paired conversation in front of the teacher, like the ones they had practiced in class, or a final party in which they were expected to sing one of the songs in front of the other students. Three to five of the students chose the latter method. This activity motivates students in non-English-speaking countries who are fulfilling a course requirement in English but see no immediate need for or applications of English in their daily lives. The activity also assesses linguistic skills, such as pronunciation, intonation, and use of reduced forms, and pragmatic skills, such as the ability to understand and effectively interpret and convey emotion in English.

Procedure

1. In advance, find a suitable location (a karaoke bar or a room with the appropriate equipment at school).
2. Two classes before the evaluation date, pass around a sign-up sheet (see the Appendix) on which the students can mark their first, second, and third choices for songs to sing. Be sure to provide space for the students to indicate any special considerations (e.g., whether they have to arrive late or leave early on that date).
3. In the class before the evaluation date, provide the students with a list of songs they will be responsible for and the order in which they will be expected to sing.
4. Gather in the designated place at the designated time, and let the show begin!

Feedback and Scoring

1. I evaluated the students on the following factors: pronunciation (20%); liaison, reduction, intonation, and rhythm (30%); delivery (eye contact, voice projection, stage presence) (20%); and expression of content, meaning, and emotions conveyed in the song (30%). These criteria were consistent with rating sheets often used for marking students' performances in recitation and speech contests.
2. Incorporate peer evaluation into the assessment procedure.

Caveats and Options

1. This activity is most suitable for beginners and false beginners. However, with any of the following modifications it could be used with intermediate- or advanced-level students:
   - Require memorization.
   - Have the teacher (or other students) choose the song, using a lottery-style selection process.
   - Include a follow-up question-and-answer or short speech period.
   - Require all participants to use English exclusively throughout the evening.
2. The addition of alcohol to the evening may successfully lower affective filters.
3. I highly recommend using this procedure in conjunction with another assessment option, as karaoke is not everyone's cup of tea!

References and Further Reading

Kanel, K. R. (1995). *Pop song listening.* Tokyo, Japan: Seibido.

Appendix: Sample Sign-up Sheet

Your name _____ Your number _____

Please circle either 1 or 2.

1. I plan to take the English song test. I will sing (Mark your first, second, and third choices with 1, 2, and 3.)
   - _____ 1. "Love Me Tender"
   - _____ 2. "Be My Baby"
   - _____ 3. "Imagine"

_____ 4. "Locomotion"
_____ 7. "Yesterday Once More"
_____ 8. "Hard to Say I'm Sorry"
_____ 9. "I Just Called to Say I Love You"
_____10. "Help"
_____11. "Sailing"
_____14. "Faith"
_____15. "Let It Be"
_____17. "Woman"
_____19. "Are You Lonesome Tonight?"
_____20. "Bridge Over Troubled Water"

You will be graded on the following:
- Pronunciation (20%)
- Liaison, reduction (20%)
- Delivery (30%)
- Expression (30%)

Singing ability will *not* be evaluated. If you feel more comfortable chanting the words, that is fine.

Any notes, questions, or comments?_____

_____

_____

2. I plan to take the conversation test with (name of partner) _____, Student Number _____.
    I (will/will not) _____ come to the karaoke party on July 7.

Contributor

Judy Yoneoka teaches at Kumamoto Gakuen University in Kumamoto, Japan.

Assessing Production and Reception of Minimal Pairs

Levels
Beginning–intermediate

Aims
Be motivated to
produce well-formed
minimal pairs
Understand breakdowns
in attempts to produce
and interpret minimal
pairs
Rapidly demonstrate
pronunciation

Class Time
50 minutes

Preparation Time
15 minutes

Resources
None

Some classes are too large to permit one-on-one assistance with pronunciation, yet many students really need help on basic sound formation. Lost in a sea of badly produced words, students compound their misunderstanding and make few attempts at nativelike pronunciation. If this situation is familiar, then this assessment activity is for you. It will provide students with enjoyable practice in minimal pairs, as participants can give each other feedback on performance and demonstrate to the class how poor pronunciation can greatly affect communication.

Procedure

1. Decide on the minimal pairs you wish to contrast (e.g., *ship/sheep*; *right/light*; *heart/hat*; *rocket/racquet*). Devise a picture to represent each word in each contrast (e.g., ♥ for heart, ∏ for hat; ⇑ for rocket, ¶ for racquet; → for right, Ω for light. Think of a lexical set that needs reviewing (e.g., *shops: bank, café*).
2. Make a diagram as follows (see the Appendix), and make copies for the students.
   - On a piece of paper, make a 1-inch border on all sides. Prepare a binary tree in the center:
   - Place an arrow labeled *Start* pointing at the root node of the tree.
   - From this node make two branches that each lead to an alternative in the first minimal-pair contrast (e.g., *heart/hat*; see the Appendix, Diagram 1).
   - Give these two nodes (*heart* and *hat*) two branches that lead to the alternatives in the second minimal-pair contrast (e.g., *right/light*; see the Appendix, Diagram 2).
   - Give each of the lowest nodes two branches that lead to the alternatives for the next minimal-pair contrast (e.g., *rocket/racket*).

Include one alternative only at the end of each branch (see the Appendix, Diagram 3).

- Repeat until all the minimal pair contrasts have been diagramed.
- In the margin around the tree, write down members of the lexical set that the students need practice with. Connect every lexical item in the set (e.g., shop) to a different one of the lowest nodes.

3. Present the minimal pairs in class as usual, remembering to practice perception before production. When necessary, illustrate good and bad habits.

4. Give the students the handouts. Give the L1 equivalent or a definition for one of the words in the margin, and ask the students to find the word (e.g., for *bank, a place to keep money* or the Japanese *ginko*). Tell the students to write the name in their L1 above the English version.

5. Repeat this process for all the other lexical items. Provide remedial help on vocabulary as required.

6. Direct the students' attention to the *Start* arrow in the center. Explain that the students must listen carefully, follow the lines with their finger, and find out where you are going. For example, if you call out one alternative from each of the minimal pairs in turn (e.g., "heart," "right," "rocket"), the students must follow the line from the last node to the shop and then call out the shop's name when asked where you are.

Feedback and Scoring

1. Some students will take the wrong path through the tree. By tracing the path they have taken and seeing where it diverges from yours, note where the student's perception was faulty.

2. Give feedback as necessary, showing where your path and theirs diverged and offering helpful suggestions (e.g., lip-read). Repeat Steps 5 and 6 until the students are familiar with the procedure.

3. Divide the group into pairs. Have the students take the role of listener or speaker, freeing you to circulate and give personal assistance as required.

Caveats and Options

1. Review any number of phonemes in this manner.
2. At the beginning of a course, use this assessment activity diagnostically to swiftly assess which of a group's problem areas most needs attention.

References and Further Reading

Avery, P., & Ehrlich S. (1992). *Teaching American English pronunciation.* Oxford: Oxford University Press. (Treatment of the sound system and specific problems)

Appendix: Sample Diagrams

Diagram 1

Diagram 2

Diagram 3

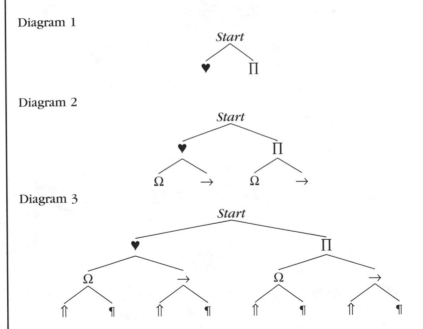

Contributor

Neil McPhee teaches in the Department of English at Gakushuin Daigaku, in Japan.

Key to Activities

Part, section, and activity	Portfolio	Journal	Conference	Self-assessment	Peer assesment	Group work	Pair work	Test taking	Test making	Grading	Evaluating curricula	Reading	Vocabulary	Writing	Grammar	Listening	Note-taking	Speaking	Pronunciation
Part I: Alternative Methods of Assessment ◆ **Portfolios**																			
Valdez Pierce, L.: Planning Portfolios	✓		✓	✓	✓														
Wolfe-Quintero, K.: ESL Language Portfolios: How Do They Work?	✓																		
McNamara, M. J., & Deane, D.: Self-Assessment: Preparing an *English* Portfolio	✓			✓										✓					
Asbjornson, B.: Portfolio Assessment of Newscast Listening	✓															✓			
Cummins, J. E.: The Process of Business Communication	✓						✓									✓		✓	
Freeman, R. F.: Pretty Popular Pupil Portfolios	✓													✓					
García, J.: Using Portfolios in the EFL Reading Class	✓					✓						✓		✓					
Pettys, D. K.: Writing Pictures	✓													✓					
◆ **Journals, Logs, and Conferences**																			
Blankmann, J.: Using Journals for Self-Evaluation at Midterm	✓		✓							✓	✓			✓					
García, J.: Don't Talk About It, Write It Down		✓										✓		✓					

Part, section, and activity	Portfolio	Journal	Conference	Self-assessment	Peer assessment	Group work	Pair work	Test taking	Test making	Grading	Evaluating curricula	Reading	Vocabulary	Writing	Grammar	Listening	Note-taking	Speaking	Pronunciation
McNamara, M. J., & Deane, D.: Learner Self-Assessment: Keeping a Language Learning Log		✓		✓									✓						
Tovar, J.: Passport: A Log		✓												✓					
Neill, D. R.: Eat, Drink, and Be Merry: Lunchtime Student Assessment			✓											✓					

Part II: Alternative Feedback Perspectives
♦ **Self-Assessment**

Part, section, and activity	Portfolio	Journal	Conference	Self-assessment	Peer assessment	Group work	Pair work	Test taking	Test making	Grading	Evaluating curricula	Reading	Vocabulary	Writing	Grammar	Listening	Note-taking	Speaking	Pronunciation
Tomlinson, D.: Assess It Yourself				✓															
de Moaes Menti, M.: Learner Access to Assessment				✓								✓		✓		✓		✓	
Murphey, T.: Self-Evaluated Video				✓			✓											✓	

♦ **Peer Assessment**

Part, section, and activity	Portfolio	Journal	Conference	Self-assessment	Peer assessment	Group work	Pair work	Test taking	Test making	Grading	Evaluating curricula	Reading	Vocabulary	Writing	Grammar	Listening	Note-taking	Speaking	Pronunciation
Johnson, J.: So, How Did You Like My Presentation?				✓												✓		✓	
King, K.: Teachers and Students Assessing Oral Presentations				✓	✓													✓	
Lee, J.: Active Book Report				✓								✓		✓		✓		✓	
Mansour, S., & Mansour, W.: Assess the Assessors				✓										✓				✓	
Richardson, C. A.: Test Your Talk						✓	✓										✓		✓

Part, section, and activity	Portfolio	Journal	Conference	Self-assessment	Peer assessment	Group work	Pair work	Test taking	Test making	Grading	Evaluating curricula	Reading	Vocabulary	Writing	Grammar	Listening	Note-taking	Speaking	Pronunciation
◆ **Self-Assessment Combined With Peer Assessment**																			
Blankmann, J.: Oral Presentations: How Did I Do?				✓	✓													✓	
Christianson, M.: I Said What?				✓	✓		✓									✓		✓	
Gallo, P. B., & Jacobs, G. M.: Gradually Growing Presentation Assessment				✓	✓													✓	
Ho, B.: How Well Did I Communicate?				✓	✓											✓		✓	
Lau, G.: Self-/Peer/ Teacher Assessment of Group Performance				✓	✓	✓												✓	
Murphey, T.: Walk-Talk Oral Tests				✓	✓		✓									✓		✓	
Norris, J. M.: Interviews and Presentations for Clarifying Authentic Public-Speaking Needs			✓	✓	✓	✓										✓		✓	
Poulshock, J. W.: Peer Evaluation of Natural Communicative Behaviors With Dialogues				✓	✓	✓												✓	
Valdez Pierce, L.: Activating Self-Assessment			✓	✓	✓		✓							✓					
Progosh, D., & West, R.: Self- and Peer Assessment of Group Participation				✓	✓	✓						✓		✓		✓		✓	

Part, section, and activity	Portfolio	Journal	Conference	Self-assessment	Peer assessment	Group work	Pair work	Test taking	Test making	Grading	Evaluating curricula	Reading	Vocabulary	Writing	Grammar	Listening	Note-taking	Speaking	Pronunciation
Part III: Alternative Groupings for Assessment ◆ **Group Work**																			
Wilhelm, K. H., & Rivers, M.: Author, Author! Guided Reader Response					✓	✓						✓		✓					
Berridge, R., & Muzamhindo, J.: Group Oral Tests						✓												✓	
Carroll, M.: Putting It Together: A Jigsaw Task						✓										✓		✓	
Garman, K.: How Many Words Is a Picture Really Worth?						✓							✓						
Ikeguchi, C. B.: Mini–Talk Shows in Classroom Assessment						✓										✓		✓	
Ohtani, M.: Run and Win						✓							✓	✓					
Russ, R.: Let Me Explain						✓												✓	
Valdez Pierce, L.: Reciprocal Teaching: Reading Strategies at Work			✓			✓						✓							
◆ **Pair Work**																			
Bulach, J. J.: Face to Face							✓						✓					✓	
Nakamura, Y.: Three-Sentence-Speech Speaking Test (TSSST)							✓											✓	
Norris, J. M.: The Audio Mirror: Reflecting on Students' Speaking Ability			✓				✓			✓								✓	

Part, section, and activity	Portfolio	Journal	Conference	Self-assessment	Peer assesment	Group work	Pair work	Test taking	Test making	Grading	Evaluating curricula	Reading	Vocabulary	Writing	Grammar	Listening	Note-taking	Speaking	Pronunciation
Okano, S. F.: Using the Science and Art of Colors to Teach ESL							✓						✓					✓	
Rodriguez, I. A.: Organizing Ideas With Pictures							✓								✓			✓	
◆ Group Work Combined With Pair Work																			
Paltridge, B.: Observation, Feedback, and Individual Goal Setting			✓			✓	✓											✓	
Samsell, C.: Consolidate Yourself						✓	✓											✓	
Stafford, M. D.: Whose Shoes Do You Use?						✓	✓								✓				
Part IV: Alternative Ways of Doing Classroom Chores **◆ Preparing Students for Tests**																			
Allan, A.: Test-Wiseness Minitest								✓											
Deane, D.: "Now You're a Professor!" Anticipating Essay Exam Questions								✓					✓						
Wilhelm, K. H.: It's OK to Argue								✓										✓	
◆ Creating Assessment Procedures																			
Gonzalez, D.: U Test U							✓		✓			✓	✓						
Gorsuch, G. J.: Let Them Make Quizzes: Student-Created Reading Quizzes						✓			✓			✓							
Power, M. A.: Developing a Student-Centered Scoring Rubric						✓			✓										

Part, section, and activity	Portfolio	Journal	Conference	Self-assessment	Peer assesment	Group work	Pair work	Test taking	Test making	Grading	Evaluating curricula	Reading	Vocabulary	Writing	Grammar	Listening	Note-taking	Speaking	Pronunciation
Progosh, D.: A Continuous Assessment Framework							✓		✓	✓									
◆ Making Grading Easier																			
Bulach, J. J.: Raise Your Hand and Be Counted										✓		✓		✓		✓		✓	
Lyddon, P.: Course of Events										✓		✓		✓					
Grove, R.: Getting the Point(s): An Adaptable Evaluation System										✓								✓	
◆ Evaluating Curricula																			
Becker, C. A.: Thermometer											✓								
Murphey, T.: Multiple Assessment Action Logging											✓			✓					
Murphey, T.: Wow! Marvelous Task											✓								
Part V: Alternative Ways of Assessing Written Skills **◆ Reading**																			
Berridge, R., & Muzamhindo, J.: Taking the Speed out of Reading Tests												✓							
Jungheim, N. O.: Keeping Track With Free Readin'												✓							
Norris, J. M.: The Reading Beat: Investigative Questioning and Reading Comprehension										✓		✓		✓					

Part, section, and activity	Portfolio	Journal	Conference	Self-assessment	Peer assesment	Group work	Pair work	Test taking	Test making	Grading	Evaluating curricula	Reading	Vocabulary	Writing	Grammar	Listening	Note-taking	Speaking	Pronunciation
Rosenkjar, P. A.: A Window on the Reading Process												✓							
Tondolo, Z. G.: Sort It Out												✓		✓		✓			
◆ Reading and Vocabulary																			
de Aguerrevere, B.: Have You Seen My Brother?												✓	✓						
Bartelen, H.: Extra! Extra! Read All About It!												✓	✓						
MacLennan, C.: On the Spot!												✓	✓						✓
Malagarriga, E.: Definition-Resource Cloze												✓	✓						
◆ Vocabulary																			
Albers de Urriola, M. I.: Going to the Supermarket												✓	✓					✓	✓
Bame, J.: Party or Test: Who Cares? Let's Eat!													✓					✓	
Bricault, D. R.: The Price Is Right													✓		✓				✓
Bricault, D. R.: Color-Coordinated Quiz													✓						
Fisher, R.: Vocabulary Information-Gap Electronic Discussion													✓						
Uhr, J. A.: A Vocabulary Quiz Given by Students to Themselves													✓			✓		✓	

Part, section, and activity	Portfolio	Journal	Conference	Self-assessment	Peer assesment	Group work	Pair work	Test taking	Test making	Grading	Evaluating curricula	Reading	Vocabulary	Writing	Grammar	Listening	Note-taking	Speaking	Pronunciation
◆ Writing and Grammar																			
Mulling, S.: Check It Out: A Library Research Checklist														✓					
Ballance, T.: Tense Excitement Throwing a Die														✓	✓				
Kirimura, M.: Who Is He?															✓				
Part VI: Alternative Ways of Assessing Oral Skills **◆ Listening and Notetaking**																			
Arnold, S. L.: We Are Here to Communicate!																✓		✓	
Bartelen, H.: The Traveling Teacher Listening Assessment Tour																✓			
Bricault, D. R.: Get the Picture																✓			
Brown, J. D., Hilferty, A.: Reduced-Forms Dictations																✓			✓
Browne, C.: Watch Your Listening																✓			
Golden, S.: The Couch-Potato Diagnostic Listening Test																✓			
Tatsuki, D.: The Laser's Edge: Assessing Listening With Laser Disc Video																✓			
Wilhelm, K. H., & Caldwell, C.: Colors Galore!																✓			

Part, section, and activity	Portfolio	Journal	Conference	Self-assessment	Peer assesment	Group work	Pair work	Test taking	Test making	Grading	Evaluating curricula	Reading	Vocabulary	Writing	Grammar	Listening	Note-taking	Speaking	Pronunciation
Wilhelm, K. H.: LSS: Listen and Skim/Scan														✓		✓	✓		
Plakans, L. M., & Myers, C. L.: Welcome to English 101																✓	✓		
◆ **Speaking and Pronunciation**																			
Mckay, E.: What Can You Do?																		✓	
Progosh, D.: Presentation Check				✓	✓													✓	
Shimazaki, R.: Guess What My Favorite Animal Is							✓												✓
Yamashita, S. O.: Skit Assessment			✓		✓	✓												✓	
Zhang, X.-R.: Assessing Spoken Language Proficiency			✓															✓	
Yoneoko, J.: Karaoke-Dokey				✓														✓	✓
McPhee, N.: Assessing Production and Reception of Minimal Pairs																			✓

Also available from TESOL

E-Mail for English Teaching:
Bringing the Internet and Computer Learning Networks
Into the Language Classroom
Mark Warschauer

More Than a Native Speaker:
An Introduction for Volunteers Teaching Abroad
Don Snow

New Ways in Teaching Adults
Marilyn Lewis, Editor

New Ways in Content-Based Instruction
Donna M. Brinton and Peter Master, Editors

New Ways in Teacher Education
Donald Freeman, with Steve Cornwell, Editors

New Ways in Teaching Grammar
Martha C. Pennington, Editor

New Ways in Teaching Listening
David Nunan and Lindsay Miller, Editors

New Ways in Teaching Reading
Richard R. Day, Editor

New Ways in Teaching Speaking
Kathleen M. Bailey and Lance Savage, Editors

New Ways in Teaching Vocabulary
Paul Nation, Editor

New Ways in Teaching Writing
Ronald V. White, Editor

New Ways in Teaching Young Children
Linda Schinke-Llano and Rebecca Rauff, Editors

New Ways of Teaching Culture
Alvino E. Fantini, Editor

New Ways of Using Computers in Language Teaching
Tim Boswood, Editor

New Ways of Using Drama and Literature in Language Teaching
Valerie Whiteson, Editor

Tasks for Independent Language Learning
David Gardner and Lindsay Miller, Editors

For more information, contact
Teachers of English to Speakers of Other Languages, Inc.
1600 Cameron Street, Suite 300
Alexandria, Virginia 22314 USA
Tel. 703-836-0774 • Fax 703-836-7864
e-mail publ@tesol.edu
http://www.tesol.edu

Founded 1966